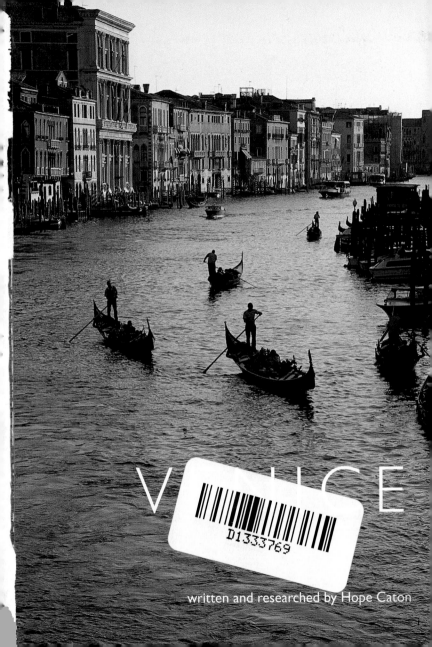

VENICE

written and researched by Hope Caton

www.purpleguide.com

The Purple Guide: Venice
Credits

Writer: Hope Caton
Editor: Robin Bell
Design: Sharon Platt
Cartography: Anderson Geographics Ltd
Sub-editor: Jon Stanhope
Translator: Isabella Lofiase
Contributors: Cesare Battisti, Nino Artale, Nini Morelli, Robin Bell, Sharon Platt
Photography: All photographs by Hope Caton, except:
Bridgeman Art Library: 105,119,125,132,136,179; Italian Tourist Board: 205;
Robin Bell: 8,18,19,32,85,112-113,138,148,153,162,168,187,194,211,234,236,239,242,
252,259,261,263,271; Museum of the Hellenic Institute of Byzantine and
Post Byzantine studies:177

Publishing Information

First published in the United Kingdom in 2004 by:
The Purple Guide Ltd,
Teddington Studios, Broom Road
Teddington Middlesex, TW11 9NT
Second Edition 2007

ISBN 978-0-9547234-5-3
Printed in Slovenia
Maps © 2007 Anderson Geographics Ltd. Used under licence.

Sales

For information, telephone our sales department on 020 8614 2277
or email: **sales@purpleguide.com**

Write to Us

We welcome the views and suggestions of our readers. If we include your
contribution in our next edition, we will send you a copy of the book, or any other
Purple Guide that you would prefer.
Please write to us at the address above or email: **feedback@purpleguide.com**

The publishers have done their best to ensure that the information found in
The Purple Guide: Venice is current and accurate. Some information may be liable
to change. The publishers cannot accept responsibility for any loss, injury or
inconvenience that may result from the use of this book.

thepurpleguide
the inside story

'a winning formula' The Sunday Times

Unlike most traditional guide books, The Purple Guide provides a wealth of surprising and entertaining stories and secrets, anecdotes and facts, adding a whole new dimension to the Venetian experience that might otherwise be missed.

We aim to make your holiday relaxed and fun. As well as offering tips and advice that can only be gleaned from years of living with the locals, we give you **the inside story** on:

- navigating in Venice, you won't be lost unless you want to be.
- the city's unique districts, with introductory pages to help you choose your own itinerary.
- eating well in Venice, with 36 pages on food & drink, and restaurant recommendations that are personally researched.
- the most interesting shops in Venice, with a special section on local artisans.

www.purpleguide.com

We constantly update our website with useful information to support each guidebook we publish. Before you travel, pay a visit to our website for our hotel recommendations, new information on restaurants, shopping and special events in Venice.

With many thanks to …

Our on-the-ground team of contributors including **Nino Artale**, a Venetian chef and food writer; **Nini Morelli**, a painter and sculptor with a thorough understanding of Venetian crafts and artisans; and **Cesare Battisti**, a tourism professional with 37 years of experience at the Italian Tourist Board in Venice. *Mille grazie!*

CONTENTS

The story of Venice begins with *la Laguna*, the Lagoon. Initially, it was a hiding place, a refuge from barbarian invasions. Repeated attacks drove the early settlers onto the islands of the lagoon permanently. They established villages, and then united as a republic that would last for over a thousand years. A great city was built, the home of an enormous trading empire, that would dominate the eastern Mediterranean for over 400 years.

La Laguna covers the 189 square miles of water that surround the city of Venice. It is bordered on three sides by the Veneto mainland, and on the east by the Adriatic Sea. A narrow strip of two islands, Lido and Pellestrina, form a fragile barrier between the lagoon and the open water. There are three entrances from the Adriatic: the gates of Lido, Malamocco and Chioggia.

The islands of the lagoon are made of mud and silt that is transported by rivers originating in the Dolomites and the Alps. Maintaining the correct balance is crucial or the build-up of silt could increase to the point where the lagoon becomes mainland. The rivers of the Veneto have all been diverted to empty directly into the Adriatic, in an effort to manage the waters of the lagoon.

On the bottom of the lagoon are alternate layers of compacted clay and sand, which provide a stable base for building. Timber piles, driven 25 feet into the ground, rest on solid compressed clay known as *caranto*. Closely packed piles do not rot in the waterlogged subsoil. And the deep layer of watery sand, below the clay stratum, creates a hydraulic resistance to the downward pressure of the buildings. Istrian stone from the Dalmatian coast was used to make damp-proof foundations.

In the centre of the lagoon, connected to the mainland by a causeway four kilometres long, is one of the world's most beautiful and visited cities. Here, on a cluster of 120 small islands, linked by nearly 450 bridges over some 150 waterways, and now home to approximately 65,000 permanent residents, is the city of Venice.

CAMPO SAN GIACOMO DELL'ORIO, SANTA CROCE

Watching a tourist hike up his trousers and tip toe through high water is a comical experience. A Venetian will stop, consider his options, and then calmly and gracefully walk through the water as though it isn't there.

Clever and adaptable, the Venetians first were sailors, then merchants, artists, engineers and inventors. They developed a society that was, like their city, completely unique. Today their descendants manage to live in a place where everything is complicated by water – from below and from above. High tides bring flooding with increasing regularity. But if a leaky roof needs fixing, the repairman will likely come from nearby Mestre because he cannot afford to live in Venice. Everything is more expensive in Venice because of the water, the source of her beauty.

Venetians often complain and say: *'we need a butcher shop, not another mask shop.'* They are concerned that if tourism becomes the only business, their town will die. Foreign ownership is a big worry, but Venetians have always stuck together and they are forming consortia to protect themselves. Even though the population has shrunk by 50 per cent over the last 50 years, there are still strong and vibrant communities, often invisible to a tourist. These are centred around the local *campo*, which is much more than a town square. It is the place where children play and mothers watch, where people go to shop, socialise, drink, gossip and be entertained.

Refuge

Before the fall of the Western Roman Empire in 476 AD, northern Italy was subject to invasion by a succession of Goths, Visigoths, Huns and Vandals. The people of the Veneto learned to use the lagoon as a means of protection. When invading hordes arrived, they escaped on rafts to the safety of the marshland in the middle of the lagoon. The tall grasses on the small islands provided a hiding place and were also useful as building material for emergency lodgings and fuel for fire. The waters were full of fish and clams, so the people did not starve.

Soldiers, accustomed to fighting on land, were ill-equipped to follow the fleeing villagers through the water. War galleys could not enter the shallow waters of the lagoon and a strip of islands at the entrance offered protection from attack from the Adriatic. For centuries the lagoon was populated only in times of war. When the armies retreated, the refugees abandoned their temporary homes and returned to the mainland.

Attila the Hun invaded Aquileia in 452. The town was sacked and villagers fled once again to the lagoon, but this time they planned to stay. They started a community on a cluster of islands in the centre known as *Rivo Altus*. In 638 the citizens of Altinum, an important *Patriarchate* (seat of the Roman church), received a dire warning: the divine voice of heaven was heard, telling the people to flee. The much-feared Lombards were advancing so the

Altini loaded their treasures of Christian faith in makeshift boats and searched the lagoon for a new home. They chose an expanse of mudflat in the north, which they named *Turricellum*.

As invasions continued, the lagoon became home to many more refugees. Rome was weak, so the citizens sought protection from the Lombards by placing themselves under the authority of Byzantium, the Eastern Roman Empire based in Constantinople. In 697 the first *duca* (imperial magistrate, or *doge*), Paoluccio Anafesta, was chosen with the approval of the Byzantine Emperor. The most Serene Republic, *La Serenissima*, was born.

Byzantium versus Rome

Rome was determined to wrest control of the Italian peninsula from Byzantium. The Pope crowned the French king, Charlemagne, Holy Roman Emperor in 800. French armies, fighting for Rome, had seized the Veneto and were threatening the lagoon. Venice was caught in the crossfire. For commercial reasons, the fledgling city-state was dependent upon the Byzantine Empire. Peace was declared in 812 with a compromise: Venice resumed her trade relations with Byzantium but offered spiritual loyalty to the Pope in Rome. In 828 she traded

her Byzantine patron saint Theodore for St Mark. The latter was a saint of much higher status. Mark's bones in the new Basilica of San Marco would ensure Venice's position as a religious power, and they would aid her in commerce too.

The city developed a navy that was the envy of the medieval world. She became the gateway to the *Levant*, a region encompassing Lebanon, Syria, Israel, Egypt and parts of modern Turkey. Merchants from all religions traded comfortably in Venice: Jews, Muslims, and other traders from the Orient, brought their goods. All were welcome to invest in the markets and banks of the Rialto. Marco Polo's travels to China in the 13th century opened new trade routes for valuable spice and silk.

Empire

The sack of Constantinople in 1204 marked the beginning of the Venetian Empire. After defeating hated rivals the Genoese in 1380, Venice extended her domains. Over time she would control the Veneto and Emiglia Romana, her lands reaching as far as Ancona in the south, Milan in the west, and Friuli in the east. She was *Queen of the Adriatic* and ruler of the Dalmatian coast, Apuglia, the Ionian Islands, Crete, Cyprus and Beirut.

Hers was a mercantile empire. Venetians had little desire to convert the world to their cause or to dominate vast tracts of mainland. It was commerce they sought. The existence of so many Venetian ports meant that every landing stage for ships bound for the east belonged to Venice. From the Lagoon to the Black Sea, merchants could sail with confidence knowing that their enterprise would never have to dock at a foreign harbour. Their humble beginnings as refugees on lagoon islands were just a memory.

The end of the 15th century saw the climax of Venetian success; she was the envy of Europe. But with riches came pride and arrogance. Venetian merchants boasted that they were the true successors to Rome and the world belonged to them. The Grand Canal was considered the world's most beautiful thoroughfare and the grand palazzos lining its banks were proof of Venetian supremacy. Moreover, Venice's artists, especially her painters, were the equals of any in the Renaissance.

Disaster struck in 1498. Three Portuguese ships docked at Calcutta inquiring about the Spice Islands. Venetian bankers flew into a panic. It was the worst possible news! A new trade route had opened. Portugal had discovered a sea route around Africa, bypassing Venetian and Muslim middlemen without involving a gruelling overland trek. Soon much of the lucrative spice trade was flowing into Portugal. It was the beginning of the end of the Empire.

Venice's relationship with Rome was often turbulent. In 1508, Pope Julius II united Urbino, Mantua, Ferrara, Aragon and France in the League of Cambrai in order to suppress the *'insatiable cupidity of the Venetians and their thirst for domination'*. Venice was excommunicated in 1509 and again in 1606. These papal decrees were usually ignored, but La Serenissima had another, more dangerous enemy. Venice was repeatedly stricken by plague – the worst in 1500, 1575, 1616 and 1630.

While Venice was arguing with Rome, the Ottoman Empire had built up a powerful fleet. Turks seized Venetian ports in the Mediterranean and in the Adriatic. Venice fought and won her last great sea battle at Lepanto in 1571, but her territories were already severely diminished. She was being outflanked by the superpowers of east and west.

Decadence and decline

Venetian nobles turned from investment in trade to speculation in real estate. Industry and banking now proved more profitable in the new Rialto than ships and trade. Venice loved luxury and the city of theatre and *carnevale* – that so attracted the English on their Grand Tour – emerged in the shadow of the Empire.

In the 17th and 18th centuries, Venice was the pleasure capital of Europe. People came from all over the world to gamble and party in the atmosphere of a masked carnival that lasted for six months of the year. Venice was now famous for her courtesans and sexual freedoms. Fortunes that had taken centuries to acquire were lost at the gambling tables. This period saw the last great flourishing of the arts in Venice, with paintings by the Tiepolos and the Guardis, and music by Albinoni and Vivaldi. Moreover, Venice was the first home for a new musical genre – *the opera.*

The end of the Republic

In the Napoleonic wars, Venice claimed neutrality and allowed both Austrian and French ships to pass through her ports. Napoleon wanted to use Venice as a bargaining chip with Austria, to avoid another winter campaign in the Alps. He also saw her as a huge treasure trove to help fund his ambition. When the Venetians were foolish enough to be provoked into attacking a French ship, he announced, *'I will be an Attila to the Venetian state.'* Napoleon declared war on 1st May 1797.

Doge Ludovico Manin surrendered without a fight. On 12th May 1797, the Grand Council assembled for the final time for a vote to eliminate the Ducal government of the Republic. The vote passed with 512 in favour and 20 opposed. The governing elite had voted themselves and 1,000 years of Republican rule out of existence. Venetians were so angry when the news was circulated that they burned the Golden Book and the Ducal Insignia in a bonfire at Piazza San Marco. (see p.62)

The French methodically stripped Venice of treasures, doing unto her what she had done to Constantinople. Then, after only five months, Napoleon used his chip and ceded Venice to Austria on the 17th of October.

Venetians hated the Austrian occupation. Daniele Manin and Nicolo Tommaseo, a Dalmatian writer, printed a call to arms. Venetians rose up in a general strike and

Manin raised a civic guard of 4,000 men, who successfully challenged the Austrian occupying force. Manin was named President of Venice on 21st March 1848. On 2nd April 1849, Austrian troops encircled the lagoon. Venetians vowed to fight. A pitiless bombardment was followed by a long siege and cholera spread through Venice's starving population. On 23rd August 1849, Manin and Tommaseo were exiled. Venice was desolate.

Nationalist fever continued to spread throughout Italy. Vittorio Emanuele II defeated the Austrians and united the country in 1866. Venice and the Veneto together voted overwhelmingly in favour of the new Italy.

The completion of a rail bridge in 1846 linking Venice with the mainland ended her maritime isolation. When the Suez Canal opened in 1869, it was the beginning of a new era of prosperity. With a new harbour built for ocean-going ships, Venice became Italy's second largest port in 1881. By the early 20th century she was fashionable again and new hotels were built on the Lido.

Modern Times

A period of fascism, beginning in 1922, saw an oil refinery and tanker port completed in Marghera. Deep shipping canals were dredged in the lagoon and a road bridge was built in 1931. Industry in Marghera and nearby Mestre made those cities a target for Allied bombers in World War II but Venice emerged unscathed.

Today the delicate ecology of the lagoon and damage caused by industry are big political issues. The floods of 1966 raised global awareness of the fragile nature of Venice. In 2006, forty years after the flooding, the MOSE project was approved: three mobile flood barriers are being constructed at Lido, Malamocco and Chioggia. The barriers are designed to be water-filled gates that rest in housings on the lagoon bed. During extreme tides, an emission of compressed air will force the water out, causing the gates to rise and block the flow of sea water into the lagoon. The project is highly controversial but everyone agrees that Venice needs protection.

VENICE

THE GRAND CANAL

Navigating in Venice

Getting around Venice may seem daunting at first. The layout is complicated and random with no apparent logic to the place. The Grand Canal offers a central link to most destinations, but finding your way through the maze of streets, canals and bridges can pose a real challenge.

However, there is a Venetian logic to the city and understanding a few key elements will aid you in finding your way: the *sestiere* (districts); the address system (unique to Venice); the parishes; and the waterbuses (*vaporetti*).

Getting lost in Venice is one of life's great pleasures. Do not be afraid to go off and wander around the city, the worst that will happen is that you will walk down an alley that leads to a canal instead of a bridge. *Piazza San Marco* (St Mark's Square) and *Ponte Rialto* (the Rialto Bridge) are excellent landmarks to help you get your bearings. Once you have established the route back to your hotel from San Marco or Rialto, it should be possible to find your way even in the dark. Being aware of the Grand Canal in relation to your position also helps when trying to find your way out of the winding lanes.

Venice is compact; it is possible to walk the length of the city in just over one hour. Signs directing you *per Rialto, per San Marco, per Accademia* are common and plentiful in all tourist areas. Graffiti directions are usually a result of building works and can be trusted.

There are some streets that become so crowded with other tourists that you may become frustrated, particularly if you are in a hurry. The Venetians have an expression: *anddare per le fodre,* which means 'going in the lining of the coat'. To avoid the crowds they take the lesser-known streets. Stepping off the beaten track will instantly afford more space, and more peace and quiet.

Names

Piazza San Marco is the only square in Venice that
is designated a *piazza*. Every other square is called a
campo, which means 'field' in Italian. The narrow lanes
and streets in Venice are called *calle*; wider pavements
alongside a canal are often called a *fondamenta*. *Rio terrà*
signifies a pavement that was once a waterway; a canal
that has been filled in.

In the early days of the Republic, it was only the *Doge*
(Ducal Magistrate) who was allowed a *palazzo*. All other
places of residence were to be called a *casa* (house), with
the prefix *Ca'*. Therefore, *Ca' Rezzonico* and *Ca' d'Oro*, are
palazzi in reality, but it was not until Venice sold official
titles to its nobility, in a bid to raise finance in the 17th
century, that a *casa* was allowed to be renamed a *palazzo*.

The Venetian dialect, different from standard Italian, is
often used for street names. Many streets and churches
are therefore known by at least two names. For example:
San Giovanni e Paolo becomes *San Zanipolo* in Venetian;
San Angelo is shortened to *L'Anzolo*. This happens with
common names as well; the Italian *Guiseppe* becomes
Isepo, *Eustachio* becomes *Stae*, and *Giovanni* becomes
Zuan or *Zan*. This explains why you may find yourself
standing in a *campo* with three names.

As a general rule, most major monuments and sights are
named in Italian (for example: *Piazza San Marco, Palazzo
Ducale*) and many street names and local names are in the
Venetian dialect. In 2007, with the singular exception of
San Marco, most Italian street names and signage have
been replaced by Venexiàn. Fortunately, Venetians will
know the Italian name as well as the Venetian one, so
they will be able to help if you are in doubt.

FINDING YOUR WAY AROUND

Safety

Venice is a safe city even at night, but pickpockets have been known to favour the waterbuses where people tend to stand close together. Also be aware of personal security when in the Piazza San Marco. Wear a comfortable pair of shoes, take your camera, set out through the *calles*, and do not be afraid to walk off the commonly used tourist trails. You will always be rewarded with a sight of unexpected beauty.

Glossary of Venetian Street Names

calle	street or lane
campo	square
campiello	tiny square
corte	courtyard
fondamenta	street alongside a body of water
piscina	square formed by filling in a place where boats turned
ramo	small street
rio	canal
rio terrà	street formed by filling in a canal
riva	very large street beside a body of water
ruga	major street
salizzada	main street of a parish
sottoportico	covered entrance to a street or courtyard (also called a *sottoportego* or *sottoporto*)

FONDAMENTA DELLA MISERICORDIA, CANNAREGIO, *PREVIOUS PAGE RIGHT*

Sestieri

The islands of central Venice are divided into six administrative districts, each known as a *sestiere* (derived from the Italian *sei,* meaning 'six'). In the year 1171, Doge Vitale Michiel defined the *sestieri,* three on each side of the Grand Canal: *Dorsoduro, San Polo* and *Santa Croce* on the west; *Cannaregio, Castello* and *San Marco* on the east. There is no sestiere named Rialto, the district is part of San Polo.

In general, Venetians tend to live in the west side of Dorsoduro, Cannaregio and the east side of Castello. San Marco, Rialto and parts of Dorsoduro are largely given over to tourists.

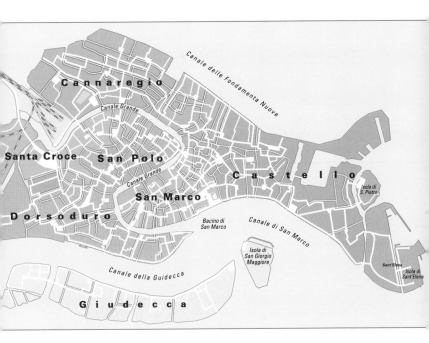

THE SESTIERI OF VENICE

San Marco

This is where most of the essential sights are clustered and as such is the most expensive and crowded part of the city. San Marco is the location for the majority of luxury hotels, shops and restaurants. Venice's grand showpiece, Piazza San Marco, was conceived as a vista for the Doge's Palace and the Basilica. The Piazza was described by Napoleon as '*the most elegant drawing room in Europe*' and it has always been a magnet for visitors. San Marco was the home of early opera and it includes the famous theatre, *La Fenice*.

San Polo

The Rialto markets are located in San Polo. When they were first established in the 11th century, this sestiere became the commercial hub of Venice. The recent opening of the (formerly wholesale only) Erbaria food markets to the public has created a canal-side terrace that, together with the adjacent campo, is one of the liveliest spots in Venice. This formerly industrial area has no residents to complain if loud music is played long into the night so open-air concerts happen frequently.

Santa Croce

For the most part, this is a sestiere of very narrow, tightly packed streets and squares where you will see the humbler side of Venetian life. Its grandest palazzi lie along the Grand Canal. Venice's two car parks are in Santa Croce: at Piazzale Roma and at Tronchetto. The cruise ship terminal is also located in this sestiere.

Dorsoduro

The home of several major art collections, most notably the Accademia Gallery and the Peggy Guggenheim Collection. The churches in this district are rich repositories of paintings and sculpture: *San Sebastiano* has fine paintings by Paolo Veronese while the *Scuola Grande dei Carmini* and the church of the *Gesuati* both have ceilings painted by Giambattista Tiepolo.

Cannaregio

The name of this district derives from either the Italian *canne* (meaning cane or reeds) or from *Canal Regio* (Royal Canal), now known as the *Canale di Cannaregio* - the second largest canal in Venice. This waterway was the main entry to Venice before the advent of the rail link with the mainland. Cannaregio extends from the Santa Lucia railway station to the Rialto Bridge. *Vaporetti* (waterbuses) to the islands of Torcello, Burano and Murano depart from the Fondamenta Nuove. Thirty per cent of Venice's population live in Cannaregio.

Castello

Extending from San Marco and Cannaregio in the west to the modern blocks of Sant' Elena in the east, this sestiere contains Venice's largest public gardens. The industrial hub of Castello was the *Arsenale*, where the great shipyards produced Venice's fleet of warships and merchant vessels. Castello's most popular area is the *Riva degli Schiavoni* promenade. Behind the waterfront it is comparatively quiet and is characterised by narrow alleys, elegantly faded palazzi and fine churches, including the great *Santi Giovanni e Paolo*, also known as *San Zanipolo*.

Addresses

Knowledge of the sestieri is a valuable navigating tool and it is essential when searching for an address in Venice. Occasionally a street will share the same name as another street in a different sestiere. The address numbering system will change when you cross into another sestiere (even within the same sestiere, numbers will not always make sense).

The problem for the traveller is that a Venetian postal address does not include the name of the street. Addresses are listed by sestiere and number: for example, San Marco 2285. This can make it very difficult to locate a hotel, shop or restaurant when these establishments do not provide the name of the street.

Although there is a Venetian convention that an address should be written as street name, followed by sestiere, followed by number, you will see every permutation.

WHEN YOU FIND A PLACE YOU WANT TO RETURN TO, IT HELPS TO MAKE A NOTE OF THE STREET NAME OR THE NAME OF A NEARBY CAMPO OR CHURCH.

The Purple Guide has researched the street names for all monuments, galleries, restaurants and shops listed in this book. These are cross-referenced to the detailed maps at the back of the book.

Parrocchias (Parishes)

Within each sestiere there are many parishes. Venice is comprised of some 120 islands, each of which began as a parish. The city developed parish by parish, finally becoming the grand city of Venice. Understanding the parish church and the campo may assist you in finding your way around.

Every island had its own well and water supply, and its own church and bell tower centred around the campo. A shopping street would lead off the campo and be connected to the next parish by a wooden bridge. Following the shopping calles will usually lead to a bridge and the next parish. There are more than 70 churches in Venice.

In the 9th century, there were only a dozen parishes. By the 11th century there were more than 50 churches, and many other convents, monasteries and *scuole*. In the 13th century, the population in Venice had soared to 120,000 residents in over 70 parishes. The church was at the centre of a cohesive neighbourhood, a little world within a larger civic world through which the Republic was able to control its citizens.

Each parish had its wealthy families who would dispense patronage and judgment over their parishioners. They often paid for the construction of the church and built their large homes opposite to prove their status.

Even if the surrounding community was poor, the inside of the church would be lavishly decorated. When benefactors endowed churches with the richest and rarest adornments, the poor cherished them as communal possessions. Churches were 'public palaces' for the parishioners; the richness of the interiors was a relief from the endless poverty suffered by many in the congregation. Mass was held several times per day and the church was always open.

A parish church in Venice will often have a special painting, a frescoed ceiling, or an outstanding woodcarving or sculpture. If you are passing an open church it is worth taking a moment to explore and take relief from the hot or rainy weather. Opening hours vary and the church may not be open when you next pass by. Some churches close on Sunday after mass.

Most Venetian churches give away cards (in English) that explain the contents of the church, each artwork, the artists, the year it was finished, and perhaps a plan of the church.

MADONNA DELL'ORTO

'Venetian first, Christian second'

Although Venetians were capable of deep religious feeling, the Republic of Venice had absolute authority over any papal interference in the affairs of government. The doge considered himself equal to the pope. This attitude resulted in Venice being excommunicated at least six times during the thousand-year Republic. Venetian rulers often dealt with the interdict by refusing to acknowledge it and banning priests from informing their parishes, forcing them to continue saying mass, their parishioners none the wiser. Negotiations would then be carried on in secret to have the interdict withdrawn.

There is a story of Doge Francesco Dandolo (1329-1339) who succeeded in having the excommunication of Clement V withdrawn by hiding under His Holiness' dinner table in Avignon, embracing the pope's knees and refusing to let go until he got what he wanted.

Underlying trade disputes often caused considerable tension between the doge and the pope. When Leonardo Donà met the young Cardinal Borghese in Rome on a diplomatic mission, the dislike was instant and mutual. Borghese said, '*If I were pope, I would excommunicate you*'. Donà replied, '*If I were doge, I would laugh at your excommunication*'.

These words proved to be prophetic. Pope Paolo V (Borghese) issued an interdict against Venice in 1606. Doge Donà banned the circulation of the papal decree and mass was said as usual. The majority of the clergy remained loyal to Venice and continued to administer sacraments and hear confession. In a public display of defiance, the doge continued to hold the celebrations of Corpus Christi, publicly partaking in the Eucharist (communion). In this case it took the diplomatic intervention of the King of France for the interdict to be withdrawn.

Scuole

Located near the parish church, there was a *scuola* (literally meaning 'school'). This was a uniquely Venetian institution: a cooperative, independent guild or confraternity that could be founded on religious, charitable, political, work, or special interest grounds. Glassmakers, fruiterers, and even foreigners belonged to a scuola, which was much like a modern day guild, club, or community group.

Each scuola had its own constitution and a body of electors who decided what was best for its members, maintaining standards, regulating wages and settling disputes. The scuola maintained a hospital and a school for its members and provided them with a pension. Venetian wages fluctuated in accordance with how many dependants the worker had to feed and house. The member paid dues calculated on earnings and had the security of knowing that upon his death or incapacitation, the scuola would care for his wife and children.

Each scuola had its own headquarters. Buildings were used for prayer in addition to serving as charitable administration offices and social clubs. Most of these buildings were small, but if the fraternity was wealthy, a *Scuola Grande* was constructed. Members would donate vast sums to their scuola for the beautification and commissioning of what remain Venice's most precious art treasures. Even the Republic was known to borrow money from a *Scuola Grande*.

Napoleon disbanded the 300 plus *Scuole* in favour of a strong, central government. To Venetians, it was tantamount to tearing the heart out of their communities.

Vaporetti (water-buses)

Vaporetto means 'little steamer', as the original *vaporetti* were steam-powered. Today they are diesel motorboats and, as well as being the only means of getting to certain destinations (without engaging a taxi or private boat), they are an excellent way to see the beautiful facades of the palazzi that line the Grand Canal.

Strictly speaking, there are three different types of boat, all of which are commonly referred to as vaporetti: the large, wide boats used on the slow routes (such as Line 1) are vaporetti, the smaller, sleeker vessels used on routes with less traffic volume (such as Line 52) are called *motoscafi,* and the two-tiered ferries that go to the Lido and outlying islands are *motonove.* This knowledge is useful for disabled travellers, because the motoscafi cannot accomodate wheelchairs (*Travel Basics,* p.280)

The water-bus system may seem confusing at first but it is actually very easy to use. Vaporetto stops (indicated on our maps) are dotted along both sides of the Grand Canal, and they have clearly visible route maps. The route of the approaching boat is also shown on a digital sign above the entrance platform. A common mistake is to take a boat travelling in the wrong direction, so be sure you are on the correct platform.

Allow passengers to disembark first through the exit before boarding. Try to put any luggage in the marked luggage area or, if it is full, out of the way of passengers trying to get on or off. If you have a particularly large suitcase, you may be asked to pay a supplement up to the amount of your ticket. If you are carrying a backpack, you should take it off before you get on the boat.

If you are near the exit on a crowded vaporetto, it is a courtesy to step off and let passengers disembark and then step back on to continue your journey.

The service is every 10 to 20 minutes depending on your destination. In peak season and rush hours, additional water-buses run on the main routes. The night service runs every 20 to 40 minutes.

Tickets

Tickets should be bought in advance from the ticket office on the landing stage, from a tobacconist (*tabacchi*), at shops displaying the ACTV sign, at the airport, Piazzale Roma or from the main tourist office in San Marco. If this is not possible (for example in the evening, or at a remote stop) then the conductor will sell tickets on board at the regular price, providing you speak to him immediately. There is a fine in the region of €23 plus the cost of the ticket, if you are caught without one.

There are a number of single and return tickets: the cost depends on whether or not you will be travelling on the Grand Canal. Most are poor value and should be purchased only if you plan to use the system once.

The best value is to get a *biglietti turistici* – either a one-day (12 hr) travel card for €13 or a three-day card for €30 (at the time of printing). These allow you unlimited access to the ACTV system.

If your ticket does not have a date/time stamp on the top, it must be validated in the yellow box on the landing stage before use. Travel cards only require validation the first time they are used.

A detailed list of routes is in *Travel Basics* (p.278).

Water taxis

Water taxis in Venice accept payment in cash only and they are very expensive.

All licensed water taxis have a yellow stripe or box clearly displaying their number from one to three digits. The numbers should be displayed either side of the taxi. Beware of illegal taxi drivers, mainly at Tronchetto near the car park. There is a vaporetto into Venice (line 82) from Tronchetto.

Your hotel may be able to book a water taxi for you if you contact the concierge.

Traghetti

Traghetti are old gondolas that ferry passengers across the Grand Canal between special piers at six crossing points. The gondolier offers his elbow to help passengers board. Venetians tend to stand during the crossing but there is a seat for those without sea-legs. The sound of the gondolier's oar dipping in the water and the gentle motion of the gondola make this a fun way to cross the Grand Canal and, as there are only three bridges, this is also a practical method of getting across the canal.

Most traghetti only operate until 14.00 but the Rialto/Ca d'Oro operates all day. The fare to row you from one side to another is very reasonable: just 50 cents.

VIEW OF THE GRAND CANAL FROM SCALZI BRIDGE, *NEXT PAGE*

Canale Grande (Grand Canal)

Venice's main waterway winds its way through the centre of the city and follows the course of an ancient riverbed. Great galleys and trading vessels used to make their stately way towards the Rialto, but now the waterways are busy with vaporetti, traghetti, gondolas, barges, launches and rowing boats. The annual *Reggata Storica*, held in September (p.213), pays tribute to Venice's glorious past: a large parade of historic vessels manned by crews in traditional costume is followed by boat and gondola races.

The famous *Ponte di Rialto* (Rialto Bridge) was built in 1588 and is one of only three bridges crossing the canal. The other two are the *Ponte Accademia* (Accademia Bridge) in Dorsoduro and the *Ponte dei Scalzi* (Scalzi Bridge) near the train station.

Palazzi

For a span of over 500 years, the basic plan of a Venetian palazzo changed very little from the characteristic Venetian-Byzantine house, first built in 1100-1200. Homes were designed to be light in weight because the entire structure rested on piles sunk into the silt bottom of the Lagoon. The exterior facades changed over time, but for practical reasons the essential design remained the same, as can be seen from the harmonious view along the Grand Canal.

Early Venetian architects took their inspiration from Byzantium (p.56), making use of loggias, arcades and courtyards. These continued to be an integral part of the Venetian palazzo through the Gothic (1200-1450), Renaissance (1450-1600) and Baroque (1600-1750) periods. The term *Venetian Gothic* refers to the intricate Byzantine-influenced window decoration that is unique to Venice.

Because palazzi were both homes and warehouses for merchandise and trading, the ground floor was reserved for storerooms and offices. Goods and visitors arrived by boat, so this floor included a landing stage, which was also the front door. Since the public entrance overlooked a canal, this frontage became the focus of decorative attention and expense. The side facing the street would be much less elaborate.

The family entertained on the *piano nobile* (first floor), which was lavishly decorated and located above ground level to avoid any danger of flooding. The upper floor housed the family and the servants slept in the attic.

A list of the finest palazzi on the Grand Canal includes the *Ca' d'Oro*, the most beautiful Gothic palace in Venice. *Ca' Foscari* and *Ca' Loredan* are fine examples of 15th century palazzi; *Ca' Vendramin-Calergi* (now the casino) and *Palazzo Grimani* are Renaissance palaces built in the 16th century; *Ca' Pesaro* and *Ca' Rezzonico* are 17th century Baroque palazzi; *Palazzo Grassi* dates from the 18th century.

Throughout history, the rich and famous have lived along the canal: Turner, Verdi and Proust stayed at the *Palazzo Giustinian*, now the headquarters of the Biennale. Lord Byron swam naked up the Grand Canal, his servant (and his clothes) in the gondola behind. Pen Browning bought Ca' Rezzonico with his American wife's money. Pen's father, Robert Browning, lived there for a year before succumbing to bronchitis. Ca' Rezzonico is now a museum allowing a rare glimpse inside one of Venice's grandest palaces.

The modern white facade of the *Palazzo Venier dei Leoni*, home of the Peggy Guggenheim Collection (p.138) stands in stark contrast to its Venetian neighbours because it has no upper floors. Nearby is the ancient and pretty *Ca' Dario*, said to bring ill-luck to its owners. Stories of suicide, murder and bankruptcy circulate – most recently the suicide of industrialist Raul Gardini in 1992.

The Gondola

Gondolas are hand-crafted from eight types of wood: elm, oak, fir, lime, larch, walnut, cherry and mahogany. The oars are made of beech and the curved oar-rest, or *forcola*, is made from a solid piece of walnut, oiled and carved to suit each gondolier. The forcola allows the oar to be used in eight different positions. The asymmetrical shape of the gondola counteracts the force of the oar. Without the leftward curve to the prow, 24 cm wider on the left than right, the boat would go around in circles. It also serves to counteract the weight of the gondolier.

Black pitch was originally used to make the vessel watertight. This gave way to bright paintwork and gilding which was banned in the anti-sumptuary laws of 1562. Today the hull is protected by seven coats of black paint and its flat bottom enables the boat to navigate shallow waters with greater speed. Less then half the hull is in contact with the water, providing a pivot that permits the gondola to turn sharply on its axis.

FOLLOW FOUR MAIN RULES WHEN BARGAINING FOR A GONDOLA:

- AGREE THE ROUTE
- AGREE THE TIME IT WILL TAKE
- AGREE THE COST
- AVOID THE GONDOLIERS IN THE MAIN TOURIST AREAS

The Gondolier

According to a Venetian poem, the gondola was created when a crescent moon tumbled from a starlit sky to shelter a pair of lovers. In truth, it evolved gradually to adapt to the shallow and angled waterways of the Venetian lagoon. Legend has it that the gondolier also adapted to Venice's watery life by growing webbed feet. The gondolier's intimate knowledge of the waterways is passed on from father to son; women have yet to establish themselves in this strictly male profession. That said, in 2007 a 'license to operate a gondola' was awarded to a German woman. However, since she did not pass her exams to join the guild of gondoliers, she may not wear the uniform.

Being a gondolier is expensive: a new gondola takes three months to build and costs £10,000. They need to earn a year's living during the months of the high season. Their uniform must conform to exact specifications: the jumper must be obtained from one outlet, the striped t-shirt from another. They require a black, pom-pom hat in winter and a Venetian straw boater, also traditional and very expensive, in the summer. The gondola needs to be maintained and cleaned every three weeks and can warp beyond repair in five years, whereupon they are pensioned off as traghetti to cross the Grand Canal.

Gondoliers stand upright and push on the oar to row in the direction they are facing. Legend says this is because Venetians are a suspiciously watchful race, but in fact standing helps the oarsmen to manoeuvre through Venice's treacherous mudflats. They use their oars like punting poles in the shallower canals. Only two canals are too shallow: near La Fenice and near San Stae.

Gondolas have absolute right-of-way in Venice. Should you see another vessel accidentally strike a gondola, be prepared to witness a most humble and abject apology.

GONDOLIERS CAN BECOME BAD-TEMPERED DURING PEAK SEASON WHEN ASKED TO BE PHOTOGRAPHED BY TOURISTS WHO HAVE NO INTENTION OF TAKING A RIDE.

In the days of the Republic, gondoliers formed a homogenous and powerful group, the second most important after the nobility. Gondoliers took an oath that obliged them to keep absolute secrecy about what they had seen and heard while transporting passengers. If a gondolier was discovered by his colleagues to have revealed an amorous confidence or political intrigue, he could be drowned in the canal.

The gondola was sacrosanct as a place of pleasure or asylum, or both, as in the case of Casanova who was aided in his escape by a gondolier. With their intimate knowledge of Venice, gondoliers were often relied upon to know the location of a secret staircase leading to a lady's bedroom, and to sing out a warning of the husband's unexpected return.

Songs of the gondoliers have a special name, *barcarolle,* and a unique history. The lyrics of these songs, *Canzoni da battello,* were first published in 1753, followed soon after by an English translation that was as popular during the Grand Tour as Murano glass trinkets are today.

From the 15th century lyrical poetry flourished in Venice, especially that of Leonardo Giustinian, a poet, musician and statesman born to a noble family. His poetry was popular among gondoliers who would sing stanzas to each other in passing and then reply from one gondola to the next; then six or twelve would follow each other exchanging stanzas as long as memory and distance (and echo) would allow.

The songs themselves often followed one of three themes:

Happy lover: *I'm totally happy in sunshine or in rain, everything is love.*

Naughty lover: *I have never been weaned, I'll never tire of your breasts.*

Desolate goodbye: *Farewell my love, I am dying because I must leave you.*

It is easy to imagine how the passionate songs of the gondoliers could have influenced the beginnings of opera, first performed publicly in Venice in 1637.

Venetian Air
Thomas Moore (1779-1852)

Row gently here, my gondolier;
so softly wake the tide,
That not an ear on earth may hear,
but hers to whom we glide.
Had Heaven but tongues to speak,
as well as starry eyes to see,
Oh! think what tales 'twould have
to tell of wandering youths
            like me!

Now rest thee here, my gondolier;
hush, hush, for up I go,
To climb yon light balcony's height,
while thou keep'st watch below.
Ah! did we take for Heaven above
but half such pains as we,
Take day and night for woman's
love, what angels we should
            be!

SAN MARCO

BASILICA SAN MARCO

San Marco glitters like a jewel in the heart of Venice. It is here that you can fully appreciate the splendour that was *La Serenissima*.

The centre of San Marco is the *Piazza*, a good navigational base from which to begin your explorations of Venice. Many key sights are in the vicinity and visitors will find expensive designer shops and boutiques in the surrounding streets and campos. If the crowds become too much, take a break in the *Ex Giardini Reale* or find refuge in the *Museo Correr*. There isn't enough time to see everything in one go; choose your sights carefully and make sure to visit other parts of Venice.

Piazza San Marco
Venice's most famous
public square
Basilica San Marco
extraordinary mosaics
Doge's Palace the
splendour of the Republic
• the Secret Itinerary tour
Museo Correr museum
of Venetian culture
• the Bellini room
Campanile
tallest bell tower in Venice
Museo Fortuny
1920's fashion museum

Ex Giardini Reale
A garden tucked away behind
Piazza San Marco near the
water.

restaurants p.224
shopping p.256
nightlife p.227

**Did you
know that..?**
Every year on
April 25th the doge
would eat a soup of
rice and peas called
risi i bisi.

Campo San Stefano
charming cafés and a
temporary market during
Carnevale.

SAN MARCO

45

Piazza San Marco (St Mark's Square)

vaporetto San Marco Villaresso or San Zaccaria
map 10, F2

Piazza San Marco has been the centre of Venetian pomp and ceremony for over a thousand years and it is still the most popular sight in Venice. Early mornings and late afternoons are the best time to visit for those wishing to avoid crowds.

In the 12th century, Doge Sebastiano Ziani requisitioned the land to build the Piazza. Between the years 1500-1600, the Piazza and the adjoining *Piazzeta* assumed their definitive form. The Piazza is bordered on three sides by galleries and government buildings, and on the fourth side by Basilica San Marco and the Palazzo Ducale (Doge's Palace). The lagoon here is known as the *Bacino San Marco*.

The south building is named the *Procuratie Nuove* and the west, *Ala Napoleonica*, so called because Napoleon demolished a Renaissance church to build a grand ballroom. These two buildings contain the *Museo Correr*, the entrance to which is found at the north end of Ala Napoleonica. This is also the entrance to the *Museo Archeologico* and the *Biblioteca Marciana*. On the north side of the Piazza is the *Procuratie Vecchie* and the *Torre dell'Orologio*, the clock tower that has reopened after a fifteen-year restoration. The *Campanile* (bell tower) is Venice's tallest structure.

Caffè Florian, under the arcades on the south side, has been an institution in Venice since 1720. This is where Casanova, Byron and Goethe all sipped the most expensive coffee to be found in Venice. One evening, during the Austrian occupation, Wagner and his friends were dining at the Florian whilst listening to his overtures being played by an orchestra; not one single Venetian in the Piazza applauded his music.

At *Carnevale*, the Piazza becomes the setting for a masked parade. It is the place to walk and display one's costume and has been known to attract over 100,000 people.

In the Piazzetta, guarding the entrance to the city, are two tall granite columns; the winged Lion of St Mark crowns the eastern column. This three-ton bronze was restored by the British Museum in London and returned with great ceremony in 1990.

Standing on the western column is Theodore, a Byzantine saint. Theodore was the patron saint of Venice before being superseded by the arrival of the relics of St Mark. That Theodore and Mark continue to stand together is a symbol of the Venetian relationship with both western and eastern forms of Christianity, the Roman and the Byzantine.

Theodore

Venice's first patron saint Prince Theodore Shatebi was born in 281 in Achaera, a port on the Black Sea. Baptised at the age of 15 and filled with the Holy Spirit, he became famous for his faith and his bold courage in battles. He fought and defeated the Persians, was proclaimed *Hero of the Roman Empire* by the Emperor Diocletian, and appointed ruler of the city of Otichos.

A demon-possessed dragon (depicted in statues as a crocodile) lived in the nearby mountains. The fearful populace were sacrificing their children to appease the beast. A Christian widow, who had been called upon to give her own two children, wept and prayed to God. She heard a voice say: *'Fear not, Theodore will save your children.'* With the help of the Archangel Michael, Theodore fought and killed the dragon. Later his piety and devotion became too much for his superiors; he was beheaded and martyred in 313.

Mark

Two Venetian merchants were visiting Alexandria in 828 and overheard a few local toughs threatening to destroy the tomb of Mark the Evangelist, located in a nearby church. The merchants decided to steal the bones and take them to Venice. Aided by the churchwarden, the apostle's mummified body was removed and substituted with bones from a nearby grave. To evade Muslim customs inspectors, the relics were boarded on ship hidden in the belly of a pig, unclean for a Muslim to touch. A storm blew up during the crossing: the ship was being tossed against treacherous rocks when the spirit of St Mark appeared. The vision led the awestruck sailors through the rocks and safely homewards.

Venice claimed St Mark as her patron saint and adopted the winged lion as her symbol. The lion is often seen holding a book displaying a greeting in Latin, saying: *'Peace be unto you, Mark my Evangelist.'*

Basilica San Marco

vaporetto San Marco Vallaresso
map 10, G2
09.45-16.30 daily, Nov-Mar
09.45-16.00 daily, April-Sept
14.00-16.00 festivals and holidays
mass said nine times per day
admission free, restricted during
mass.
Mosaics are lit:
11.30-12.30 weekdays
14.00-16.00 Sundays and holidays

Museo della Basilica (also known
as the Museo Marciano) and the
Loggia on the facade
10.00-16.00 daily
admission charge

Pala d'Oro & Treasury
09.45-16.45 daily, Nov-Mar
09.45-17.45 daily, April-Sept
14.00-16.00 festivals and holidays
separate admission charges

Entry to Crypt, Baptistery, Capella Zen by appointment only.

The interior of the Basilica lies in perpetual twilight,
except during the hours when the mosaics are lit. It
can be disorientating to enter the church from bright
sunshine. Visitors are herded through a portion of the
church on a designated route; a walk down the carpeted
path takes a mere ten minutes. Independent exploration
is not encouraged.

As the light changes throughout the day, it will reveal
some mosaics and hide others. Most of the windows have
been covered to make more room for additional mosaics.
Currently, the only source of natural light is a ring of
windows around the base of each of the five domes, and
three windows behind the altar.

It is worth planning to arrive when the mosaics are lit.
The effect is stunning: every available inch of wall space
is encrusted with mosaics, some of them brought from
Byzantium, but most completed by Venetian artists.

The plan of the Basilica is based on the 6th century
Justinian Church of the Holy Apostles in Constantinople.
The Basilica is a fusion of Byzantine, Gothic and
Renaissance restoration and improvement projects
carried out under the watchful eye of the *Proto* (church
architect). Venice's best architects served as Proto:
Bergamo Bon, Jacobo Sansovino, and Baldassare

Longhena. The Basilica is the third church to stand on the site: the first was built in the 9th century and was destroyed by fire; the second was pulled down in the 11th century to make way for a more spectacular building reflecting the escalating power of the Republic.

The five domes are Byzantine in origin. Keeping them waterproof is crucial as the cupolas beneath them house priceless mosaics. Over the centuries they have suffered during restoration. Various projects have seen the domes bound with iron hoops, raised up on drums, windows added, and in the 18th century, chains were placed around them.

The Miracle of San Marco

The first church of San Marco was consecrated in 832 to enshrine the body of St Mark, which was stolen from Alexandria. Unfortunately, two hundred years later the bones were lost during the reconstruction of the Basilica. They had been stored in a safe location known only to the Doge and the *Primercerius* (the highest ecclesiastic of San Marco) who had both died. When the day arrived for the rededication of the new church, the bones were nowhere to be found.

Three days of fasting and prayer were ordained. Then, miraculously, a surviving pillar of the old church opened of its own accord, disclosing the sarcophagus of the Saint. Witnesses claimed a beckoning hand attracted their attention. The Basilica was reconsecrated in 1094 with the bones placed in the crypt. St Mark was subsequently moved to the altar in 1835.

Relics were *de rigueur* in medieval Europe. As befitting its status, San Marco has several: drops of the Sacred Blood of Jesus Christ; a piece of the True Cross; a fragment of the skull of John the Baptist; and an arm of St Pantalon. Many other relics perished in the fire that destroyed the first church: a bone of St Philip; a hair of the Virgin; a rib of St Peter; and four of St Biagus' teeth.

Politics

The Basilica did not become the cathedral church of Venice until 1807. Until that time it was the doge's private chapel. As such, it was a political as well as a religious institution. San Pietro di Castello (p.187) was the seat of the Patriarchate of Venice and therefore held the authority of the Roman church in Venice. However, the bishops of San Pietro were considered far too subservient to Rome so the doge, along with the Senate, nominated and invested the *Primicerius* of San Marco as the head of the Venetian church. He was always a Venetian nobleman and subject only to the doge.

It was at the Basilica where the doge was presented to the city after his election. This is also where heads of state, popes, princes and ambassadors were received. Emperor Frederick Barbarossa and Pope Alexander III agreed to peace here in 1177: a lozenge in the atrium floor marks the spot just inside the entrance. This was a turning point as Venetian allegiance shifted from Byzantium to Rome.

Mosaics

The mosaics of Basilica San Marco were created over a 500-year period during the height of the Venetian Empire. Early mosaics trace the history of Venetian art and its Byzantine influence: they include references to the Orient and Islam. Later mosaics were inspired by Renaissance art, finally developing into a uniquely Venetian aesthetic.

A mosaicist drew the outline (copying a cartoon supplied by the artist) on the first layer of cement, then applied a second layer of marble dust and pebblestone lime. The whole scene was painted in colour and, while the cement was soft, the master and his men stuck in the appropriate *tesserae* (tiny, irregular and chipped fragments of jagged, coloured stones). Some were tilted in the wet cement to catch the light from a certain window.

The mosaics evolved, with human emotion and facial expressions becoming more developed over time. All of the great Venetian artists throughout the centuries, from Veneziano to Tiepolo, contributed to the mosaics in the Basilica. They saw it as their duty to Venice.

The lunette above the *Porta di Sant' Alipio* on the left side of the exterior facade depicts the *Translation of the Body of St Mark to the Basilica.* This mosaic dates from 1260 and shows the Basilica as it must have looked at the time.

Interior mosaics illustrate stories from the Bible. Inside the Basilica in the *Narthex*, or atrium, is a charming series depicting the life of Noah. Next to it, in the *Genesis Cupola*, are illustrated scenes of the *Creation of the World*, featuring Adam and Eve and Cain and Abel.

Through the Narthex and over the entrance to the main church is the *Great Arch of Paradise* mosaic, which includes the *Damnation of Evil-doers*, taken from a cartoon by Tintoretto.

The mosaics in the *Dome of the Pentecost*, (first large cupola nearest the entrance) depict stories featuring the Holy Spirit, with *Christ Orders the Apostles to Baptise* and *Apostles Baptising* dating from the 12th century. In the central cupola, the *Ascension Dome* shows *Christ in Glory Surrounded by the Nine Celestial Orders*. From the 13th century, it illustrates Christ's ascension into heaven, surrounded by angels, the 12 apostles and the Virgin.

The *St John the Baptist* cupola is above the left transept, with mosaics based on drawings by Jacobo Tintoretto, Paolo Veronese and Giuseppe Salviati. In this area the developed Venetian painting style becomes more obvious. In the third chapel of the left transept is the iconic painting *Madonna of Nicopeia*. This painting is from Constantinople where it was carried at the head of battles to inspire the soldiers to greater courage.

Jacopo Sansovino designed the baptismal font and carved the doors to the Tabernacle and Sacristy. On the Sacristy door (always locked) is a self-portrait of Sansovino with fellow artist Titian.

Pala d'Oro

Be sure to see the blinding screen of gold and precious gems behind the high altar. There may be a queue and there is a small charge but the Pala d'Oro is worth the effort. Originally from Constantinople, the gem-encrusted screen has been renewed and enriched by various doges; each addition can be dated by the architectural style of the miniature arcaded panels.

The bejewelled side faces the high alter and though the overall size may seem small, the sheer number and size of the jewels is awesome: rubies, emeralds, diamonds, amethysts and topaz; some as large as two square inches. The Pala d'Oro is so detailed, so fantastically embellished with gold and gems, that Venetian officials were able to convince Napoleon's generals it was not genuine. French soldiers worked with vandalistic fury melting down gold and silver vessels, removing precious gems and sending the booty to Paris. Had Napoleon's generals been apprised of its true value, the Pala d'Oro would no longer exist.

Treasury

The entrance to the treasury is off the right transept and through the ticket office. The treasury holds one of the world's most important collections of Byzantine art, most of it taken from Constantinople in the fourth crusade (p.183). The icons of *St Michael the Archangel* and those of the *Crucifixion* are worth seeing: they are richly gilded with gold and jewels. The galleries are full of silver gilt altarpieces and beautifully crafted candelabra. There is also a rare 10th century chalice that belonged to the Byzantine Emperor Romanos.

Galleria, Loggia dei Cavalli, Museo della Basilica

Enter through the door at the far right of the Narthex and take the stairs to the *Galleria* and the *Loggia dei Cavalli*.

The **Galleria** offers wonderful views of the inside of the Basilica and contains the Museo and the bronze horses *(Quadrigo)*. The **Loggia**, on the exterior of the Basilica, contains copies of the horses, and offers views over the Piazza.

Quadrigo

The four gilded bronze horses originate from the 2nd century AD and are attributed to Roman artists. They were so admired in ancient Rome that they decorated monuments to three different emperors before being taken to the Hippodrome in Constantinople.

Doge Dandolo secured the horses for Venice as part of the concessions after the surrender of Constantinople and the fall of the Byzantine Empire. Their triumphant arrival at San Marco in 1204 signalled the beginning of the Venetian Empire.

In 1797 Napoleon shipped the four horses to Paris, marking the end of both the Empire and the Republic. The sculptor Antonio Canova is rumoured to have negotiated their return to Venice in 1815. The horses were subsequently removed to Rome for the duration of the two World Wars.

Pala Feriale

This painted wooden altarpiece is in the second room of the Museo. It was used to cover the ornate golden jewels of the Pala d'Oro on weekdays, when it was deemed improper to view such splendour.

Painted in 1345 by Paolo Veneziano and his sons Luca and Giovanni, it represents the stories of St Mark set below icons of Christ and the Saints. Veneziano began the development of a unique Venetian style by using rich colours and animated gestures to depict the stories of the saints.

THE DOMES OF THE BASILICA

Byzantium

The roots of the Byzantine Empire go back to Constantine, on duty in Britannica in the year 306. When the Emperor Diocletian died and Rome was for the taking, Constantine marched south and, within the year, his armies had conquered the Italian peninsula. He installed himself as Emperor.

Constantine's gradual conversion to Christianity began sometime around 310, and in the year 312 he issued the Edict of Milan, a charter of toleration allowing each Roman citizen to *'choose and profess his own religion'*, thereby ending the persecution of Christians under

Diocletian. Constantine made it legal for Romans to bequeath their estates to the church and decreed that clerics should be paid, establishing the priesthood as a viable career.

A new imperial capital located in the eastern part of the Empire was needed for trading purposes. In 330 Constantine chose the ancient city of Byzantium (now modern Istanbul), located on the Bosphorus. The government of Rome was moved to the new city, renamed Constantinople. The decision had serious implications for an empire that encompassed the Danube and Euphrates rivers, Antioch and Alexandria, and included Crete, Cyprus and Jerusalem, the jewel in the crown.

When Constantine died in 337, his city was only half built. His son, Constantius, finished construction and established a senate on a par with Rome. In 381 Emperor Theodosius proclaimed Christianity the religion of the Roman Empire and named Constantinople as one of the five Patriarchates, giving it the same status as Jerusalem. Constantinople had superseded Rome, it was the new Jerusalem. After the fall of Rome and the Western Empire in 476, Byzantium became the most powerful empire in the Mediterranean.

Venice was dependent upon the Byzantine Empire for commercial and trading interests. However, by 800 many Venetians favoured an alliance with Rome over Constantinople. Venetians took sides and bloody quarrels erupted between factions: island against island, parish against parish. Peace was declared between Rome and Byzantium in 812 and Venice resumed her position of dependence on Constantinople. She had learned a valuable lesson: Venetians continued to trade with Byzantium, but also offered spiritual loyalty to Pope Leo III and to Charlemagne, the Holy Roman Emperor. Gradually, Venice would transform her position and became her own master: she would gain complete independence and aquire her own empire.

PALAZZO DUCALE, *NEXT PAGE*

Palazzo Ducale (Doge's Palace)

Piazza San Marco
vaporetto San Marco Vallaresso or San Zaccaria
041 271 5911
09.00-19.00 daily, April-Oct
09.00-17.00 daily, Nov-Mar
single admission €12, see Churches and Museums p.262 for
information about the Chorus Pass and Museum Card.
advance booking 041 520 9070
map 10, G2

The palace can be a pleasant place to visit if you arrive
early, or later in the day. Expect a lot of tour groups in
the high season. An audioguide with commentary can be
hired. Guided tours of the palace (often very good) cost
an additional €7. There are explanatory name boards in
English throughout the palace.

FOR AN INSIGHT INTO THE INNER WORKINGS OF VENETIAN
GOVERNMENT, THE SECRET ITINERARY IS HIGHLY
RECOMMENDED, BUT BOOK WELL IN ADVANCE (P.68).

The Doge's Palace was not just the residence of the doge,
it also contained the seat of government, law courts,
prisons, and offices for the civil service. This was where
all power was concentrated during the Republic. The
palace is a testament to the enormous wealth amassed by
the Venetian Empire, displaying the magnificence of La
Serenissima in its glory.

Begun in the 9th century as a fortified castle, the original
buildings were destroyed by a series of fires. The exterior
of the existing palace dates from the 14th century,
with work ongoing to the 1500s, and is a synthesis
of Romanesque, Gothic and Islamic architecture.
Displaying a combination of lightness and strength,
this truly is *Venetian Gothic*. The upper storeys are clad
in pink Verona marble and stand on columns of white
Istrian marble. The columns on the base appear too short,
but they were once taller: the level of the pavement has
been raised over the years to compensate for rising water.

The corners have interesting sculptural groups, intended to provide moral instruction: the one nearest the Basilica is *The Judgement of Solomon*, with the *Archangel Gabriel*. On the corner of the Piazzetta are *Adam and Eve* with the *Archangel Michael. The Drunkenness of Noah* is on the corner near the Ponte della Paglia, with the *Archangel Raphael and Tobias.* The Apochryphal story of *Raphael and Tobias* concerns a young boy leaving home, which resonates with Venetians, who are often forced to leave Venice in search of income. (p.149)

Beside the Basilica, and above the doorway of the *Porta della Carta,* is a figure of the Doge Foscari kneeling before the winged lion of St Mark, symbolising his stature as a servant of Venice. Once the grand entrance to the palace, today it is the exit. The entrance is found on the side facing the Riva degli Schiavoni.

The Doge

Unlike monarchs of the day, the doge did not have absolute power, but he was much more than a mere figurehead. Privy to all state secrets, he sat on all major councils and was therefore able to influence policy.

The first doge was appointed in 697, later doges were elected by a complicated balloting system. It was a dangerous job: of the first fifty, twelve were assassinated, three were exiled, four deposed and three judicially blinded, a favourite punishment of the Venetians. Doge Candiano's attempt to make the title hereditary led to rioting and the issuing of decrees to prevent nepotism.

Elected for life, the doge was always a man over 70 years of age because the Republic considered that old men were less corruptible. Since the doge was such an old man (when average life expectancy was 45 years), his time in office was short, sometimes less than two years. A doge was never allowed to travel (except on state visits) could accept no gifts but flowers or rosewater, could not visit a café or theatre, and was expected to pay for his own robes and banquets.

The government of the Republic

Enshrined in the constitution of the Republic is the belief that: *'The state is all; it is for the individual unconditionally to serve the state. No person may rise above others, no cult of personality will be tolerated'.*

Venice functioned as a police state, except that instead of worshipping power, she sought to control it and refused power to any single citizen. Should a citizen achieve greatness and garner popularity, he was at once humiliated to prevent the emergence of a powerful dictator. This also included those who won great victories at sea or in battle. A returning hero had to be humble and watch his back, or he could find himself falsely accused of any number of violations.

Initially democratic, the government of the Republic evolved over time until, by the end of the 13th century, it had become an oligarchy (rule by the elite). In 1297 a list of patrician families was compiled, effectively excluding the public from government. These members of the Venetian nobility, most of them wealthy traders, accounted for three or four per cent of the population of Venice. From this point onwards, there were never more than 1,200 to 2,000 men eligible to serve in government or be elected doge. The list was succeeded by the *Libro d'Oro* (Golden Book), a registry of births and marriages that determined any claim to membership of the elite. By 1310 the constitution and government were structured in a way that would last, more or less, until the fall of the Republic.

The *Maggior Consiglio* (Great Council) was both an electorate and legislative body, numbering some 500 members of the elite. They elected the doge, the *Minor Consiglio* (Small Council, with six members to advise the doge) and the *Senato* (Senate). The Senate elected the *Collegio dei Savi* (College of Wise Men), the *Quarantie* (three law courts comprised of 40 members) and the *Consiglio dei Dieci* (Council of Ten).

Executive power rested with the *Signoria* (Lords), comprised of the Minor Council, three heads of the Quarantie, and the doge. Legislative power was vested in the Great Council, the Senate and the College. The Council of Ten (and their offshoot, the Council of Three), held judicial power, along with the Quarantie and other officials.

Even though 97 percent of the population was excluded from government, it functioned rather well and, after three revolts in the 1300s, there were no serious uprisings. This was because the governors were also businessmen and employers, interested in policies that benefited themselves and their employees. Elected offices were not held for long periods of time, keeping the worst effects of nepotism in check, and there was an elaborate and frightening system of state security.

Procurator of San Marco

A *procurator* was responsible for the upkeep of San Marco and the administration of other government owned properties. Their offices were situated in the *Procuratie Vecchie* and later, in the *Procuratie Nuove*. Procurators were second in position only to the doge and there were never more than nine at any one time. They were elected for life from the list of noble Venetian families contained in the *Libro d'Oro*. The *Grand Chancellor* and the doge were the only other Venetian officials elected for lifetime terms.

Many noble families had members that served in the government of the Republic through succeeding generations. Certain names reoccur throughout the history of Venice: there were four Dandolo doges, three Tiepolo, seven Contarini, three Morosini, three Donà, three Loredan, two Falier and one Faliero.

Council of Ten

The reforms of 1297 caused unrest among the middle and lower classes who were now formally excluded from government. Merchants and tradesmen were suffering in an economic crisis caused by the war against Genoa. The people of Venice were also angry at the insolent and provocative attitude of the younger members of the aristocratic families. The discontent led to three attempted rebellions: the first, in 1300, led by Marin Bocconio, was immediately suppressed; the second, in 1310, was led by the Tiepolo and Querini families, who were outnumbered by the Doge's soldiers; the third, in 1355, was led by Faliero, a doge himself.

Faced with unrest, the government took precautions. In 1310, they revived the Council of Ten to deal with insurrection, and oversee courts and state police. Created a few years previously for exceptional circumstances, it was now granted sweeping powers and authority for the purpose of exposing plots, preventing acts of terrorism and maintaining peace.

The Council of Ten constituted a supreme criminal tribunal whose harsh and feared methods gradually dissipated the wise distribution of work and power that had existed among various governing bodies. They began to interfere in other departments and abused their ever-increasing powers. Soon the *Dieci*, as they were known, became the highest ranking state body with almost unlimited authority.

Venetians had a saying: '*Under the Ten, torture, under the Three, death*'. The Council of Ten appointed the Council of Three. Initially created as a constitutional court responsible for checking the legality of decisions taken by the Senate, the Great Council and other legal bodies, the Council of Three evolved into a secret body with supreme power over life and death.

Inside the palace

From the ticket office, a tour begins with the **Museo dell'Opera**, with models of the palace and original capitals from the columns of the lower and upper loggias. At the end of the courtyard opposite the ticket office is the **Scala dei Giganti**, a 15th century staircase by Antonio Rizzo, with sculptures of *Neptune* and *Mars* carved by Sansovino in 1566.

A tour of the upper rooms begins with a climb up the **Scala dei Censori** to the loggia and then up to the *primo piano nobile* and the chamber of the Great Council. On this floor are the doge's apartments, special exhibition galleries, and access to the Bridge of Sighs .

The main staircase, Sansovino's **Scala d'Oro**, leads up to the *secondo piano nobile*, and the Chamber of the Council of Ten. In many of the allegorical paintings throughout the Palace, Venice is depicted as a buxom blonde.

The **Atrio Quadrato**, with a ceiling painting of *Justice* by Tintoretto, leads into the first of the great public spaces, the **Sala delle Quattro Porto**. After 1574, this room was where ambassadors would await their summons to meet with the doge and other officials. The next room, the **Anticollegio**, is well regarded, with four Tintorettos hanging on the door walls, including *Bacchus and Ariadne Crowned by Venus*. Look for Veronese's *Rape of Europa*.

The **Sala del Collegio** was the meeting place of the *Collegio*. A full Collegio included the Signoria and 16 members of the Collegio dei Savi. This was the cabinet of Venetian politics, where major policy decisions were taken. Veronese painted the picture over the throne, *Doge Sebastiano Venier Thanking Christ for Victory at Lepanto*.

Next door, the **Sala del Senato** was the meeting place of the Senate. Over the years they numbered from 60 to 300 members. Paintings are by Tintoretto and his pupils.

Sala del Consiglio dei Dieci (Chamber of The Council of Ten) This was the office of state security. There is a cycle of allegorical paintings depicting the functions of the councillors. The central ceiling painting is a copy of a Veronese which now resides in the Louvre.

Sala del Maggior Consiglio (Chamber of the Great Council)

Meetings of the Great Council were held in this chamber on Sundays. Members were called to meetings by the ringing of the bell of San Marco.

At the time of the Republic it was the largest room in Europe, able to accomodate the burgeoning number of council members, far exceeding 500, who were later able to buy their way into the nobility.

The seating plan was unusual. Members were seated in two rows, back-to-back. Armed guards insured that no weapons were allowed into the chamber, the doors were closed, and all discussions were kept secret.

In the frieze just below the ceiling are portraits of the first 76 doges. One is painted black with an inscription instead of a portrait. This is the memorial to doge Marin Faliero (1354-1355). Doge Faliero was accused of plotting to take control of the Republic. The conspiracy was discovered and Faliero executed. The inscription translates: *This is the place of Marin Faliero, beheaded for his crimes'*.

At one end of the chamber is *Paradiso*, the longest canvas painting in the world at 25 metres. Paolo Veronese won the competition for the commission of the painting but then died; the commission went to Jacopo Tintoretto who completed it with the aid of his son, Domenico.

From the Chamber of the Great Council, follow a trail of corridors leading to Venice's second most famous bridge: the **Ponte dei Sospiri** (Bridge of Sighs). Completed in 1614, it takes its name from the sound made by prisoners as they had a last look at freedom before being led to the *Prigioni Nuove* (New Prisons) across the canal. It is possible to visit the prisons. Exit the Doge's Palace from the Porta Della Carta.

Itinerari Segreti (Secret Itinerary)

Doge's Palace
041 271 5911
Must be booked one week in advance, longer during busy times
English language tour: two per morning
€16

Tickets are only good for the tour and admission to the Doge's Palace. They do not include admission to the other museums of San Marco. Pick up your tickets from the ticket office in the Doge's Palace.

Well worth the effort, this 90 minute guided tour takes you through the various rooms of the palace that are not open to the public. This fascinating tour provides an insight into the inner workings of Venetian government and an account of Casanova's escape from prison. It also includes a visit to the torture chamber.

First stop on the itinerary is the **Bocche di Leone** (Lion's Mouth), a letterbox for denunciations. Every crime had its own Bocche di Leone: there were 72 boxes placed throughout Venice. Polluting water was a serious crime, and there were other boxes concerned with reporting health matters. One box was for reporting ostentatious displays of wealth: it was a principle of Venetian society to respect poor people and not indulge in public display of luxuries. There was also a box for reporting communications with foreigners, as Venetians could only associate with them for the purposes of commercial activities.

The denunciations were opened and read by the fearsome Council of Ten. Initially, denunciations were anonymous but after discoveries of abuse, the law was changed. Letters had to be signed and if it was found that the accusation was false, then the accuser would face charges.

During *Carnevale*, nobles had to be very careful not to mistakenly engage in conversation with a masked individual who was foreign. If by accident, a nobleman was seen speaking to a foreigner for a non-commercial purpose, he was best to confess it at once to the Council of Ten rather than risk a denunciation.

The secret itinerary really begins at the top of the **Scala d'Oro**, but instead of turning right and proceeding to the public state rooms, you pass through a door on the left. The scale of grandeur is immediately reduced. You are no longer in areas intended for public display: this is where the business of the Republic was conducted.

You enter a number of small wood-lined rooms that served as offices for magistrates. There were 300 magistrates in Venice, governing every area of commercial and civic life. To avoid corruption they presided for only three months, while secretaries (like today's civil servants) remained constant with their office.

There is a nautical theme in the decoration of these rooms: as you enter the **Hall of the Chancellery**, you will be told that it was built to resemble the inside of a wooden ship, with swinging doors that close on their own. This is where important documents were stored. Venetians kept records of everything: at the end of the Empire there were three large warehouses full of documents.

The Great Chancellor was a supreme civil servant who came from the middle classes: he was not an aristocrat. Holding one of only three lifetime positions (the others being the doge and the procurators), he was chief administrator with responsibility for all documents and archives. For this he was paid a substantial salary in the region of 3,500 ducats (equivalent to €500,000). There was a risk: if he lost a document he had three days to find it or face the death penalty. It was possible to buy the title of Great Chancellor because during wartime the state needed money and would sell titles as a way of paying for imperial ambitions.

Next you proceed to the **torture chamber**. The favoured torture was to tie the arms behind a prisoner's back and then, using a system of hoist and pulley, lift him above the floor, suspended by his wrists. Prisoners were forced to participate in another's torture in the hope that they might recant and confess before undergoing their own physical torment. Torture took place at night so visitors to the palace would not hear screaming. Three *Signori della notte dei criminali* (judges of the night of the criminals) sat and questioned the accused.

It all sounds very gruesome but in reality, Venice was a relatively progressive state during medieval and Renaissance times. Prisoners had a right to a lawyer, had to be brought to trial within a month, could not be arrested without evidence, and search warrants were issued by committee. Torture was actually abolished in the early 1700s. It was mostly the fear of denunciation and dreadful punishment that kept Venetians in line during the Republic.

There were two kinds of prisons in the Doge's palace: the **Piombi** and the **Pozzi**. From the word 'lead', because the cells were lead-lined, the Piombi are above the offices and torture chambers. These were the prisons for nobility and those whose crimes were of a less serious nature. The lead in the Piombi was insulation from the damp. The *Pozzi* (or 'wells') are found in the lower part of the palace. Dank, dark and cold, these were for those who had committed murder or given away a state secret.

The tour continues with a visit to Casanova's cell in the Piombi and the story of his escape. Casanova was arrested for practising alchemy, a crime against the church. While in his first cell, he managed to conceal a piece of marble and a piece of metal he found when taking his exercise on the roof. He used these to scrape a hole in the floor of his cell. Then, to his frustration, he was moved to a new cell in the attic. His priest, Father Balbi, would visit him and take messages away in the

Bible he always carried. He used the same book to bring Casanova a piece of metal. Over time, Casanova was able to cut a hole in the roof and, in 1756, both he and Father Balbi escaped over the rooftops. They managed to crawl down to a waiting gondola and disappear from Venice.

In the attic, above the **Sala del Maggior Consiglio** (Hall of the Great Council) you will see another Venetian state secret: the ceiling is suspended from the top of the palace. A remarkable achievement, given that the dimensions are 53 by 25 metres.

The tour will likely conclude with an entrance through a secret door to the **Office of the Three Inquisitors of the Nation**. This was where the most feared Council of Three pronounced death sentences. And it was here that Casanova would have landed on his first escape attempt, having scraped a hole through the floor of his cell located immediately above.

Giacomo Casanova (1725-1798)

In their own lifetime, few historical figures have earned the reputation of libertine, seducer, gambler, spy, forger, man of letters, musician, poet, slanderer, traitor, cardsharp, cheat, atheist, blasphemer and alchemist.

The symbol of Venetian decadence was born on April 2nd, on the *Calle della Commedia* in San Marco, near San Samuele. His mother Zanetta was an actress, who left her young son with his grandmother while she and her husband went to London for her theatrical debut.

As a child, Casanova suffered from constant serious nosebleeds. His grandmother, fearing for his life, called in the services of the local witch. The young boy was anointed and locked in a chest while the witch chanted over him. A vision of an angel appeared: a dream mother who kissed him and restored him to health. He was cured and forever initiated into the world of magic and the power of women's arts.

Zanetta decided on an ecclesiastical career for her son. She obtained a position for him with the Bishop of Martirano, in Calabria. But Casanova swiftly grew bored in rural Italy and went to Naples. There, he lied about his ancestry to obtain favour with aristocrats on the Grand Tour. In what was to become a pattern in his life, Casanova left quickly when threatened with exposure.

While in the service of Cardinal Acquaviva in Rome, Casanova became embroiled in a scandal. Dismissed, he returned to Venice where he fell in love with the *castrato* Bellino. Correctly suspecting that the singer was in reality a woman, he unmasked her and then proposed marriage. Casanova later cancelled the nuptials, claiming he could not endure a life of poverty.

In 1746, Casanova was supporting himself as a violin player in the Teatro San Samuele when he met Count Matteo Bragadin. He used his knowledge of alchemy to heal the Count after he had suffered a stroke. The grateful Bragadin adopted Casanova and gave him a generous allowance. For three years Casanova played the extravagant nobleman, until his sexual proclivities and his practise of alchemy brought him to the attention of the Council of Ten.

In 1750 Casanova left Venice quietly, travelled to France and became a Freemason in Lyons. The secret society was very popular at the time and he gained a network of prosperous contacts. Later joining Zanetta at the court in Dresden, he completed his first play *La Molucheid.*

Returning to Venice in 1753, he had a torrid affair with Caterina Capretta. Caterina's father immediately placed her in a nunnery on Murano. There she befriended the nun known as MM, who was having an affair with the French Ambassador. The four become a *menage a quatre,* establishing Casanova's reputation as a lover who preferred the company of nuns.

The State Inquisitors did not approve and were suspicious of his close relations with the French Ambassador. Casanova was arrested on 26th July, 1755. He was denounced as a magician and alchemist and sentenced to five years' imprisonment in the Doge's palace. (p.60)

After his daring escape he travelled across Europe, socialising in the court of Louis XV and befriending Madame Pompadour. In 1761 he met the gambling and party set in London and became infatuated with Marie Charpillon. She swindled him out of a great deal of money, causing him to flee England in March 1764. Between 1774 and 1782 Casanova is rumoured to have worked as a spy for the Venetian Inquisitors. In 1787, he attended the first performance of Mozart's *Don Giovanni* in Prague and may have helped revise the libretto.

Casanova wrote his memoirs *Histoire de ma vie* in the castle of Count Waldstein, at Dux in Bohemia, where he was hired as the curator of the library. He died there, at the age of 73. His last words were: '*I have lived as a philosopher and die as a Christian.*'

Torre dell'Orologio

Visits are only permitted as part of a guided tour. Book at the ticket desk of Museo Correr. This is also the meeting point.

English language tours: every hour, on the hour:
09.00-11.00 Mon-Wed
13.00-15.00 Thurs-Sun
tour length: 45 minutes
€12
includes Museo Correr / Museo Archeologico complex.
adults only, children under 12 and disabled not permitted

Please note the inside of the tower is cramped, and stairs between the five levels are both narrow and steep.

The tower was begun in 1496 by Mauro Coducci with additions by Pietro Lombardo, who was also building the church of Santa Maria dei Miracoli. He used the same marble in both structures. At the top is a large bronze bell with two figures who strike the hours. These were cast in 1494 and were known as Moors because of their dark patina. The clock face is in gilt and blue enamel, with the hours, phases of the moon and movement of the sun depicted in relation to the signs of the zodiac.

Venetian Time

Public clocks in Venice were divided into 24 sections instead of the usual 12. This came about because the calculation of time was based on a Byzantine system whereby 00 hour was established at sunset. The first hour of the day moved in relation to sunset and would change daily with the seasons. Therefore, assuming a 6pm sunset, an evening performance beginning at 03.00 Venetian time would actually start at 9pm.

Imagine the confused traveller arriving in Venice at noon and being told the time was 6pm! Conversion tables from the 17th century show that on 8th June one year, midnight occurred at 03.45 Venetian time but on the 8th January, midnight occurred at just past 07.00.

Venice kept to the Julian calendar, establishing 1st March as New Year's Day, until 1797, long after other regions in Europe had made 1st January the beginning of the year.

Museo Correr (Correr Museum)

Piazza San Marco
vaporetto San Marco Vallaresso
041 240 5211
09.00–19.00 daily, April-Oct; 09.00-17.00 daily, Nov-Mar
single admission €12, see p.272 for museum pass information

PIAZZA SAN MARCO

Enter from the *Ala Napoleonica* at the west side of the
Piazza. The entrance to the Correr is also the way into
the Museo Archeologico and the Biblioteca Marciana
(also called the Libreria Sansoviniana). Entrance to all
is covered by a Museum Pass or a Museum Card. The
Museo del Risorgimento is closed and there are no plans
to reopen it in the future.

The galleries in the Correr occupy the Ala Napoleonica and the adjoining *Procuratie Nuove*. Don't miss the *Museum of Venetian Life and Culture* on the first floor (ballroom level) and the *Quadreria* (painting gallery) on the second floor.

Ballroom

Napoleon noticed that there was no grand ballroom on the Piazza, so he demolished the beautiful Renaissance church of San Geminiano in order to build one suitable for his court. Rectangular in shape, it features a loggia with gilded and curved balustrades that make the room appear oval-shaped. Here is where the musicians would sit, looking down upon the dancers in the ballroom. The sculpture grouping, *Orpheus and Eurydice*, is by the 18th century artist Antonio Canova. Other Canova works on display in the rooms leading off the ballroom include a figure of *Paris*, *Daedelus & Icarus*, and *Venus Italica*. There is also a model for what Canova had planned to be a memorial to the painter Titian. The actual pyramid-shaped tomb became Canova's own, and is installed in the Frari.

Canova's genius lay in his carving, his ability to make marble appear as soft as skin. The pieces displayed here are all in gypsum, the second stage of the creative process, preparatory to the actual carving of the precious stone or marble. The pin marks on the *Paris* are to enable Canova's studio assistants to transfer the sculpture accurately to marble.

Museum of Venetian Life and Culture

With a carded guide system available in four languages, the museum has some fine exhibits, in particular the maps dating from the 16th century, all hand-drawn and beautifully executed. **Room 13** displays a large map of the Arsenale, providing a rare insight into the great shipyard where the methods of galley construction were a state secret. **Room 14** has a collection of Venice city plans from the 16th and 17th centuries.

Rooms 17 and 18 are devoted to Francesco Morisini and his battles with the Turks. Considered a hero of Venice, Morosini is not so well regarded elsewhere: in 1687 his army managed to destroy the Parthenon during an attempt to liberate Greece.

Be sure to double back towards the entrance and you will pass through a series of small rooms that exhibit the social history of Venice. There are shoes and clothes, decks of cards, games, drawings and paintings of sporting competitions and festivals, all part of the Venetian social calendar.

There is a showcase of perilous 18-inch platform shoes worn in the 15th and 16th centuries called *ciapine*. These served a twin function for the wearer: keeping the bottom of the costume dry and eliminating the necessity for a trailing hem. Very fashionable at the time, these went against Venetian sumptuary laws which forbade excessive displays of wealth (laws which resulted in all nobles dressing constantly in black).

There are also paintings of *forze d'ercole* (labours of Hercules). This was a test of balance where several men would form the basis of a pyramid and, using a system of planks and bodies, create a human pyramid several stories high.

A more dangerous Venetian game was *guerra dei pugni* (war of fists), pitched battles fought between the *Castellani* and the *Niccoletti* usually on the Ponte dei Pugni in Dorsoduro. The object of the game was to clear the bridge by forcing their opponents into the canal. This game often resulted in many deaths by drowning and was outlawed in the 1700s.

The staircase off **Room 14** leads up to the picture gallery and a temporary exhibit area, formerly the home of the now closed Museo Risorgimento. Follow the signs from Room 17 to find the Museo Archeologico and Biblioteca Marciana.

Quadreria

Room 25 is devoted to Paolo Veneziano and other Venetian painters of the 14th century. His *St John the Baptist* begins the movement away from Byzantine iconic influences and towards a uniquely Venetian style of painting. Also see Maestro dell'Arengio's *Madonna with St Paul.*

Cosme Tura's *Pieta* (1468) is in **Room 30**. From Ferrara, Tura combined elements of northern European art with the realism of Piero della Francesca and the emotive sculptures of Donatello. This is a timeless work: modern surrealists such as Salvador Dali and Rene Magritte were influenced by Tura.

Adoration of the Magi, by Pieter Bruegel the Younger, is in **Room 33**. There is also a Lucas Cranach painting *The Resurrection.*

In **Room 34** see the powerful *Pieta withThree Angels* (1475) by Antonello da Messina, a Sicilian painter who brought Florentine ideas of perspective to Venice and introduced the Flemish technique for painting in oil. **Room 35** is devoted to 16th century Flemish painters.

Room 36 exhibits work of the Bellini family: Jacopo the father, the older son Gentile, and Giovanni, the youngest son. There was an astonishing depth of creativity in the family: here is Jacopo's *Crucifixion,* Giovanni's *Madonna and Child* and *Dead Christ supported by Two Angels* and Gentile's *Portrait of Doge Giovanni Mocenigo.* This portrait of the doge, in profile and wearing the distinctive *zogia* hat, is widely reproduced and has the immediacy of a modern image.

Room 38 contains one of Vittore Carpaccio's (1460-1525) most celebrated paintings *Two Venetian Noblewomen,* better known as *The Courtesans. Portrait of a Young Man in a Red Hat* in the next room, was once credited to Carpaccio but is now attributed to an unknown painter from Ferrara.

Biblioteca Marciana
(also known as Libreria Sansoviniana)

Piazzetta San Marco, access from Museo Correr

This was the national library of the Venetian Republic, home to many secret documents.

IF YOU WOULD LIKE TO SPEND A DAY READING UNDER SKYLIGHT, REQUEST A DAY PASS AS A RESEARCHER OR STUDENT (NOT AS A TOURIST) AND BE PREPARED TO LEAVE YOUR PASSPORT AT THE ENTRANCE.

The library was established when Cardinal Bessarione, papal legate to Venice, donated his literary collection to the Republic in 1468. Jacopo Sansovino was commissioned to design a great building to house the library. Work began in 1536 and building continued for nine years until Sansovino was committed to the Doge's Palace prisons following the collapse of the vault of the inner chamber. The architect was released but had to finance the rebuilding of what had been ruined. Vincenzo Scamozzi took over as architect in 1583 and completed the building in 1588.

The vaulted ceiling over the grand staircase leading to the library is richly decorated with paintings by Giovanni Battista and Battista il Moro. There are bas-reliefs by Alessandro Vittoria. The paintings and sculpture depict man's power to rise above matter (the planets and the elements) and attain wisdom (at the top of the first flight of stairs) through the exercise of virtues (the second flight of steps). On the first floor is a beautifully hand-drawn map from 1500, *View of Venice* by Jacopo dei Barbari.

On the ceiling of the entrance hall to the reading room is *Divine Wisdom* by Titian. Inside the large Salone are 21 canvases set in a wood-coffered ceiling. Seven artists were chosen by Sansovino and Titian to paint from twin themes of Greek mythology and the virtues of learning. *Song, Music, Honour* are by Paolo Veronese, as are the paintings of *Plato* and *Aristotle* on the side walls.

Jacopo Sansovino (1468-1570)

Jacopo Tatti, called Il Sansovino, was born in Florence. He studied sculpture in Rome but fled to Venice when the Lutherans sacked the Vatican in 1527. While in Rome Sansovino met Michelangelo, Raphael, Bramante, and Andrea del Sarto. His prowess as a sculptor led Lorenzo Lotto to declare that Sansovino was second only to Michelangelo.

Sansovino was invited to stay by the Signoria, and a mere two years later was appointed as *Proto of the Procuratori of San Marco*, architect to the Basilica. It was the highest appointment in the Republic for an architect and a major achievement for a non-Venetian.

The Proto was responsible for the Basilica and the Piazza, a demanding job that paid well at 80 ducats a year with an apartment in Piazza San Marco. Sansovino's responsibilities included acting as architect for all new building, costing any and all repairs, obtaining approvals of the Procuratie, hiring and supervising the workforce, and licensing and policing the traders doing business in the Piazza.

Handsome and well-dressed, Sansovino was a ladies man. He kept his figure by eating sparingly and would often confine his meals to three cucumbers and a lemon. He was a prodigious worker who kept the Basilica from falling into ruin for over 40 years: supporting the foundations, inserting tie-beams, erecting buttresses and binding the church with heavy bands of iron.

He also built the Procuratie Nuove and the Library, which he crowned with sculptures of classical mythological figures. Sansovino was succeeded in the post of Proto by Baldassare Longhena, architect of the Salute. His tombstone is in the anti-Baptistry in the Basilica San Marco.

Campanile

daily 09.30-16.15, Nov-Mar; 09.00-19.00 April-June and Sept-Oct
09.00-21.30, July-Aug
€6 admission

Queues for the lift to the top of the Campanile can appear long, but on a clear day the views are worth waiting for. Access is via an internal lift carrying 14 people at a time: the lift moves quickly and so does the queue. A large viewing platform at the summit provides excellent opportunities for photographs. It is a good way to see how Venice is situated in the lagoon.

The tallest bell tower in Venice stands 98.5 metres high. It was first completed in 912, with extra height added in 1156-1173. Restoration work was carried out in 1514 and the tower was made even taller. But no thought was given to strengthening the piles supporting the structure, and it finally collapsed on 14th July 1902. Fortunately there were no casualties.

During excavations, it was discovered that erosion or water damage had not affected the supporting piles; the problem occurred because they hadn't been sunk deep enough to support the height. The new tower is a structurally sound replica of the original, rebuilt in 1912 after a worldwide appeal for funds.

Only one bell survived the tower's collapse, the rest were a gift from the pope. Five bells ring out on the hour and can be heard throughout Venice. The sound can be deafening if you happen to be in the tower when they ring.

In 1609, Galileo demonstrated the wonders of the telescope to Doge Donà and the Council of Ten from the top of tower.

INSTRUMENTS ON THE SIDE OF THE CAMPANILE CONTINUOUSLY MEASURE AND RECORD TIDE LEVELS IN THE LAGOON. IF THE RED LIGHT IS ON BEWARE: AN *ACQUA ALTA* IS COMING.

Acqua Alta

Piazza San Marco has the lowest elevation in Venice. It is one of the first places to suffer *acqua alta* (high water). In 1900, Venice was flooded nine times, and by 1996 the number had risen to 99. As ocean levels rise, the 21st century will bring even more flooding. November and February are the worst months for *acque altae*, depending on the wind.

Although high water generally occurs in autumn and early winter, in the last six years it has happened in spring and as late as May. Strong tides in the Adriatic Sea are the cause and, if they are accompanied by a high wind, flooding will be worse. If it blows from the north or west the flooding won't be as serious but a southerly wind from Africa (called a *scirocco*) makes for an extreme acqua alta, with higher water levels at San Marco.

Sirens go off about two hours before an extreme high tide to warn inhabitants and give them time to raise any items that might be damaged by water. An acqua alta will last for two or three hours.

Duck boards appear in Piazza San Marco and other areas of Venice, permitting access to waterbus stops and the most frequented parts of the city. Remember that the boards are not a tourist attraction, they enable people to get to and from work. Traffic wardens can fine you for holding up the traffic to take snapshots.

IF YOU ARE IN THE CITY DURING HIGH WATER, YOU CAN BUY PLASTIC PULL-ON BAGS TO COVER YOUR SHOES. ON SALE AT KIOSKS AROUND VENICE, THEY CAN BE TIED ABOVE OR BELOW THE KNEE.

Alternatively, pay a visit to the Palazzo Ducale or the Accademia to spend a few hours until the water recedes. Unfortunately, there is no way of predicting when these high tides will take place.

Museo Fortuny

Palazzo Pesaro, Campo San Benedetto 3780
vaporetto Sant'Angelo
041 520 0995
10.00-18.00 daily, closed Monday
€4; map 9, B1

Fortuny's dresses, paintings, photographs and theatre designs are on display in the museum, which has been restored. It is advisable to check ahead before visiting.

Mariano Fortuny y Madrazo (1871-1949)

Fortuny or Don Mariano (his preferred name) was born in Granada to wealthy parents. His mother endowed Madrid's Prado Museum with her family's collection. Both his father and grandfather were celebrated artists. After his father died, the family moved to Paris where Fortuny studied painting, drawing and chemistry. He was introduced into Parisian society. His mother purchased the Palazzo Pesaro and she and Fortuny moved to Venice.

After turning part of the enormous palazzo into a studio, he began painting. In 1897 Fortuny was awarded the gold medal at the Munich International Festival of Art for his painting, *The Flower Girls*. He would consistently exhibit his paintings at the Venice Biennale until his death. Fortuny was an avid photographer, taking over 10,000 photographs before turning to fashion in his early forties. Ultimately, his creative talents were best expressed in fashion and fabric design.

Fortuny kept his designs simple, minimalist, and in contrast with the period. He approached fashion like an artist, seeking inspiration from other cultures and eras. Japanese wood-cuts had been influencing Parisian artists for over half a century and Fortuny applied kimono cutting techniques to his designs. For additional inspiration he turned to classical Greek sculpture and in 1907 he produced the *Delphos* gown – a column of pleated silk with bat-wing sleeves.

Fortuny's pleated dresses were unique, no two alike. Pleats were formed by hand on wet silk, tacked in place by stitches and allowed to air-dry slowly on heated porcelain. His clinging dresses elongated the female figure and made most woman look taller and slimmer. Don Mariano was a hit: he became known for his Grecian styles and was soon designing for Isadora Duncan.

In the 1920s Fortuny's designs became more a reflection of the convergent history of Venice, featuring Persian style jackets, Moorish capes and medieval tabard gowns. Today, one can see the influence of Fortuny on the modern designer, Issey Miyake.

The model Henriette Negin was the love of Fortuny's life. His mother did not approve of the match but Don Mariano and Henriette lived together for 47 years. They did eventually marry and it was Henriette who bequeathed their home to Venice as a museum. The last Fortuny boutique closed in 1965.

Where to buy Fortuny

Trois
Campo San Maurizio 2666
041 522 2905
10.00-13.00, 16.00-19.30
Tuesday-Saturday
16.00-19.30 Monday
no credit cards
map 9, B3
Authentic Fortuny fabrics are on sale at lower prices than outside Venice. Beadwork, masks and accessories are available.

Venetia Studium
C. large XXII Marzo 2403
041 522 9281
09.30-20.00 Mon-Sat
10.30-19.30 Sunday
credit cards accepted
www.venetiastudium.com
map 9, D3
Pleated silk fabrics in the Fortuny style for dresses and luxurious printed silks and velvets for interiors. Also sells accessories.

Bevilacqua
Ponte della Canonica 7581
041 528 7581
10.00-19.30 Mon-Sat
10.00-16.30 Sunday
credit cards accepted
map 10, G1
Hand woven velvet brocades, damasks and silks in the ancient Venetian tradition.

Opera

Travellers in the 17th and 18th centuries were astonished at what they heard in Venice. There was music – not just in the concert halls and churches, but also in the streets, canals, shops and squares. According to reports, schoolgirls would walk hand in hand, singing perfect three-part harmony. Even beggars in the street could play and sing with virtuosity. Small wonder that Venice was a famous centre of music and the first home for opera.

When Claudio Monteverdi (1567-1643) arrived in 1613 to take his position as *maestro di cappella* at San Marco, he had already written *Orfeo* (1607) – the first important opera. When Europe's first public opera house, San Cassiano, opened in 1637 Monteverdi had several more of his operas performed in the theatre. Within 50 years there were six opera houses, supported by the patrician families of Venice and each producing several new operas per year.

Unlike today, opera tickets were inexpensive, so the opera was one of the few places in Venice where gentry and peasantry would mix. Nobles and workers alike were enthralled by the spectacle, and the opera was a kind of social event lasting all evening, with food and wine. Venetians attended several times a week and they were just as interested in each other as in the music. There would be a pause in the festivities for the Aria, and then everyone returned to flirting and posing.

An eyewitness account:

'Moreover, everyone wears a mask. Do not do anything wrong, because the people in the boxes, especially the upper ones, are at times so insolent they will do anything – even spit – particularly when they see someone using a small candle to read the libretto. The most insolent of all are the common folk, who stand below the boxes on all sides. They clap, whistle and yell so loudly that they drown out the singers. They pay no attention to anyone, and they call this Venetian freedom...'

La Fenice

Campo San Fantin
vaporetto: San Marco
map 9, C2
bookshop: 10.00-18.00 daily
theatre tours take place
outside of performance times.
book with Hello Venezia

Performance tickets
bookings: Hello Venezia
0039 041 2424
www.teatrolafenice.it

Tickets sell out well in advance,
however returns become
available about three weeks
before the performance date.

In 1774, the San Benedetto Theatre, Venice's leading opera house for more than 40 years, burnt to the ground. No sooner had it been rebuilt than a legal dispute broke out between the management company and the owners, the Venier family. The issue was decided in favour of the Veniers so the theatre company decided to build its own opera house on the Campo San Fantin.

Completed in 1792, it was named *La Fenice* (The Phoenix) alluding to the company's resurrection from the ashes. La Fenice was at its height in the 19th century when Rossini mounted two major productions and two operas by Vincenzo Bellini had their premiere. In December 1836 the theatre burned down again. It re-opened on the evening of 26 December 1837. Verdi's *Attila*, *Rigoletto*, *La Traviata* and *Simon Boccanegra* all premiered at La Fenice. In 1930, the Biennale initiated the International Festival of Contemporary Music, and brought Igor Stravinsky and Benjamin Britten to Venice.

La Fenice was again destroyed by fire in January 1996; two electricians, Carella and Marchetti, were convicted of arson and sentenced to seven years' imprisonment. They set the fire because they were unable to complete a rewiring project on schedule. The rest of the accused, including Massimo Cacciari, mayor of Venice, were acquitted.

By 2001 only 10 per cent of the new building had been completed. After a change in construction firms, La Fenice finally reopened in November 2004 with *La Traviata*, first performed here in 1853.

SAN POLO

& SANTA CROCE

THE GRAND CANAL, SAN POLO

Good shopping, restaurants and wine bars make San Polo popular with locals and tourists alike. Santa Croce is a quieter sestiere where many Venetians live.

The markets of Rialto are the place to buy everything you need for a great picnic, or to purchase delicacies to take home. San Polo has Venice's oldest wine bar, *Cantina Do Mori*, and its only Michelin starred restaurant, *Osteria da Fiore*. It is also possible to gorge on Tintoretto and Titian on the same day, by visiting the *Scuola di Grande San Rocco* and the *Frari*. Nearby artisan shops are exceptional. A walk through the neighbourhood of Santa Croce is a good way to get to Cannaregio. Those with children will appreciate the local friendliness of *Campo San Giacomo dell'Orio*.

Map labels

CAMPO S. MARCUOLA

Canale Grande

STRADA NOVA

CAMPO S. FELICE · STRADA NOVA · CAMPO DEI SS. APOSTOLI

Ponte d. Scalzi

Santa Croce

Ca' Pesaro · Ca' d'Oro

Stazione Ferrovie dello Stato S. Lucia

CAMPO NAZARIO SAURO · CAMPO S. GIACOMO DELL'ORIO · CAMPO S. CASSIANO · CAMPO D. PESCHERIA · **Rialto Market** · Erbaria

Piazzale Roma

Giardino Papadopoli

PIAZZALE ROMA

San Polo

Ponte Rialto

CAMPO S. POLO · RIVA DEL VIN · CAMPO S. BARTOLOMEO

S. Maria Gloriosa dei Frari · CAMPO D. FRARI · **S. Polo** · RIVA D. FERRO

Scuola di S. Rocco · CAMPO S. ROCCO · CAMPO S. TOMA

Canale Grande

Museo Fortuny · CAMPO MANIN · C. DEI FABBRI

R. TERRA D. PENSIERI

Rio del Tintor

Pal. Mocenigo

CAMPO S. MARGHERITA · **Ca' Rezzonico**

CAMPO SANT' ANGELO · CAMPO S. FANTIN · PIAZZA S. MARCO · CAMPO S. MOISE

Rialto Bridge Venice's most famous bridge

Rialto markets fruit, vegetable and fish market

The Frari
• Titian's masterpiece

Scuola Grande di San Rocco filled with paintings by Tintoretto

Ca' Pesaro modern art museum

Giardino Papadopoli
A small green space located across the Grand Canal from the train station.

restaurants p.228
shopping p.258
nightlife p.230

Artisans of San Polo
An area near the Frari where you can find some of the finest work in Venice. p.112

Erbaria
Formerly a wholesale only food market, this is where young Venetians go in the evenings to meet friends.

Did you know that..?
San Polo resident, Aldus Manitius invented *italics* and printed the first semicolon in 1494.

Ponte di Rialto (Rialto Bridge)

map 4, I4

Rialto derives from *Rivo Altus* (high bank) and was the name of the earliest settlement in the lagoon until the 12th century, when the name Venice was formally adopted. This area has always been the commercial centre of Venice and the setting for its busiest markets.

Stone bridges were built in Venice as early as the 12th century, but it was not until 1588, after the collapse, decay or sabotage of earlier wooden structures, that a solid stone bridge was designed for the Rialto. One of the early wooden crossings collapsed in 1444 under the weight of spectators at the wedding ceremony of the Marquis of Ferrara. The fourth bridge was an unreliable looking structure with a drawbridge to allow the passage of galleys with tall masts. This bridge can be seen in Carpaccio's painting, *Healing of the Madman*, at the Accademia.

By the 16th century the bridge was in a state of decay and a competition was held for the design of a new bridge to be built in stone. Michelangelo, Andrea Palladio and Jacopo Sansovino were among the eminent contenders, but it was Antonio da Ponte who won the commission. The Rialto bridge was completed in 1591 and it remained the only way of crossing the Grand Canal on foot until 1854, when the Accademia Bridge was constructed.

Rialto Markets

map 4, H3

Fruit and vegetable market	The Pescaria, fish market
07.00-13.00 Monday-Saturday	07.00-13.00 Tuesday-Saturday

Italians prefer their food fresh and Venetians are no exception. Many will do their daily shopping at the Rialto Market, a veritable bounty of fruit, vegetables, herbs and flowers. Meat and cheese can be purchased at nearby specialty shops where you can buy a bottle of Veneto wine to accompany a meal or picnic.

From San Marco, walk over the Rialto Bridge and swerve to the right for the outdoor markets. Walk past the *Erberia* (vegetable market) to find the *Pescaria*, the impressive fish market facing the Grand Canal. The larger streets and squares of the Rialto are named after the merchandise that is still sold there: *Casaria* (cheese); *Speziali* (spices); *Erberia* (vegetables); *Naranzeria* (oranges); and *Vin* (wine). Some of the narrow calles are named after bars.

San Giacomo di Rialto

In the heart of the Rialto market is a small church known as *San Giacometto* (little St James). Popular tradition has it that this is the oldest church in Venice. The original church was built by the first settlers in the lagoon in 421 to fulfil a vow made by a carpenter from Crete. The outer portico with its sloping roof is characteristic of the oldest Christian churches. However, this feature was retained by the builders when the church was rebuilt in the 11th century. Restored several times since then, it is worth a visit. There is a warmth in the building, a feeling that people have sought comfort here for a very long time. Many would have been merchants. On the rear pediment is written the following prayer, translated from Latin: *May thy Cross, oh Christ, be the salvation of this place. May the law of the merchants around this temple be fair, the weights just, the contracts honest.*

Gobbo di Rialto (The Rialto Hunchback)

There is a 16th century sculpture of a kneeling figure (the Gobbo) supporting a staircase in the Campo di Rialto, which is opposite the church and behind the fruit stalls. This was a welcome sight for minor offenders who were forced to run naked from San Marco to the Rialto – often under a rain of blows – to the sound of a jeering crowd. The statue marked the finishing line of the obstacle course.

THE RIALTO MARKETS, *NEXT PAGE*

Masters of Trade

The market culture of the Rialto goes much deeper than food. The earliest of all state banks, the *Banco Giro*, was opened in the 12th century. For the next 300 years the Rialto dominated all exchanges. The world came here to exchange currencies, invest funds, rent ships, talk diplomacy and war, learn news from the east, and buy and sell exotic fabrics and spices.

The Rialto was the principal financial exchange between East and West and the real power of the Venetian Empire – as formidable a presence as the World Bank and Wall Street are today. This is where Shylock demanded his pound of flesh from Antonio to settle a debt in Shakespeare's *The Merchant of Venice*.

Trade partnerships could be entered into for the duration of one or more voyages, and were financed by individuals or by a corporation of merchants. In the most common system of credit, *colleganze*, citizens would back a trusted merchant with a two-thirds investment in his voyage and receive three-quarters of any profit. The most complicated transaction would be concluded within a few hours.

Initially, Venetian wealth came from trade in salt, essential for the preservation of meat and other food before the invention of refrigeration. A regional salt monopoly was established by the 10th century. By 1453 the annual trade was 60,000 tons per year, worth about 10 million gold ducats (£20 million). Some 44,000 tons, made in salt-pans in Chioggia, were stored in the *Magazzini del Sale* in Dorsoduro. This was a stockpile that represented nearly 10 per cent of all of Venice's income.

Marco Polo's adventures opened up lucrative spice trade routes with the Orient. Venetians bought spices from the East, and sold textiles and metals from the West. Their trading network extended from the Alps in the north, southwards along the Italian, Dalmatian and Greek coasts, and included the whole of the eastern Mediterranean and parts of North Africa. At the height of her empire in the 15th century, it was possible to sail from Venice into the Black Sea, docking at a Venetian port at every stage of the journey.

A network of mercantile agents in foreign ports organised the sale and exchange of goods. These agents constituted a vast intelligence service and were experienced in the affairs of the Levant and Byzantium. Venetian knowledge of eastern trade routes, and of Islam, meant that the agents were consulted whenever western Europeans wanted to do business with – or plot against – people of the eastern Mediterranean.

Providing services for pilgrims and crusaders was a lucrative business in Venice. The first 'package tour' was arranged here: pilgrims paid a set fee for a journey to Jerusalem, including the sea voyage and transfer by donkey for the trip overland. Crusaders were charged top rates: first by merchants for supplying the fleet, and then by Venetian moneylenders as interest for loans.

As with all trading nations and empires, Venice profited from the sale of slaves. In the 9th century, Venetians were selling Slavic eunuchs to sultans in the East. Later, young Russian girls between the ages of 12 and 16 were brought into Venice as concubines. By the 14th century, the trade in slaves from the Caucasus was a big industry. Purchased at Black Sea ports, slaves were carried away in Venetian ships to be sold to the Muslim rulers of Egypt and North Africa. This traffic was tolerated, even though the slaves were Christians, because their orthodox beliefs were considered heretical by the papacy in Rome.

Several Rialto banks failed in 1499 when the news of Vasco da Gama's landing at the Spice Islands reached Venice. Thus the lucrative Venetian spice trade was lost to the Portuguese.

Marco Polo (1254-1324)

In the early 1200s, Asia and Europe reeled under invasions from the Tartars of Mongolia. Armies on horseback swept over the Steppes and across Eurasia as far west as Germany and Poland, commanded by a ruthless and gifted overlord known as Ghengis, the first Great Khan. At his death in 1227, his territory reached westward into Poland, north to Russia, south to the Crimea and east to Persia and China. The kingdom was divided amongst his grandsons: Mangu Khan became Great Khan, Hulagu Khan ruled Persia and another brother, Kublai Khan, ruled China.

The port of Sudak, on the Black Sea, had a colony of Venetians. Two brothers, Niccolò and Maffeo Polo, owned a house there. In 1260 they journeyed overland across the Steppes to the court of Barka Khan, brother of Hulagu, who met them with great pomp and ceremony. They were the first Venetian merchants to establish commercial connections with the Tartars.

Barka granted them trading concessions for the entire Khan territory and they enjoyed 12 months of lucrative business. When war broke out between Barka and Hulagu, the Polos were prevented from returning to Venice and took refuge in the trade centre of Bukhara.

After being stranded for three years, the brothers were offered safe passage eastwards to the court of Kublai, who was now the Great Khan. They crossed the Gobi desert and travelled through China, south of the Great Wall, to Peking. Kublai was very interested in religion and wanted to learn all about Christianity; the Polo brothers were the first Latin Christians he had ever met. He kept them answering questions for more than a year.

When Kublai finally granted them leave to return to Venice, it was to escort a Tartar ambassador to meet with the Pope. The Great Khan had determined that this was the best way to establish relations with Europe. If all went well, he would open the doors of China to the West, and to Christianity. The Polo brothers would emerge as the greatest missionaries who had ever lived. The journey home took three years, and just after their arrival in Venice the Pope died, with no one to succeed him for two years. The brothers waited for his successor, and Niccolò's son, Marco, heard of their adventures.

Marco Polo was born in Cannaregio near the Rialto. His mother died in childbirth and he was raised by the extended family. At the age of 17 he joined his father and his uncle on their journey back to the court of Kublai Khan. They travelled for more than three years by horseback through some of the world's most rugged terrain, including the Pamir Mountains and the Gobi desert – trekking through Islamic lands that few European Christians had seen.

Upon their arrival in Cathay, Kublai Khan appointed the Polos as military advisors to his court. Marco was sent across China and India with instructions to report back on the customs, trade and defence capabilities he encountered. The Great Khan held the Polo family in such esteem that he would not let them return home. It was only when Kublai was close to death that he let Marco leave China to escort a Mongol princess on a wedding voyage to Persia.

After returning from his travels in 1295, Marco Polo lived in the Rialto in two little courtyards: *Calle del Milione, Corte 1* and *Corte 2*. Venetians nicknamed him *Il Milione*, 'of the million lies', because they did not believe the claims of his book, *Description of the World.*

Taken prisoner in the trade wars between Venice and Genoa, Marco had relayed his adventures to his cellmate who was a writer. Credible or not, the book was a bestseller, and the adventures of the Polos opened up trade routes that would increase Venetian wealth for over four centuries.

FRARI ALTAR

Santa Maria Gloriosa dei Frari (Frari Church)

Campo dei Frari
041 275 0462
vaporetto San Toma
09.00-17.30 Monday-Saturday, 13.00-18.00 Sundays and holidays
closed Christmas and New Year's Day
admission charge unless attending mass chorus pass
map 3, D5

The church belongs to the Lesser Friars of the Franciscan order known as *Frari*, who came to Venice in 1250. Doge Jacopo Tiepolo gave them the campo to build a church. Completed in 1338, it originally faced the opposite direction. Two years later, the idea of building a bigger, more imposing church took hold and work began. It took more than a century to complete the new church.

The Franciscans and the Dominicans were both *mendicant orders*, meaning that they were dependent on alms for their survival. They needed big churches that could accomodate large, alms-giving congregations. The two orders were competitive and so the construction of the huge Dominican church in Castello, Santi Giovanni e Paolo, may have generated a building frenzy amongst the Franciscan Friars of San Polo. The Frari is similar in size and construction to Santi Giovanni e Paolo. Both churches have the distinction of containing monuments to the heroes and rulers of Venice.

In addition to magnificient altarpieces by Titian, the Frari has works by Donatello, Bartolomeo Bon, Jacobo Sansovino, Giovanni Bellini, Bartolomeo Vivarini and Antonio Canova.

The Titian altarpiece *Assumption of the Virgin* is spectacular. Outside of mass, visitors are given ample time to linger in one of the pews and appreciate the masterpiece. Clad in scarlet and blue, the Madonna is lifted heavenward by winged cherubs towards the loving face of God; while the Apostles gather below in various attitudes of amazement. The Friars expressed shock and dismay at the roughness of the apostles when the altarpiece was unveiled on 18th May 1518. Titian ignored their requests for modifications to the painting.

In a small Florentine chapel next to the altar stands the powerful carving of *St John the Baptist* by Donatello. The Baptist's wild-eyed expression, straggling hair and tattered wool garment was probably imbued with much of the artist's own personality. Donatello was known for refusing to wear fine clothes; his friend Masaccio portrayed the artist as a hobo in his fresco cycle of *St Peter*, found in the Brancacci Chapel in Florence.

In the sacristy to the far right of the altar is the triptych *The Virgin and Child with Saints Nicholas, Peter, Mark and Benedict* by Giovanni Bellini. Giovanni was at the height of his fame when he completed the work in 1488. The frame is original, designed by Bellini and carved by Jacopo da Faenza.

The ornately carved Friars' choir, said to be the most beautiful in the world, is the only one located in the centre of a church nave. It was carved in the Venetian

Gothic style under the direction of Pietro Lombardo, and completed in 1475. Within each stall is a panel representing a saint. There are 124 in all.

To the left of the choir is Titian's *Madonna di Ca' Pesaro,* which depicts the Pesaro family paying tribute to the Virgin Mary. Titian spent many years wrestling with the painting. To compensate for the location of an altar on the left aisle of the Frari, and the problem of a diagonal view, Titian placed the Virgin to the right of centre, with saints as active participants in the scene. The painting was considered audacious by Titian's contemporaries. Titian also broke with convention by painting Lunardo Pesaro, on the lower right, looking directly at the viewer instead of venerating the Madonna. Titian's wife was the model for the Madonna.

A gigantic carved monument dedicated to Doge Nicolo Tron dominates the left side aisle of the church. Tron's wealth exceeded his achievements as a doge because he only held the position for two years. Antonio Rizzo Veronese supervised the carving.

The white marble pyramid, near the entrance of the church, is the tomb of Antonio Canova, who died in 1822. During Canova's lifetime, secret societies were popular and numerous in Venice. Napoleon used the Freemasons to gather information about Venice before his invasion, and he continued to do so during the occupation. Masonic symbolism is very obvious in this sculpture. A gypsum model is found in the Correr Museum (p.76). Designed by Canova as a monument to Titian, it became instead a model for his own tomb.

Across the aisle is a monument to Titian, completed in 1853 by Canova's students. Titian negotiated a special concession to be buried here before dying of plague in 1576. The monument rests upon his tomb.

Claudio Monteverdi, composer and inventor of opera, chapel master at San Marco, died in 1643 and is also buried in the church.

THE PESARO ALTARPIECE

Titian (1490-1576)

Tiziano Vecellio, nicknamed Titian, was born in Pieve Di Cadore in the Dolomites. At the age of ten he was sent to Venice to apprentice as a painter. His first position was with Gentile Bellini, followed by a stint with Bellini's brother Giovanni. He then joined the studio of Giorgio da Castelfranco, better known as Giorgione, with whom he painted frescoes on the exterior of the Fondaco dei Tedeschi. Giorgione died of plague in 1510, Giovanni Bellini in 1516. Titian was named official painter to the Republic of Venice at the age of 26. By his mid-thirties Titian had surpassed his masters to establish his own distinctive style. He not only dominated Venetian art, but influenced the whole course of European painting.

Titian was a contemporary of Leonardo da Vinci, Michelangelo and Raphael. In 1545, while the artist was in Rome painting portraits of the Pope and his family, Michelangelo visited him and later commented: *'It was a pity that in Venice they did not learn to draw properly right from the start.'* The battle lines were drawn: Tuscan draughtsmanship versus Venetian colour.

Venetian painters considered drawing as a means to establish the initial idea, the broad outline of the painting. Then they developed the image on the canvas. Indeed, Titian had abandoned all graphic preparation, considering it a limit on his creative imagination. After completing a rough sketch, he painted both his landscapes and his portraits directly on the canvas. When something didn't work, he merely painted over the offending figure in grey; this is apparent in *The Holy Family with Saints Catherine and John* at the Accademia.

Titian's mastery lay in his handling of paint: in mixing deeply saturated colours, especially reds, and he invented a rich colour still known as *Titian Red*. To solve his composition problems, Titian increasingly broke conventional rules and relyed on colour to achieve harmony. Titian also was the first artist to depict candlelight in a nocturnal scene in *The Martyrdom of St Lawrence*. Later, his experiments in *chiaroscuro* would greatly influence Michelangelo Merissi, known as Caravaggio.

Returning to Venice, Titian was invited to Augsburg in 1548 to paint Charles V, the Holy Roman Emperor. In Milan the same year, he did a portrait of Philip II of Spain, Charles' heir and successor. After 1552, Titian stayed in Venice, living very comfortably and surrounded by friends, including Sansovino.

Titian's wife Cecilia bore him two sons, Pomponio and Orazio. She died during the delivery of their daughter Lavinia, in 1530, shortly after modelling for the Pesaro Madonna. Titian died in the Great Plague of 1576, tragically preceded by the death of a son. Titian's final painting *Pieta* was a response to his overwhelming grief. It was painted for the Frari; an exchange for special dispensation to be buried inside the church, and is now on display at the Accademia. (p.118)

Titian in Venice

Frari
Assumption of the Virgin 1518
Pesaro Altarpiece 1519-1526

Scuola di San Rocco
The Annunciation 1526

Gallerie dell'Accademia
Raphael and Tobias 1507
Holy Family with saints 1528
St John the Baptist 1532
Presentation of the Virgin 1538
Pieta 1576

Santa Maria della Salute
St Mark Enthroned 1511
Pentecost 1540
The Sacrifice of Abraham 1545
David and Goliath 1549
Cain slaying Abel 1553

San Sebastiano
St Nicholas 1563

Doge's Palace
St. Christopher 1524

Biblioteca Marciana
Divine Wisdom 1564

San Salvatore
The Annunciation 1556
Transfiguration of Christ 1560

San Giovanni Elemosinario
St John the Almsgiver 1540

Ca' d'Oro
Venus at the Mirror 1550
Titian's frescoes

San Marziale
Raphael and Tobias 1530

Gesuiti
St Lawrence 1555

Scuola Grande di San Rocco

Campo San Rocco
vaporetto San Tomà
041 523 4864
09.00-17.30 daily, April-Oct; 10.00-16.00 daily, Nov-Mar
closed Christmas, New Year and Easter
€7 adults, €5 students
map 3, C6

Around the corner from the Frari is the largest and best preserved of Venice's six *Scuole Grande*. Those with an interest in Tintoretto will be thrilled; he painted for the Scuola from 1564-1588 and the building is full of his work.

In 1315, *San Rocco* (Saint Roche) left his comfortable home in Montpellier to work amongst plague victims in Italy. The story is that when he contracted the illness himself, a divinely inspired dog arrived, who licked his wounds clean and brought him bread, causing a miraculous cure. San Rocco returned home to be spurned by his wealthy family and died in prison at the age of 32. After his death the intervention of San Rocco was believed to cure the bubonic plague. In 1527, the Scuola's treasury filled with gifts from people seeking his protection.

The cornerstone of the Scuola Grande was laid 1515, with Bergamo Bon as the first architect. The work was continued by Scarpagnino and finally completed by Giangiacomo dei Grigi in 1560. Shortly afterwards, the Brothers of San Rocco held a competition to determine which artist would get the commission to decorate the Scuola. Tintoretto was clever: he completed the central painting of San Rocco, *St Roch in Glory,* and installed it in the ceiling of the Sala dell'Albergo before the deadline for submissions. Once the painting was actually *in situ* the Brothers acclaimed him the winner of the competition. Tintoretto later became a Brother himself.

There are three rooms to visit: the ground floor hall, the upper hall and *Sala dell'Albergo*. Entrance is via a grand ballroom with a little gift shop on the ground floor. As a suggestion, proceed immediately upstairs to the Sala dell'Albergo to see Tintoretto's *St Roch in Glory*, spend time in the grand upper hall and then return to the ground floor.

TO HELP VIEW THE CEILING PAINTINGS, USE ONE OF THE MIRRORS AVAILABLE ON THE GROUND FLOOR.

Sala dell'Albergo

The entire back wall is taken up with Tintoretto's *Crucifixion*. Tintoretto placed himself at the scene: he is the bearded man just above the man digging in the lower right foreground. On the entrance wall, to the right, is *Christ Before Pilate*, above the door is *Jesus Shown to the People*, with *Ascent to Calvary* on the left.

Upper Hall

The upper hall is sumptuous and perhaps a little overwhelming: 23 enormous paintings by Tintoretto cover the walls and ceiling. With the exception of *San Rocco* and *San Sebastiano*, opposite the altar, there are New Testament stories rendered on the walls; while the ceiling paintings show scenes from the Old Testament.

The altarpiece is Tintoretto's *The Glorification of San Rocco*. Providing an opportunity to compare the styles of the two great masters, Titian's *Annunciation* is displayed on an easel by the altar. A piece by Giambattista Tiepolo, *Abraham Visited by the Angels*, is nearby on another easel.

There are some extraordinary wood carvings in the Upper Hall. Twelve figures by Francesco Pianta occupy the wall opposite the grand staircase. Carved in the 17th century, they are allegories of ignorance, avarice, melancholy, science, theatre, music, war, painting, liberty, honour, curiosity and integrity. *Painting* is a caricature of Tintoretto with his pallets and brushes.

Ground Floor

Paintings by Tintoretto based on the New Testament.

Tintoretto (1518-1594)

Jacopo Robusti was nicknamed *Il Tintoretto* because of his father's occupation as a dyer of cloth.

Venice's most successful painter after Titian, he was happily married with eight children. A son Domenico and daughter Marietta were among his many assistants. Born in Cannaregio, he lived and died there, never travelling. The family is buried together in the Madonna dell'Orto.

Tintoretto studied briefly with Titian (some reports say as little as ten days), but the animosity between the two vastly different painters lasted throughout their careers. Titian was establishment; Tintoretto the underdog. Methodical by nature, Titian preferred to work on several pictures at the same time: leaving each painting untouched for weeks, to allow each successive coat of paint to completely dry and harden before applying the next.

In contrast, Tintoretto was a painter of action who loved writhing bodies and theatrical settings. He was spontaneous and liked to improvise, often beginning to paint on half a canvas without the least idea as to how the other half was to be filled. He rarely waited for layers to dry before continuing and, as a result, the colours in some of his early paintings are dark and muddy.

Tintoretto's avowed ambition was to combine the colouring of Titian with the design of Michelangelo. To understand complex poses, he made wax models and arranged and lit them with spotlights. Then he would paint the same figures from different angles.

Being a superb draughtsman, Tintoretto experimented with daring foreshortenings and spatial illusions. He was the predecessor of Rembrandt in expressing moods of passion and emotion by using candlelight, luminous half-shadows and semi-opaque darkness.

Tintoretto loved to portray the messiness of life, in all its gory detail, choosing to depict members of the Holy Family as real people leading ordinary lives. He included himself and his wife in the sea of foreshortened limbs in *The Last Judgement*.

When Ruskin's wife Ellie first viewed the painting in the Madonna dell'Orto, she fled from the church and later recalled: *'to see a death's head crowned with leaves gave me such a shiver that I ran out of the church and I do not intend to return.'*

There is a story that one day in the Doge's Palace, while Tintoretto was painting the *Paradise* with his usual artistic frenzy, he was approached by a couple of prelates and a senator. On seeing Tintoretto at work with such amazing rapidity, the senator was heard to remark that painters like Giambello painted slower and were more accurate. Tintoretto replied: *'That may be, but he has not so many tiresome persons around him.'*

Whatever the senator's opinions of the artist, the Doge's Palace has at least one Tintoretto in almost every public gallery; Veronese is the only other artist so well represented.

Tintoretto was a prolific painter; he hated bare walls. He was so anxious that the presbytery and walls of his parish church, the Madonna dell'Orto, should be filled that he donated his own paintings.

Because Tintoretto's work was produced almost entirely for the churches, confraternities and rulers of the Venetian state, it is usually a part of the building in which it is exhibited. Therefore the majority of the great artist's work must be viewed *in situ* in Venice.

There is a tiny museum in Tintoretto's house in Canareggio at:

Fondamenta dei Mori 3399
map 2, H4

Artisans of San Polo

Near the Frari is a cluster of streets featuring Artisan shops.

map 3-4, E5

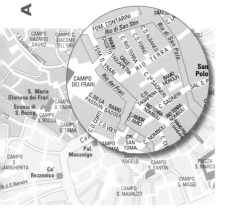

LAURA PINATO

La Zanze Venexiana
Calle 2a Saoneri 2657
041 523 7983
Everything Laura Pinato sells is hand-made. There are masks, decorative boxes, bookmarks and beautiful icon paintings. A very special little shop.

Defina Ennio
Calle Saoneri 2672
041 373 43
Impressive wood carvings, with imaginative picture frames and animal figures. Ennio also does furniture restoration.

A Mano
Rio Terrà 2616
041 715 742, phone ahead
www. amanovenezia.com
The shop has moved to San Marco (p.256) but the workshop is still here. It is open most mornings when you can see the lamps being made and you can make a purchase.

A MANO

Amadi
Calle Saoneri 2747
041 523 8089
Animals, vegetables and seashells, all beautifully made in glass. Incredible.

Gilberto Penzo
Calle Seconda dei Saoneri 2681
041 719 372
www.veniceboats.com

Lovers of model boats and ships must visit this shop. Gilberto Penzo makes accurate replicas down to the planks and nails. He uses computer scanning technology to create plans and then proceeds to a completely accurate miniature. Gilberto is reputed to be the best model boat-maker in Italy. He also sells some very nice books on gondolas, naval vessels, and Venetian boats, all well illustrated and written in Italian and English.

La Bottega dei Mascareri
Calle Saoneri 2720
041 524 2887
Ruga della Orafici 80
041 522 3857
Venetians Sergio and Massimo Boldrin keep the traditional mask-making craft alive. Watch the mask makers at work in the studio on calle Saoneri or pop into the shop near the Rialto bridge.

Franco Furlanetto
Rio Terrà dei Nomboli 2768/B
041 520 9544
08.30-13.00, 14.30-18.00 Mon-Fri
Franco provides an essential product in Venice; he makes the oars and rowlocks (fòrcole) for gondolas and other boats. Each is custom made and some are elaborately carved.

Atelier Pietro Longhi
Rio Terrà 2604/b
041 714 478
www.pietrolonghi.com
Just off the Campo dei Frari, Francesco and Anna Briggi make some of the best costumes in Venice. They offer tailor-made theatrical outfits, for sale or rental. This is the place to go if you're in Venice for Carnevale and you want a costume. Large sizes available.

FRANCESCO BRIGGI

DORSODURO

This pretty sestiere has a broad promenade where you can find fresh air and a feeling of space. A centre for students and artists, Dorsoduro has several excellent galleries, some fine restaurants and a lively nightlife.

Venetians call the eastern side of Dorsoduro *la zona Americana* because of the large numbers of American visitors.

Go to the *Salute* for the view across the canal and, if you are in a hurry, the splendid *Peggy Guggenheim Collection* and the *Accademia* can be visited on the same day.

Canals are lined with picturesque residences belonging to wealthy foreigners, but further west is where Venetians live. *Campo Santa Margherita* is the best place to meet them. If you are young or young-at-heart, this is where you should go in the evening.

SANTA MARIA DELLA SALUTE

Dorsoduro

Accademia · world's best collection of Venetian art
Ca' Rezzonico museum of 18th century Venice
Peggy Guggenheim Collection museum of modern art · very special
Santa Maria della Salute Baroque church and Venetian landmark
San Angelo Raffaele paintings of Raphael and Tobias

Zattere
Promenade with excellent views across to Giudecca. Take a walk or sit and enjoy a gelato while the sun sets.

restaurants p.234
shopping p.260
nightlife p.237

Campo Santa Margherita
A vibrant meeting place for students and locals with bars that are open late.

Did you know that..?
Cats are revered in Venice because they helped to rid the city of plague.

Gallerie dell'Accademia (Accademia Art Gallery)

vaporetto Accademia
041 522 2247
08.15-19.15 Tues-Sun, 08.15-14.00 Mon
last entrance 30 mins before closing time
€6.50
map 8, H5

The Accademia contains the largest collection of Venetian art in existence, displaying the complete spectrum of the Venetian school, which spans five centuries from the medieval Byzantine period through the Renaissance to the Baroque. The gallery is located in the former church of Santa Maria della Carita and the Scuola della Carita, founded in 1260 as one of the great Venetian schools.

The *Accademia di Belle Arti* (Academy of Fine Arts) was formed in the early 19th century when Venice was a prize being passed between the Austrians and the French. According to the Treaty of Presburg in 1805, all public palazzi and religious buildings were closed and some destroyed. This law particularly affected the scuole, who were among Venice's most generous patrons of the arts. Paintings and other art works that were rescued from destruction (and not shipped to Vienna or Paris) were placed in the church and the Scuola della Carita.

To create the gallery, the two buildings were joined. The church was completely gutted and subdivided into five large rooms. Gothic windows were walled in, a new passageway at the back of the first floor connected the buildings, and a stairway linked the foyer to the galleries. The plan of the Scuola was not drastically altered. The carved ceiling found in room 1, completed by Marco Cozzi in 1484, is the original from the Church of La Carita. The 15th century wooden ceiling in the Albergo room (24) is from the Scuola.

Many of the paintings in the galleries were created as altarpieces. They were meant to be considered uniquely, to assist the viewer in his or her spiritual journey or Christian education. And when the works were moved from their original location in churches to the relative sterility of the exhibition space, the viewer's experience of the art was inevitably affected. Looking at dozens of pictures of saints, gazing upwards at the ubiquitous Madonna, causes the paintings to lose their meaning and power.

The layout is odd and it is easy to miss some galleries. The list overleaf will provide a quick tour of some of the best paintings in the Accademia. However, to really appreciate 500 years of Venetian art, we recommend you spend a rainy day here.

TITIAN: *RAPHAEL AND TOBIAS*

Room 1

Altarpiece from the Church of Santa Chiara, Paolo Veneziano

The beginning of a Venetian story-telling style of painting is evident in this Byzantine altarpiece. A devotee of Saint Francis, this piece illustrates certain incidents in the life of Santa Chiara, a devotee of St Francis.

Room 2

Madonna on the Throne with Child, with Saints and Angels, Giovanni Bellini

Presentation of Christ in the Temple, Vittore Carpaccio

These two altarpieces, painted by rival artists, share a similarity of style. Both paintings originally graced the altars of the Church of San Giobbe in Cannaregio. The influence of the Tuscan Renaissance is visible here.

Room 5

La Tempesta, Giorgione

This famous painting is much smaller than you would imagine and is easy to miss if you are not looking for it.

Room 8

Raphael and Tobias, Titian

Titian has painted this theme more than once, but this is his most sensitive interpretation. The gallery is adjacent to the excellent bookshop and there is a bench conveniently located just opposite the painting. The story of Raphael and Tobias is on p.149.

Room 10

Christ in the House of Levi, Paolo Veronese

The painting includes portraits of Michelangelo and Titian, which are given equal positions near the ends of the table. Veronese paints himself, in the role of host, leaning against a marble pillar in front of the banquet.

Transport of the Body of Saint Mark, Tintoretto

Painted for the Scuola Grande di San Marco later in Tintoretto's life, this piece depicts the story of the dramatic rescue of Saint Mark's body from Alexandria. This is Tintoretto at his most theatrical.

Pieta, Titian

Titian uses a restrained palette in this moving piece, painted in exchange for burial concessions at the Frari Church. The old man kneeling at the feet of the Madonna is Titian.

Room 11

Discovery of the True Cross, Giambattista Tiepolo

A large ceiling painting made for the church of Le Cappuccine in Castello. The painting was saved when the church was destroyed by Napoleon to build the Via Garibaldi.

Room 17

Portrait of a Young Man and *Self-portrait*, Rosalba Carriera

Two pastel portraits by the most sought-after artist in Venice by travellers on the Grand Tour. (p.134)

Room 19

Healing of the Madman (Miracle of the Cross at the Rialto), Vittore Carpaccio

The old wooden Rialto Bridge is illustrated here, with scenes of Venetian pageantry. The painting narrates the story of the miraculous healing of a possessed man, in three stages.

Room 20

Procession in Piazza San Marco, Gentile Bellini

This is another wonderful Bellini narrative, giving insight to Venetian religious life. The painting depicts a procession for the Feast of Saint Mark, held in the Piazza San Marco, whereby Venice's scuole and churches would parade around the square displaying their relics.

Room 21

The Cycle of Saint Ursula, Vittore Carpaccio

The Saint Ursula cycle of eight paintings, completed between 1490 and 1495, were originally in the Scuola di Sant' Orsula, an institution devoted to the care of orphan girls. Ursula was the daughter-in-law of the King of Brittany and was sought in marriage by the King of England for his son.

The first picture represents the ambassadors arriving from England. In the second, Ursula accepts the offer, but only if her betrothed would provide her with an escort of 11,000 virgins for a pilgrimage to Rome. The ambassadors depart in the third painting. The fourth picture is divided: on the left we see the Prince depart England; on the right the Prince meets Ursula; and on the extreme right, Ursula and the Prince kneel before the King of Brittany. In the fifth, the Pope blesses Ursula and the Prince in Rome.

The sixth represents Ursula's dream of the violent death awaiting her at Cologne. The seventh depicts the Pope and others who accompanied Ursula to share her martyrdom. The eighth picture shows the dream's reality, the massacre by the Huns, with Prince Julian aiming an arrow at Ursula's breast.

Paint and Canvas

Venice's wealth and status as a trading port gave Venetian artists privileged access to the best materials. Rare and expensive minerals were available to create certain pigments for paint. Warm yellows and burnished orange colours were made from minerals that came from Persia. Ultramarine blue was made from lapis lazuli, a gemstone found in Badakhshan, northern Afghanistan. This colour was a huge luxury; lapis lazuli was more expensive than gold, and it was used for the heavens and the Virgin's mantle.

Trusted apprentices ground the pigments and mixed the paint by hand in accordance with special recipes. A 15th century Venetian manual gave more than a hundred recipes for the colour red – a colour that Titian used to great effect.

Prior to the introduction of oil paint, artists mixed pigment with egg and water to make tempera. This was applied to treated wood panels for altarpieces or to wet plaster to create frescoes. Because of the saline atmosphere of the lagoon where the damp and the salt air tended to corrupt the plaster, many Venetian frescoes are painted on ceilings.

In the early 15th century, Venetian painters followed the early Dutch masters by embracing oil as a medium for paint. Oil paints were more luminous than egg tempera and the medium was much more flexible, with greater layering and blending options open to the artist.

Venetian and northern Italian painters were the first to use canvas, a commodity that was in plentiful supply in a maritime port. Canvas was more economical and lighter than wood, hence artists could make larger paintings. Paint could be scraped off canvas, so the artist could begin a section again. Canvas stimulated a whole new approach to art and it continues to be the most popular surface for painting.

Painters

Veneziano, Paolo (dates unknown)

Painting in the Byzantine iconic tradition, Veneziano painted in the early 1300s and was one of the first artists to develop a unique Venetian sensibility. His *Pala Feriale* in the Museo della Basilica (p.55) is notable for its confident rendering of space and imaginative way of narrating the story of Saint Mark.

Giotto, the father of Renaissance painting, lived nearby in Padua at around the same time, but it is not certain that the two artists ever met. However, one can see the influence of Giotto in Veneziano's work. The solidity and humanity of the figures, the composition and use of perspective in narrative scenes, are key elements of Renaissance painting.

The Bellini Family

Bellini, Jacopo (1400-1470)

Court painter for many years at Ferrara before settling down in Padua, where he founded an art studio, Jacopo gathered many young artists around him. One of them was Andrea Mantegna from Vicenza. When Jacopo was invited to contribute to the Doge's Palace, he moved his family to Venice. He had two sons: Gentile and Giovanni.

Bellini, Gentile (1429-1507)

Gentile developed the distinctiveVenetian style of narrative painting. His masterpiece in the Accademia, *Miracles of the Relic of the True Cross*, was painted for the Scuola di San Giovanni, a wealthy fraternity who claimed to possess a fragment of the true cross. The painting is of significant historical interest: it shows the Basilica San Marco in the 15th century, with the original Byzantine mosaics on the exterior. The Procuratie Nuove later replaced the buildings adjoining the Campanile, shown on the right of the painting.

Gentile was Venice's official painter; the highest paid

PAINTERS

artist ever to decorate the Doge's Palace. When the great Sultan asked the Venetians to send a skilled portraitist, Gentile was selected. The portrait of *Mohammed II* hangs in London at the National Gallery.

Bellini, Giovanni (c.1430-1516)

When people say Bellini, they usually mean Giovanni. He was the youngest and most prolific of the Bellini painters and he is considered the father of Venetian painting. Giorgione and Titian were apprentices in his studio. Giovanni was the first painter in Venice to use oil paint, and the first to adopt Renaissance rules of perspective to his altarpieces. He is especially renowned for his incomparable Madonnas: the *Frari Madonna*, the *Madonna of San Zaccaria* and the *Madonna of the Trees*, all found in the Accademia. Giovanni's Virgin is round and earthy, a real woman, in stark contrast to the iconic Byzantine image. Giovanni never completely abandoned tempera and is famous for his ability to achieve a purity of colour in either medium.

Albrecht Durer visited Venice in 1506. He later paid tribute to Giovanni: *'whereas the painters of Venice were hostile to, and envious of, distinguished painters who visited them from abroad, and were divided among themselves by petty jealousies, Giovanni Bellini was entirely immune from these weaknesses.'*

Mantegna, Andrea (1431-1506)

Mantegna joined Jacopo Bellini's studio in Padua after falling in love with his daughter Nicolasia, whom he ultimately married in 1453. Despite possessing a quarrelsome disposition, nothing ever clouded the affectionate intimacy between himself and his brothers-in-law Gentile and Giovanni. Mantegna was known for the pure colours in his painting and for depicting a profound feeling for humanity. He continued to live and work in Padua, but exercised influence over Venetian artists through his connection with the Bellinis.

Carpaccio, Vittore (1465-1522)

Venice's other master of narrative painting was Gentile Bellini's rival. Carpaccio's paintings are invaluable as pictures of contemporary Venetian life. They convey an immediacy missing in Gentile's grander pieces. Carpaccio's special talent lay in knowing better than any other artist how to represent the personality of Venice. In his narratives, details were not merely incidental decoration, but were specifically calculated to enhance the physical reality of the subject of the painting, be it a miracle or a gambling den. Carpaccio's paintings, together with Marin Sanudo's journals provide the best picture extant of the Venetian Empire's golden age.

Carpaccio established the rules for creative colour, which were applied by subsequent generations of Venetian artists. Given the amount of detail in his work, it is interesting to note that the artist's preparatory drawings were mere sketches. He preferred to build the image using colour and paint, picking out each lock of hair, every gleam of light, with an agile use of the brush.

Carpaccio created paintings for two scuole in particular: Scuola di San'Orsolo (now in the Accademia) and the Scuola di San Giorgio degli Schiavoni (in Castello). He had a great affection for dogs and seldom painted a picture that did not include one.

Giorgione, Giorgio da Castelfranco (1477-1510)

Born in Castelfranco Veneto, Giorgione was very influential for an artist with such a short lifespan. He was painting when art was just beginning to emancipate itself from the exclusive service of religion and the state. One of the first artists to choose his subjects based on his personal taste, Giorgione would represent a single mood, combining colour and pattern to no other end but sheer beauty. Giorgione was only thirty-three when he died of the plague and most of his works have perished. Of the many paintings attributed to him, only three are not disputed: one of these is *The Tempest* at the Accademia.

Titian
(p.106)

Tintoretto
(p.110)

Veronese, Paolo (1528-1588)

Paolo Caliari was born in Verona and moved to Venice at the age of 27. Nick-named *il Veronese* by the Venetians, Paolo had an essentially decorative painting style, basing his art on colour and perspective. He avoided shadow and dramatic gestures or lighting, preferring to charm the eye with his palette. Veronese portrayed Venetian life as a gorgeous vision of luxury and ease. He enjoyed good wine, loved the company of handsome men and lovely women, and gloried in all the pomp of triumphant aristocracy.

Indifferent to spiritual matters, Veronese's painting of the *Last Supper* got him into trouble with the Holy Orders. The artist was called to account for depicting the sacred event as an orgy of vulgarity. As a concession, he removed a man bleeding from the nose and a pair of drunken German soldiers engaging in licentious behaviour. To avoid further trouble, Veronese changed the picture's title to *Christ in the House of Levi*. Since Levi ran a pub, drinking and carryings-on might be expected. The piece hangs in the Accademia.

Veronese's major innovation was in the technique of ceiling painting. The problem of representing vertical standing figures on a horizontal ceiling had long perplexed painters. He invented the balcony device: the spectator looks up through an apparent opening in the ceiling to a magnificent upper storey, which is surrounded by a balustrade. Painted figures look down at the viewer from this false balcony.

Canaletto, Antonio Canal (1695-1768)

In 1720 Canaletto began to produce meticulously detailed paintings of Venice, filled with Venetians going about their daily lives. Called *vedute* (views), they were developed out of landscape painting, but depicted urban rather than rural scenes. Canaletto used a *camera obscura*, an apparatus that projects an image on to a sheet of paper or a canvas, in order to obtain the greatest fidelity. Having established the main lines of composition and perspective, he would then finish the painting in his studio. Canaletto would rearrange the buildings of Venice to suit his own spatial requirements. In one of his paintings, the Piazza San Marco has been reversed.

By 1740 Canaletto was a successful artist: his paintings were collected by British patricians visiting Venice on the Grand Tour. The British consul Joseph Smith became his patron. Smith persuaded him to visit London, where the artist remained from 1746 to 1755. Smith would later sell most of his Canalettos to George III. There are now only three of his paintings exhibited in Venice, one at the Accademia and two at the Ca' Rezzonico. The National Gallery in London has a large collection of Canalettos. His work can also be found in the Wallace Collection in London and in Windsor Palace.

Carriera, Rosalba
(p.137)

Tiepolo, Giambattista (1696-1777)

Best known for his frescoes, Giambattista was the most important Venetian painter of his period. He and his son Giandomenico were responsible for the resurgence of Venetian painting in the 18th century.

Giambattista was strongly influenced by Veronese, further developing illusions of perspective. His allegorical ceiling paintings use architecture, space and clouds to create a feeling of limitless sky. Greek mythological figures gaze down at us from loggias and balconies, while cupids and angels play among the clouds. Giambattista's use of colour adds to the illusion: blue for the faraway sky and warm reddish tones for subjects set closer to the viewer.

At the time, Venetian patrons were still clinging to the illusion that they were representatives of a great world power. They prevailed upon Giambattista to immortalise them in classical scenes, depicting them as Apollo or Mars, with their wives and daughters cast in the role of Cleopatra or Diana. The artist decorated some of the grand palaces and halls of Europe, spending the last eight years of his life in Madrid.

Tiepolo, Giandomenico (1727-1804)

By 1745, Giandomenico was assisting his father, but went on to develop a unique style – rejecting allegory and mythology as subjects. During a visit to Madrid, he met the youthful Goya. Influenced by his soft colour pallete and his free-flowing arrangement of figures, Giandomenico painted a series of frescoes on the life of Pulcinella for his own villa. Well worth visiting, they are now on display in Ca' Rezzonico.

Guardi, Gianantonio (1699-1760)

Brother-in-law to Giambattista Tiepolo, who married his sister in 1719, Gianantonio is credited with a cycle of paintings found in the organ loft of San Angelo Raffaele (p.148) These depict scenes from the story of Tobias and Raphael. He trained his brother, Francesco, and their individual contribution to joint works is unknown.

Guardi, Francesco (1712-1793)

The more famous Guardi brother was best known as a painter of *vedute*, although he never achieved the international success of Canaletto with his exterior scenes. His interior scenes are very revealing of Venetian life, illustrating how decadent the society had become.

Ca' Rezzonico (Museum of 18th century Venice)

Fondamenta Rezzonica 3136
vaporetto Ca' Rezzonico
041 241 0100
November-March 10.00-17.00 daily, closed Tuesday
April-October 10.00-18.00 daily, closed Tuesday
€6.50; map 8, G3

Filippo Bon di San Barnabà, procurator of Venice,
commissioned Baldassare Longhena to built a vast palace
in 1667. The entire facade was made of black and white
stone shipped across the Adriatic from Istria. However,
work proved too expensive for even a procurator's
budget and construction came to a halt. The great
architect moved on to build Ca' Pesaro and Santa Maria
della Salute. At the time of Longhena's death in 1682,
only the ground floor and the *piano nobile* of
Ca' Rezzonico had been completed.

In 1746 it was sold to an extremely rich banker from
Genoa, Giambattista Rezzonico, who had purchased his
way into Venetian nobility via 100,000 ducats deposited
in the Venice treasury. Gian's son Carlo della Torre
Rezzonico was elected Pope Clement XIII in 1758.
The Pope commissioned the best artists to decorate
the Palazzo's walls and ceilings. Giambattista Tiepolo
and his son Giandomenico contributed a great many
paintings, including a delightful series painted for their
own villa and later moved to Ca' Rezzonico. Followers of
the Grand Tour will find other works of interest: pastels
by Rosalba Carriera, two Canalettos, and paintings of
Venetian life by Guardi and Longhi.

The last remaining Rezzonico sold the palazzo to
Ladislao Zaelinski in 1837, who sold it to Pen Browning
in the 1880s. The poet Robert Browning lived here with
his son, Pen for only one year before he died on 12th
December 1889. There is a room, which is now a shrine
to the great man, containing his books and simple items
of his furniture. Robert Browning was much loved in

Venice and was often seen playing with the children in the campo. He received a state funeral in Venice before his remains were transported by rail to Westminster Abbey. Baron Hirschel de Minerbi sold the palazzo to the State in 1931. Many of the movable works of art in Ca' Rezzonico are originally from the Museo Correr.

First Floor

Room 1, Salone delle Feste

The ballroom is two storeys high with walls and ceilings entirely frescoed. The ceiling allegory is an homage to the Rezzonico family by Tiepolo's collaborator, Giovanni Battista Crosato. Ludovico Rezzonico's nomination as Procurator of San Marco was celebrated here in 1762; two years later a grand ball was given in honour of the Duke of York, brother of King George III.

Room 2, Sala dell'Allergoria Nuziale (Nuptial Allegory)

Ludovico's marriage to Faustina Savorgnan is celebrated in the ceiling fresco (the nuptial allegory) by Giambattista Tiepolo. Also in this room is *A Portrait of Clement XIII Rezzonico* by Anton Raphael Mengs.

Room 4, Sala dei Pastelli

Carriera's sympathetic portrait of *Faustina Bordoni Hasse* is just one of five portraits in this room. Don't miss Lorenzo Tiepolo's portrait of *Cecilia Guardi*

Tiepolo, wife of Giambattista and sister to Antonio and Francesco Guardi. The chandelier is 18th century Murano glass.

Room 6, The Throne Room

The ceiling fresco is *Allegory of Merit*, by Giambattista Tiepolo. *Merit*, depicted as an old bearded man, ascends towards glory accompanied by *Nobility*, who carries the Golden Book of Venetian families. The allegory is ironic, since at the time Venice was selling off her nobility to raise funds for the treasury. The gilt throne was carved for Pope Pius VI on his return to Rome from Vienna, where he had gone in vain to protest Emperor Joseph II's edicts against the authority of the church.

Room 7, Sala del Tiepolo

Nobility and Virtue overthrowing Perfidy, Giambattista Tiepolo

Painted on canvas in 1745 for the Palazzo Barbarigo at Santa Maria del Giglio, the piece then passed into the hands of the Donà dale Rosa family who sold it to the city in 1934. The painting is luminous.

Room 12, The Portego

Saturn, Tityus, Mercury, Justice, Prudence, Grace, Andrea Brustolon

These allegorical sculptures were carved from Swiss stone pine for Count Tiopo Piloni in the 1720s. Andrea Brustolon was a master Venetian wood-carver, sought after for his furniture. These sculptures show an artist at his peak.

Second Floor

Room 14, La Villa di Zianigo

It is easy to miss these two small rooms in the north wing of the second floor, found at the end of a non-descript corridor. These enchanting paintings are by Giandomenico Tiepolo, Giambattista's son. They were brought in their entirety from the Tiepolo villa in Zianigo. Painted when Venice was in decline, they possess a bittersweet melancholy.

In the highly evocative *New World*, painted in 1791, the view is from behind; a group of people are waiting their turn to gaze into a *cosmorama* or *diorama,* a new invention that showed pictures of faraway places.

In the adjacent tiny room are the *Pulcinella* frescoes, the most well-known of Giandomenico's work. Eight

paintings show scenes from the life of the clown: *Pulcinella in love; Pulcinella and the acrobats; Pulcinella carousing;* with the best one on the ceiling: *Pulcinella's swing.* Though Pulcinella comes from Naples, these clowns are distinctly Venetian, rich and poor, masked and unmasked, in attitudes both pompous and absurd.

Room 17, Sala del Ridotto

Il Ridotto and Il Parlatorio, Francesco Guardi

These paintings provide an insight into the vivacity and rather sinister undertones of Venetian 18th century life. *Il Ridotto* shows the grand hall of the gaming house in the Palazzo Dandalo. *Il Parlatorio* depicts the parlour at the San Zaccaria monastery where nuns would receive their families and friends.

Third Floor

Room 22, The *Ai Do San Marchi* Chemist Shop

Dating from around 1679, this chemist once dispensed medicines to the dei Frari convent. In 1908 it was sold to a French antiques dealer, later prevented from exporting it to Paris by the government. The gleaming hardwood cabinets, majolica jars and Murano glass bottles are all original, lovingly restored.

GIANDOMENICO TIEPOLO: *THE NEW WORLD*

The Grand Tour

The term was first coined in 1670 by Richard Lassels in what is considered to be the first guidebook in English: *The Voyage of Italy or A Compleat Journey Through Italy in Two Parts.* His book had a huge impact on a generation of upper-class young and it became *de rigueur* to take the Tour to completely absorb the *'elements and alphabet of breeding'*. The three-year journey had a strict itinerary: a lengthy visit to Florence and Tuscany was followed by Rome and then on to Naples, for Pompeii and Paestum.

The return journey was timed to reach Venice for Ascension Day and *La Sensa,* the festival of the Marriage of Venice to the Sea. British visitors to Venice on the Grand Tour were particularly impressed with the Ascension Day ceremony. Perhaps it was the shared island mentality and reliance on the sea to beget and perpetuate an empire.

A complex web of educational, social and political concerns lay behind the itinerary: Rome was where the youth was educated in the classics and appreciated his place in history; Venice was where he discovered his sexuality and immersed himself in contemporary art and literature. *Venetian Liberty* is a term used frequently in letters and reports from travellers of the day. Then, as now, Venice was a gathering place for artists and writers from around the world, and there was never a shortage of parties and festivals to attend.

Because the ability to fund such a trip was only available to a privileged few, the Tour defined an elite and unified patrician class. The Grand Tour imbued the traveller with cultural power which was proved through the art collected and displayed at home. It was compulsory to sit for a portrait while in Italy. In Rome, one sat for an oil painting by Pompeo Batoni (1708-1787); in Venice, a pastel portrait by Rosalba Carriera.

It was assumed that every well-born Englishman would

have an affair with at least one Italian countess. La Serenissima's reputation for fine courtesans was well documented, as in this letter of 1751 by Edward Thomas:

A young Gallant could not forbear offering greetings to a Lady, richly dressed and bedecked with jewels. She to our great surprise, lifted up her veil and ogled him, presenting her hand to lead him to her Gondola. The bait was took and he handed her into the gondola and the moment he was in with her she beckoned to the Gondoleers to row off with him! In view of all the people who laughed and said she was one of the greatest and most dangerous strumpets of the city. The wickedness of the place is beyond imagination.

At the height of the Grand Tour, between 1650 and 1800, the words *Venice* and *Venus* were pronounced almost identically. Alexander Pope cast Venice as an alluring Venus, both magnetic and subversive. Pope referred to the *shrine where naked Venus keeps* whose *Cupids ride the Lyon of the Deeps* (a reference to the symbol of Venice). The *Adriatic main* was the ruin for many an *enamour'd swain*, whose degeneracy would soon be imported back into England when the young patrician gentleman returned from the Grand Tour, having lost both his virginity and English morals.

It wasn't only men that took the Grand Tour. Patrician ladies constrained by rigid rules of society and unhappy marriages found freedom in Italy. It was said that gazing upon the naked statue of David caused delicate English ladies to '*swoon and some to faint*'. Regardless of the 'vapours' caused by viewing such classical artworks, women continued to travel in ever-increasing numbers, accompanied by servants and enormous baggage.

In 1775, Charles Horneck sued for divorce from Sarah Keppel (an ancestor of Camilla Parker-Bowles) who fled to Italy with publican John Scawen. Servants testified the adulterous couple passed for man and wife and '*laid in the same bed together, and their clothes lying in the room by the bedside*'.

Frances Russell, a writer of the day, stated that: '*The rich traveller on the Grand Tour would sit to Rosalba Carriera, who exercised a more direct influence on British contemporaries than any other Italian painter of the century.*'

ROSALBA CARRIERA:
HORACE WALPOLE (1741)

Soame Jenyns

The Modern Fine Gentleman (1746)

Just broke from School, pert, impudent, and raw
Expert in Latin, more expert in Taw,
His Honour posts o'er Italy and France,
Measures St Peter's Dome, and learns to dance.
Thence, having quick thro' various Countries flown,
Glean'd all their Follies, and expos'd his own,
He back returns, a Thing so strange all o'er,
As never Ages past produc'd before:
A Monster of such complicated Worth,
A no one single Clime could e're bring forth:
Half Atheist, Papist, Gamester, Bubble Rook,
Half Fiddler, Coachman, Dancer, Groom and Cook.

Rosalba Carriera (1675-1758)

Oil paintings took time to complete, sometimes as long as three years. Pastel portraits could be finished in a much shorter time and were therefore more suited to the needs of those on the Grand Tour. Rome was the city for a portrait in oil; Venice required a pastel, and not just any pastel, a Rosalba Carriera.

Rosalba was born in Chioggia, but little is known of her early life. Her English connections resulted partially from the patronage of Christian Cole and Consul Smith (Canaletto's patron). English Grand Tourists preferred Rosalba's portraits because they were informal and very flattering: subjects were softly lit against a plain dark background, with eyes looking directly at the viewer and the mouth sensually curved. The sitter was often dressed in flowing silks and lace suggesting ease and refinement, in strong contrast to the Roman oil portrait that was painted to convey the subject's status and wealth.

Carriera would place her subjects in Venice through the use of props and wardrobe, such as a Carnevale mask peaking out from beneath a richly trimmed hat. These portraits could only be painted in Venice, and as such were extremely valuable hanging on walls back home in England – confirmation of a poised young patrician's Venetian education abroad on the Grand Tour. Rosalba's British clients were also fond of purchasing series of allegory pastels featuring buxom young women, scantily clad.

Carriera not only proved the equal to any male portrait painter in Venice, but also proved pastels to be the equal of oils in their richness, colour, and handling. She was accepted as one of the few female members of the Guild of St Luke and later, the French Academy. Rosalba also painted miniature portraits in oil, the probable cause of her blindness in the final decade of life.

Peggy Guggenheim Collection

Palazzo Venier dei Leoni
vaporetto Salute
0039 041 240 5411
10.00-18.00 daily, closed Tuesday
open national holidays (including Tuesdays), closed Christmas Day
Public presentations:
11.00 and 17.00, the collection;
12.00 and 16.00, the life of Peggy Guggenheim
admission €10
www.guggenheim-venice.it
map 9, B5

Set in what was once Peggy Guggenheim's private villa
facing the Grand Canal, this is a superb collection and
well worth a visit. It is a wonderful cross-section of art
from the first half of the 20th century, exhibiting works
by most of the famous artists of the era: Picasso, Braque,
Klee, Mirò, Brancusi, Giacometti, Kandinsky, de Chirico,
Dali, Rothko and Max Ernst, who was Peggy's second
husband. There is also a room full of Jackson Pollock's
paintings. Some surprises await: two little pieces by
Henry Moore and a large Magritte, a version of his
Empire of Light.

Many of the pieces were purchased within a very short
time frame in the war years between 1939-42. Peggy was
well advised by Marcel Duchamp on what to collect

and, because of the uncertainty and conflict of the time, she was able to purchase them at bargain basement prices. Modern Art as we know it did not exist yet. This collection was Peggy's passport to acceptance, and to a relationship with society. Her investment paid off: in 1946 the collection was worth $93,000; today it is valued at $630 million.

There is a room devoted to the paintings by Peggy's daughter, Pegeen, who was a Primativist. She died tragically young, before her career became established.

A new section comprised of paintings that Peggy did not buy, the Gianni Mattioli Collection, was added in 1997. Dedicated to the Italian avant-garde, the collection displays Italian Futurists and includes a Modigliani.

The Nasher sculpture garden is in the central courtyard. Near the cafe, which overlooks the garden, is a museum shop with a good book section. It also sells souvenir copies of Peggy's outrageous sunglasses.

Peggy Guggenheim bought the palazzo in 1948 as a home and, beginning in 1949, began to open her collection to the public. After Peggy's death, restoration and conversion to a museum was made possible by a *Special Law for Venice* and by donation from Venetians and a group of Italian banks.

PALAZZO VENIER DEI LEONI

Peggy Guggenheim (1898-1979)

At the outbreak of the First World War, Guggenheim mines controlled 80 per cent of the world's silver, copper and lead. Meyer and his brother Solomon controlled the family business.

Benjamin Guggenheim was Meyer's sixth child and Peggy's father. Benjamin was a handsome playboy with little interest in the family business; he died tragically on the Titanic. Peggy received $450,000 as an inheritance. Her mother Florette got $800,000. This was a great deal of money at the time, but it was actually small change in relation to the vast family fortune.

Growing up in New York, Peggy was a misfit within the family and she was plagued with feelings of insecurity. She had a botched plastic surgery operation on her nose, causing it to swell in bad weather. In 1921 she travelled to Paris and met the artists of Montparnasse who were set to change the art world. She became friends with Man Ray and Marcel Duchamp, the man who was to provide stellar advice when she later amassed her collection.

Peggy married the sculptor Laurence Vaile in Paris in 1922 and they had two children, Sinbad and Pegeen. Theirs was a tempestuous relationship. Laurence was a violent man: he would push her around on the street, and he liked to throw her shoes out of the window after an argument. He chronicled his life with Peggy in a novel titled *Murder! Murder!* Peggy left Laurence in 1928 to live with the love of her life, the English intellectual and war hero, John Holms, who died in 1934.

The writer Samuel Beckett (with whom she had a brief affair) encouraged her to dedicate herself to contemporary art, and to establish her own gallery. In 1938 Peggy opened *Guggenheim Jeune* in London with an exhibit of Jean Cocteau's work. British customs officials objected to the nudity in one of the drawings; the exhibition received attention and controversy as a result. Her next show was the first Brititsh exhibition of Kandinsky, the father of Abstract Expressionism.

The Second World War led Peggy to return to New York, but not before she had purchased Leger's *Men in the City* on the day that Hitler invaded Norway, and Brancusi's *Bird in Space* as the Germans approached Paris. She married the surrealist Max Ernst in 1941, opened her New York gallery 'Art of This Century' in 1942, and divorced Ernst in 1943 – the same year that she gave Jackson Pollock his first show.

In 1948, the Venice Biennale invited Peggy to show her collection. This was the first time Mark Rothko, Arshile Gorky and Jackson Pollock were exhibited in Europe, and it was the most coherent survey of Modernism to be presented in Venice. Peggy was showered with accolades. She had finally established herself as a serious art collector outside of the massive shadow of her wealthy uncle, Solomon R Guggenheim.

Peggy moved to Venice in 1949 and made the Palazzo Venier dei Leoni her home. The palace, first begun in 1748, is known to Venetians as *il palazzo non finito* (the unfinished palace) because it has no upper floors. There is a story that the Corner family sabotaged its completion because it would have surpassed the grandeur of their own palace located directly across the Grand Canal. Another explanation is that construction was stopped because it was blamed for structural damage to a neighbouring palazzo. Many Venetians merely say that, 'they ran out of money'. The unusual palace was well-suited to the eccentric Peggy.

She was to live the rest of her life in Venice, continuing to fund contemporary artists until the 1960s, when high prices and a dwindling enthusiasm for the work put an end to collecting. Venetians loved Peggy affectionately naming her 'the last Doge'. Her ashes are placed in a corner of the garden, next to her beloved dogs.

Santa Maria della Salute (the Salute)

Campo della Salute
vaporetto Salute
041 274 3911
09.00-12.00, 15.00-18.00 daily
small entrance fee for Sacristy
map 9, D5

In the 13th century, anyone landing from a boat on the triangular promontory known as the Dogana di Mare, would find themselves in boggy, marshy territory, uncultivated and neglected. The land was property of the monks of San Gregorio, whose abbey was established on the west side of the *rio*. In 1256, Doge Raniero Zen cleared the ground and erected a monastery and church for the benefit of the German knights who had helped Venice defeat Genoa. The knights became known as The White Brothers of Trinity and they established a community, who built boats and traded in salt.

In succeeding centuries Venice succumbed to a series of plague epidemics: one of the most serious occurred in 1630 when nearly 80,000 people died within the year. The pestilence suddenly abated on 21st November 1631. To give thanks to the Madonna for deliverance from the disease, the *Santa Maria della Salute* was commissioned and the Monastery of the White Trinity was razed. To support the weight of the planned church, more than 100,000 timber piles were driven into the soggy ground, using heavy mallets and armies of labourers. The first stone was laid by April 1631, but it took three more years to complete the foundations and a further 20 years until work commenced on the dome.

The Architect

Baldassare Longhena, aged 32, was a short and dapper Venetian when he was commissioned as architect of Santa Maria della Salute. The son of a stonemason, he had earned a reputation as a sculptor. Although he was a follower of the Palladian school of architecture, he had yet to complete or even commence a building.

Longhena's appointment met with considerable criticism, but there were only 11 applicants to choose from because the terms of the commission were so onerous. Terms stipulated that the monument should be colossal yet cheap to build; that the inside of the church should be filled with evenly distributed light; that the high altar be the focal point of the eye upon entry to the church and dominate every other aspect of the interior; and that the whole effect create a *bella figura* or grand impression, at the entry of the Grand Canal. Baldassare designed a circular nave within an octagon, representing a glorious crown to honour the Madonna.

Longhena was *Proto* of Basilica San Marco for 50 years succeeding Jacobo Sansovino. He was responsible for the restoration of the Basilica's west facade, the north dome and the sacristy roof. The Salute was the architect's life work; it was consecrated in 1687, five years after his death.

Inside the Salute

Somehow, the building is more impressive from the outside; the interior is cold and reserved. The altarpiece features a Byzantine *Madonna* with an obscure connection to St Luke.

Be sure to visit the Sacristy where some splendid paintings reside. There are some Titians brought from Santo Spirito in 1656. The altarpiece is *St Mark enthroned with saints Cosmas, Damian, Sebastian and Rocco.* These are the plague saints: Cosmas and Damian are Byzantine; Sebastian and Rocco are Roman Catholic. On the ceiling (there are large hand-mirrors on the benches to aid viewing) are his paintings of Old Testament stories: *Cain and Abel, Abraham and Isaac, David and Goliath.* Tintoretto has included himself among the guests in his *Marriage at Cana;* (he is the first Apostle on the left).

The Plague

Plague first broke out in regions of Mongolia and the Gobi desert in early 1320 (where the disease is still endemic in the rat population) killing 65 per cent of the Chinese population between 1331 and 1353. The disease travelled overland to the Crimea where, in 1345, Genoese sailors were under siege at the port of Kaffa by the forces of Yanibeg, Khan of the Golden Horde.

The Khan's armies had been struck by plague and, in a desire to visit the affliction on his enemies, he conducted the first known act of biological warfare: catapulting the dead into Kaffa. The Genoese quickly cast the bodies into the sea but they were soon struck by pestilence. Fleeing the siege, their ships carried the disease into the Mediterranean where it arrived in Messina, Sicily in October 1347. Thus began the cycle that characterised the movement of the disease across western Europe; the disease would rage through summer months and wane in the cooler winters.

Venetian territories in the Adriatic and East Mediterranean were hit by plague as were Constantinople, Alexandria and Cyprus. The extensive network of trade routes across the Mediterranean, linked to inland cities via a system of rivers and canals, meant that the pestilence spread also to ports along the Seine, Rhine and Rhone rivers. Venice's reliance on shipping made her especially vulnerable.

Between December 1347 and May 1439, 60 per cent of the total population of 150,000 perished. Venice acted swiftly to control the epidemic; all incoming vessels were impounded for a full 40 days (hence the term *quarantine*, derived from forty). The Venetian government designated certain uninhabited islands as cemeteries, insisting that the dead be buried at least five feet deep, with no dead to be buried on the inhabited islands of Venice. But despite official precautions, the city failed to control the disease and suffered one of the highest mortality rates of any major city. By way of contrast, Milan lost only 15 per cent in a population of 100,000 because of its large rural hinterland, while Venetians were crowded together on damp islands in the middle of a lagoon. Physicians were powerless.

It was the magistrates who first noticed a pattern in the disease. They determined that the pestilence was contagious, was carried by people, and arrived with certain ships. Prevention, containment and survival took precedence over any possible curative. Italy became the strictest health territory in the world, establishing regional health and sanitation boards, while England was considered to be one of the most backward states in this regard. Venice established a board of health in 1486, which gathered statistics on the number and type of deaths. When an abnormally large number of deaths was determined on the island of Malamocco, they had the island immediately quarantined. Venice was among the first cities to recognise that quarantining the sick and the healthy together would spread the disease.

Venetian merchants who depended on the movement of trade goods were often able to prevent, or bend, the implementation of Venice's *cordon sanitaire* plague regulations. In 1630, a member of the entourage of the Mantuan ambassador to Venice was found to be infected. The delegation was allowed to enter Venice and the man placed in quarantine on the island of San Clemente. A carpenter from Venice caught the infection on the island and brought it home to his sestiere. The disease spread like wildfire and it is remembered as Venice's most disastrous plague. It did not help that ordinary people conspired to hide the presence of plague. For example, in 1630 Busto Arsizio, the doctor who gave official confirmation of plague, was shot dead.

The mask with the long beak seen at Carnevale is a legacy of plague times. Physicians would wear wax clothing and an oil-cloth mask because infections could not stick to it. The huge beak was filled with sweet-smelling herbs.

San Angelo Raffaele

Campo San Angelo Raffaele
vaporetto San Basilio
08.00-12.00, 15.00-17.00 daily
08.00-12.00 Sunday
map 7, C4

Known locally as *l'Anzolo Rafael*, the church has been resurrected four times; founded in 416, it burned down in 899, 1105 and 1149. It was reconstructed from its foundations in 1640, after decaying into ruin.

Inside, on the tribune of the Baroque organ, are beautifully painted scenes by Antonio Guardi from the story of Tobias: *The Angel Appears to Tobias, The Healing of Tobias' Father, The Departure of Tobias, The Marriage of Tobias.* Antonio, who was almost forgotten in favour of his younger brother Francesco, gives the figures a lively sense of movement as he bathes his subjects in a shimmering light.

Sally Vickers has popularized the church in a recent novel *Miss Garnet's Angel*, which interweaves the story of Tobias, the restoration of Guardi's paintings in the church, and a repressed Englishwoman discovering herself in Venice.

Raphael is the patron saint of travellers and young people leaving home for the first time. Because Venetians travelled extensively, the image of the guardian angel Raphael, together with a boy, a fish and a dog, constantly recurs in their painting and sculpture. Titian painted the following story several times.

Raphael and Tobias

From the book of *Tobit* found in the Apocrypha of the Bible

Tobit, father of Tobias, had been blind for four years on the day he prayed to God. On that same day, Sarah, his relative, also prayed. She had been married to seven husbands but the wicked demon Asmodeus had killed each of them on her wedding night. Both prayers were heard by God, who sent the angel Raphael.

Tobit remembered he had money held in trust with his kinsman Gabael at Rages in Media. He sent for his young son Tobias and commanded him to travel to Media to claim the money. Tobias needed a guide. He met Raphael in the street, but did not perceive he was an angel.

Tobias brought Raphael to meet his father who agreed to pay the angel to guide his son. They set out together: the angel, the boy and his dog. The first night, Tobias was washing his feet in the river Tigris when a large fish tried to swallow his foot. Raphael cried out, telling the boy to catch the fish and keep the gall, heart and liver.

When the travellers arrived at Rages Raphael told Tobias that he would marry Sarah. Tobias was afraid, he had heard about the fate of her seven husbands. But Raphael instructed him: enter the bridal chamber and put the fish liver and heart on the embers of the incense burner. The demon would smell the odour and flee the chamber.

Tobias asked Sarah's father Raguel for his daughter's hand. Later, everything went just as Raphael had foretold: Tobias put the fish on the burner and the demon fled. The couple then said a prayer of thanks to God and enjoyed a night of wedded bliss.

When it was time to return home with Sarah. Raphael went on ahead with Tobias and the dog. On Raphael's instructions Tobias applied the gall of the fish to his father's eyes. The medicine worked and Tobit could see once more.

A walk in Dorsoduro

**APPROXIMATELY ONE HOUR
WITHOUT STOPPING, OR A
HALF DAY WITH VISITS ALONG
THE WAY.**

Venetians love this *passeggiata
Veneziana*, both for the sense
of space it affords and
because it is not a favourite
tourist trail. Begin by taking
the No. 82 vaporetto to San
Basilio (map 7, D5). Step off
the boat onto the *Fondamenta
Zattere Ponte Longo* and turn
right to walk along the *Zattere*,
named after the timber rafts
that were used to carry salt.
Ships of all sorts can be
seen passing by as you walk
eastwards. Venice has a large
container port, cruise ship

terminal and a dock for the car
ferry to the Lido, all located at
the western end of the city. The
Canale della Giudecca (Giudecca
Canal) connects the port to the
Adriatic.

Across the water is the island
of Giudecca and the massive
church of the Redentore, built
by the architect Palladio.
In July, during Festa del
Redentore (p213) a bridge
of boats stretches across
the canal from Zattere to
the church. With few major
sites, Giudecca is currently
undergoing redevelopment.
There are wonderful views of
the city from Giudecca and
Venice's most expensive hotel,
the Cipriani, is situated on the
eastern end.

Cross the first bridge *Ponte
Longo* and look for *Santa Maria
della Visitazione* (map 7, G6).

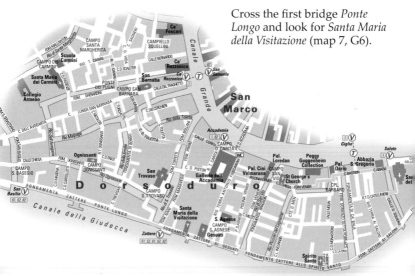

SS REDENTORE

The church has a 16th-century ceiling with saints and prophets surrounding a central medallion which represents the Visitation. Continue on the *Fondamenta Zattere ai Gesuati,* until the next church on your left, the *Chiesa Gesuati* (1736). This was founded by the Jesuits, re-consecrated by the Dominicans and is often confused with the *Gesuiti* in Cannaregio. Inside there are frescoes by Giambattista Tiepolo.

Ospedale degli Incurabili, one of the four musical *ospedali,* is further along. Once a hospital for syphilitics and then an orphanage, it is now a juvenile court. The church of *Spirito Santo* (map 9, B6) is close by. During the *Festa del Redentore* a pontoon bridge connecting Dorsoduro and Giudecca begins here. Continue past the *Magazine del Sale,* a former salt warehouse, now used as a boathouse and temporary exhibition space. The tip of Dorsoduro is known as the *Punta della Salute* and it is usually closed to foot traffic. Turn left on the Calle del Squero to reach the *Salute.* From there, cross the bridge to the *Abbazia San Gregorio* and step inside if it is open.

The walk now travels through a series of narrow lanes, past the Guggenhiem Collection and St George's church and then on to the Accademia Gallery.

CHESS PLAYERS MIGHT FIND A GAME NEAR THE GALLERY: LOOK BEHIND THE KIOSK NEAR THE GRAND CANAL.

Past the gallery on the Calle della Toletta is a series of bookshops. Continue on to Campo San Barnaba and see the San Barnaba church used as an exterior location in *Raiders Of The Lost Ark.* Cross the *Ponte dei Pugni* and complete your walk with lunch or dinner in Campo Santa Margherita, the heart of Venetian life in Dorsoduro.

CAMPO SANTA MARGHERITA

CANNAREGIO

A CANAL IN CANNAREGIO

This is a more peaceful part of Venice. The pavements are wider and the shops stock basic groceries. Bars are crowded with locals and the prices are lower than in San Marco.

A stroll through Cannaregio is a good way to way to see how a mix of faiths and cultures lived closely together in Venice. Here you will find the *Jewish ghetto* near the *Campo dei Mori* with its statues of Persian merchants. Nearby is Tintoretto's home and his parish church. Cannaregio has the last remaining cinema in Venice and a good public swimming pool. Visitors to the islands of Murano, Burano and Torcello depart from the vaporetto stop at Fondamente Nove.

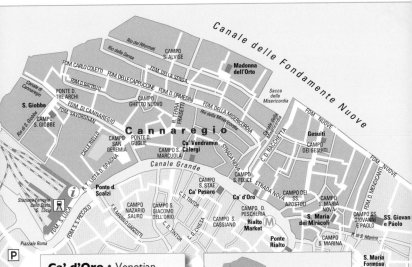

Ca' d'Oro • Venetian Gothic palazzo
Ca' Vendramin casino
Ghetto Nuovo Jewish museum and synagogues
Madonna dell'Orto Tintoretto's parish church
I Gesuiti Rococco church
Santa Maria dei Miracoli • jewel-box church with a charming campo nearby

Parco Savorgnan
This pleasant garden hidden behind a 17th century palazzo has a playground for children.

restaurants p.238
shopping p.262
nightlife p.245

Strada Nova
A broad shopping street with market stalls and good bakeries.

Did you know that..?
In the 17th century there were 10,000 gondolas in Venice. Now there are only 500.

155

Ca' d'Oro (House of Gold)

Galleria Giorgio Franchetti
Calle Ca' d'Oro 3922, off the Strada Nova
vaporetto Ca' d'Oro
041 520 0345
08.15-19.15 Tuesday-Saturday
08.15-14.00 Monday
€5; map 4, H2

Ca' d'Oro is worth visiting for the beautiful view of the canal and the photo opportunity that it affords. It is also fun to imagine what living on the Grand Canal might have been like for a nobleman living in a palazzo.

The palazzo's first owner, Marino Contarini, was a Procurator of San Marco from 1425–40. When the building was completed in 1434, the Serene Republic was at the height of her empire. Work was supervised by Bartolomeo Bon, Venice's top architect, and carried out by the best Lombard craftsmen. The facade was embellished with gold leaf and painted in ultramarine and vermilion, the most expensive pigments of the day. Over the doorway is the Contarini coat-of-arms supported in the arms of an angel.

After the Contarini, Ca' d'Oro was home to the Marcello family, the Loredan, the Bressa and then finally to Prince Trubetzkoi, who gave it to the ballerina Maria Taglioni in 1847. Taglioni remodelled the building, attempting to remove all that was Gothic. Fortunately, Baron Franchetti rescued the building and partially restored it before passing it on to the State in 1916. Restorations continued for another 12 years before Ca' d'Oro opened to the public in 1927.

Ca' d'Oro houses the Giorgio Franchetti Gallery. It is not an extensive collection, but does include *St Sebastian* by Andrea Mantegna and a sexy *Venus* by Titian. One of Titian's crumbling frescoes is also on display. There are some works by Dutch masters, including a Van Dyke and a Jan Steen, marbles by Tuscan and Lombard sculptors, as well as a graceful lunette by Sansovino.

Gambling and Ridotto

In 1638, Marco Dandolo was granted permission to turn the back section of his palazzo near San Moisè into a gambling casino. The *ridotto* (reduced quarters) was soon lavishly furnished and open for business.

Noblemen could enter barefaced, but all others were admitted only if masked. Stakes were high and both men and women sold their souls and lost their fortunes at the gaming tables. The Ridotto became so notorious that the State forced it to close in 1774. Yet this did not halt the Venetian love of gambling, which spread to salons, theatres and little private hideaways, called *casini*. Formerly used for sexual trysts, these now offered both diversions.

The Austrians put an end to gambling in the 19th century; only a lottery was allowed to continue. In 1937, as part of a scheme to show that Fascists could enjoy themselves, the Lido was developed into a playground for the gambling rich. A casino opened alongside the new Palazzo del Cinema. It became popular after the war, until the late 1950s when Ca' Vendramin opened on the Grand Canal in Cannaregio.

Crooked croupier scandals hit the Lido casino in the 1980s, along with the opening of casinos in Slovenia and the Ca' Noghera in Mestre. The Cannaregio and Mestre casinos are the most profitable in Europe. Ca' Vendramin is the classier of the two and requires customers to wear jackets.

Ca' Vendramin Calergi (the Casino)

Calle Larga Vendramin 2040
041 529 7111
www.casinovenezia.it
vaporetto San Marcuola
14.45-02.30 daily (slot machines), 15.30-02.30 daily (tables)
admission €10, credit cards accepted
map 2, F6

The Ghetto

vaporetto San Marcuola
www.ghetto.it
map 1-2, E4

This is a quiet place for a stroll and perhaps a visit to the museum. There is a kosher restaurant *Gam Gam*, an excellent kosher bakery and a highly recommended restaurant, *I Quattro Rusteghi* (p.239).

Jews in Venice

Trading in Venice from the 10th century, Jews were tolerated and welcomed, but were not allowed to become full citizens. Their choices of occupation were formally limited, but Jews could be merchants, rag traders, doctors and, from 1382, could operate legally as money lenders.

In 1509, the pressure of war was straining Venetian resources – her territories on the mainland overrun by foreign troops. A refugee crisis ensued, as Venetian citizens and Jews fled to the lagoon and the safety of a city that was excommunicated from Rome. The government reached a compromise in 1516. Rather than give in to pressures to expel the Jewish population, it was decreed that all Jews would live within the confines of a single island in Cannaregio, the *Ghetto Nuovo*. The name comes from the Venetian *geto*, meaning foundry (the island was the former home to several iron foundries).

Europe's first ghetto was reached by two bridges that were sealed off with gates. High walls were built to seal off houses overlooking the surrounding canals and all points of access to the water were blocked. The gates to the ghetto were kept by Christian guards, whose wages were paid by the Jewish community. The guards ensured the observation of a nightly curfew from one hour past sunset to dawn. Only doctors and musicians were allowed out at night, and then just for professional reasons. Two patrol boats, also financed by the ghetto's residents, circled the island. The daytime work Jews performed was too valuable to go undone, so residents were allowed to travel in the city but they were forced to wear yellow badges and hats to identify themselves as Jewish.

It all seems very punitive, but in comparison to other Italian states during the Counter-Reformation, it was relatively liberal. Venice was one of the few cities where Jews could live in peace, with laws that specifically protected them. By the end of the 16th century, the Jewish population was about 5,000. To accommodate such a large population in a tiny area, the houses in the Ghetto were the tallest in Venice, many of them rising to seven stories.

In 1797, the gates to the ghetto were taken down by the French. Jews received full citizenship at the unification of Italy in 1866. Sadly, in 1943, the fascist government deported the remaining Jewish residents.

The Ghetto today

The entire Jewish population of Venice is now just 600 people. This figure includes those living in Mestre and Treviso. Five synagogues survive but only two of them are still used by a congregation numbering about 60. The 16th century Levantine synagogue is favoured in summer, while in winter the congregation attends services in the warmer, more opulent Spanish synagogue.

Museo Ebraico

Campo dei Ghetto Nuovo, 2902B
041 715 359
10.00-19.00 daily, June to September
10.00-18.00 daily, October to May
closed Saturdays, Jewish holidays, December 25, January 1, May 1
admission €3 for museum only
Guided tours in English hourly 10.30-17.30, 15.30 Oct-May €8.50

The museum houses a collection of ritual objects in silver, sacred vestments, and other artifacts. There is also a good bookshop. The guided tour is recommended, as it includes visits to three of the five synagogues: the Schola Canton, Schola Italiana and Schola Levantina.

Madonna dell'Orto

Campo Madonna dell'Orto
vaporetto Orto
10.00-17.00 Monday-Saturday, closed Sunday
entrance fee chorus pass
map 2, H3

The delicate tracery of the facade makes this one of
the prettiest Gothic churches in Venice. Standing on a
northerly and remote part of the city, it is accessed easily
by vaporetto.

First built in 1348, to the designs of a Franciscan monk

Fra Tiberio from Parma, the church was originally consecrated *San Cristoforo* (St Christopher). The saint's kneecap is still preserved in the altar. In 1378 a great miracle was reported: a mammoth stone statue of the Madonna and Child had descended from heaven into a neighbouring orchard (*orto*). The statue was immediately taken into the church where it was duly venerated. Word spread and visitors became so numerous that the church was renamed *Madonna dell'Orto*, Madonna of the Orchard. The large statue is preserved today in the Cappella di San Mauro, on the right aisle inside the church.

From the exterior, the onion dome demonstrates a Byzantine influence that was still going strong well into the 15th century, when the church was rebuilt. Look for the statues of the *Twelve Apostles* by the delle Masegne family in the niches above the sloping wings. Over the entrance is a statue of *St Christopher* by Bartolomeo Bon.

This was Tintoretto's parish church. Ten of his paintings reside here. Over the entrance to the Cappella di San Mauro is *The Presentation of the Virgin Mary in the Temple.* In the apse of the presbytery are two large canvases, *The Last Judgment* and *The Adoration of the Golden Calf,* both painted when the artist was young. In the Cappella Morisini are two canvases by Tintoretto's son Domenico.

Madonna dell'Orto was also the parish church of the Contarini family, who held several high offices in the Republic. There is a Cardinal, a Procurator and two doges amongst the six busts in the *Cappella dei Contarini*. On the altar is another Tintoretto, *St. Agnes resuscitating the son of a Roman prefect.* In a side chapel is a jewel-toned *Madonna and Child* by the young Giovanni Bellini.

The church suffered greatly under Austrian occupation in the 19th century when it was handed over to the army to be used as stables and for storage of ammunition. Two subsequent restorations were poorly executed. Venice in Peril has been involved in two successful campaigns for restoration, in 1968-70 and 1992-96.

Campo dei Mori

map 2, H4

On the eastern wall of the campo are converted factory buildings. Embedded in the walls are statues of three men, dressed in 13th century eastern garb, who constructed the building. The men were brothers Rioba, Saudi and Afani Mastelli, silk merchants who sought refuge in Venice in 1112.

The Mastelli brothers came from Morea and were popularly called *Mori* (Moors). Each statue has a name engraved near its head. The corner figure portrays Rioba, who became the butt of jokes and the subject of lampoons. His metal nose was added in the 19th century.

The Mastelli family took part in the crusade led by Doge Dandolo. They later opened an emporium, selling spices under the sign of the camel. There is a bas-relief of an oriental man leading a camel on the exterior of Palazzo Mastelli at the end of the campo. It can be seen from the top of the bridge.

RIOBA MASTELLI

I Gesuiti (Santa Maria Assunta)

Campo dei Gesuiti
vaporetto Fondamente Nove
041 528 6579
10.00-12.00, 17.00-19.00 daily
map 5, C1

The Jesuits were not always welcome in Venice. They were expelled and re-admitted three times. In 1714, on their second return, they commissioned this church.

The architect Domenico Rossi, a Swiss of little education, was known for his wild debaucheries. He was chosen by his friends, the wealthy Manin family. The Manins were patrons of the Jesuits, they had bought their way into Venetian nobility and would ultimately supply Venice with her last doge.

The Baroque exterior facade is as imposing as the interior is opulent. Inside walls are covered by slabs of green and white marble, inlaid to create a damask effect from floor to ceiling. The pulpit is calculated to bring beauty and luxury to a poor congregation, with a gilded valance and dangling tassels. The Victorian John Ruskin was scandalized. He compared the interior of the church to 'the boudoir of an opera chorus-girl'.

In each of the four corners where nave, presbytery and transepts meet is a statue of an archangel by Torretti. These four archangels, *Michael*, *Gabriel*, *Raphael* and *Sealtiel*, are probably the most beautiful Roccoco statues by a Venetian sculptor.

Titian's *Martyrdom of St Lawrence* is found above the altar in the chapel nearest the entrance. The subject is horrific: St Lawrence is lying on a grid of red-hot coals, being prodded by a guard like a steak on a grill. Tintoretto's painting *The Assumption* hangs in the altar of the transept.

I Gesuiti is a cold place in winter, colder than being outside. Members of the congregation would carry a *scaldino*, a pot of burning charcoal, to warm themselves.

Santa Maria dei Miracoli

Campo dei Miracoli
vaporetto Fondamente Nove or Rialto
10.00-17.00 Monday-Saturday, closed Sundays
entrance fee chorus pass
map 5, C4

This gorgeous jewel box of a church is now recognised
as a model of early Renaissance architecture in Venice. A
miraculous painting led to its creation.

In 1409, a rich merchant Francesco Amadi commissioned a
painting of the *Madonna*, to be hung in a small tabernacle
on the outside corner of his palace in the Corte Nuova.
He paid the artist Nicolò di Pietro less than two ducats for
it. But by 1477, the painting was considered miraculous,
and became an object of profound veneration. An old
woman was stabbed and left for dead on 23rd August,
1480. That she survived was attributed to prayers made to
the painting by her friends. News of the miracle spread.
Soon great crowds were gathering day and night to
worship the icon.

In an effort to gain some peace, Francesco enlisted the

help of his nephew Angelo who moved the painting to the palace of his neighbours, the Barozzi. The crowds followed.

The Barozzi, in turn, threatened litigation against the Amadi if they did not remove the work. Angelo then decided to build a chapel for the *Madonna*. He solicited funds from the Barozzi, as well as providing his own. Alms and gifts from other citizens flowed in and eventually exceeded the costs of construction.

In 1481, Pietro Lombardo was commissioned as builder and he set to work immediately, dedicating his entire workshop towards completing the building. The exterior *pavonazetto* marble, found on three sides, was quarried in Greece and was favoured by imperial Rome because of its semi-transparent quality. The canal side is made from Istrian marble. The decorative roundels are carved from unused marble remnants taken from the Basilica San Marco. Some of them originate in Constantinople.

On New Year's Eve 1489, the miraculous painting of the *Madonna* was secretly transported after nightfall and installed in the high altar. Financed by public donations, the church is a symbol of Venetian pride and independence. It is also one of Venice's most popular churches for weddings. The interior is small enough for a more intimate gathering, and the canal allows the bride and groom to arrive and depart by gondola.

CASTELLO

The grand waterfront view from the Riva leads eastwards to Venice's largest public gardens. Behind it all is the Arsenale, the muscle that made the Empire.

Walk down the *Riva degli Schiavoni* past Vivaldi's church and, if it is still early, visit the *Museo Storico Navale,* a good way to understand how the little Republic became so powerful.

Via Garibaldi is Venice's widest street, full of shops and cafes. It is also where you will find the *Garibaldi monument* and a colony of turtles. From there, walk down a shady boulevard, *Viale Garibaldi,* and rest on one of the many benches.

Art lovers paying a visit to the *Scuola di San Giorgio* for the Carpaccio paintings may also want to include the nearby *Museo delle Icone.* If history is what you seek, be sure to go to *San Giovanni e Paolo* with its monuments to heroes of the Republic.

SAN GIORGIO DEGLI SCHIAVONI

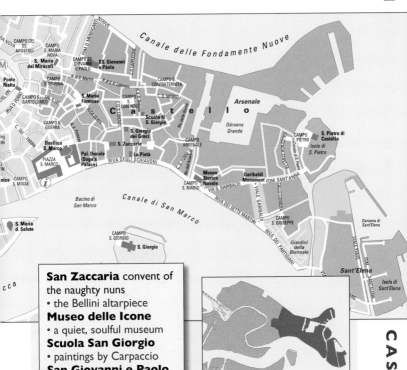

San Zaccaria convent of the naughty nuns
• the Bellini altarpiece
Museo delle Icone
• a quiet, soulful museum
Scuola San Giorgio
• paintings by Carpaccio
San Giovanni e Paolo
Venice's pantheon, many monuments to doges
Museo Storico Navale
maritime museum with Venetian ships and galleons

Riva degli Schiavoni
Promenade with excellent views to San Giorgio Maggiore.

restaurants p.242
shopping p.264
nightlife p.245

Did you know that..?
San Pietro was Venice's cathedral until the title passed to San Marco in 1807.

Giardini Publicci
Venice's largest gardens are shaded by groves of lime trees and have playgrounds for young children. The gardens host the Biennale.

San Zaccaria

Campo San Zaccaria
vaporetto San Zaccaria
10.00-12.00, 16.00-18.00 Monday-Saturday
16.00-18.00 Sundays and holidays
admission fee for Chapel and Crypt
Map 10, I1

The church was founded in the 9th century to house the bones of Zaccharias, the father of John the Baptist, buried under the second altar on the right. In the Cappella di Sant'Atanasio is *The Birth of St John the Baptist*, an early work by Tintoretto. The main altarpiece is a series of seven painted panels by Paolo Veneziano.

The main attraction is Giovanni Bellini's altarpiece *Madonna of San Zaccaria* (p.125). In the serene nobility of the Madonna and the rich colours of Bellini's palette, it is easy to see why he is credited with being the father of Venetian painting. This altarpiece was removed by Napoleon to the Louvre. It was returned to its original placement but not without some damage to the edges of the painting and to the frame.

San Zaccaria's orchards once covered the area that is now the Piazza San Marco. In the 12th century, Doge Sebastiano Ziani requisitioned the land to build the Piazza, and thereafter the Reverend Abbess of the Convent of San Zaccaria was given the privilege of embroidering the doge's cap, the *zogia*. Shaped like a horn, it symbolised power and strength. Nuns presented the doge with a new cap every Easter when he would honour the convent with a visit.

The convent

As the home for nuns from the wealthiest families, the convent attached to the church of San Zaccaria was one of the most notorious in Venice. Noble Venetian families would send many of their daughters to a convent because, with the huge dowries that were expected, marriage was exceedingly expensive. In exchange for lavish donations from their families, unmarried daughters became nuns. They were given a home and considerable freedom within the convent. Before the 16th century, nuns were permitted to receive visitors, wear their own clothes, put on amateur dramatics and even entertain in their own sumptuously decorated boudoir.

When the concept of segregation was introduced in 1506, cloistered nuns faced enclosure and separation for the first time. Suddenly all freedom and gaiety ceased: women were kept hidden behind a grille and they were expected to attend mass several times a day. Nuns who craved variety in their recreation used *Carnevale* as a good excuse to exploit the small amount of seasonal licence afforded them. They were allowed to engage in theatre during Carnevale, as long as the subject of the production was pious. As the length of Carnevale increased in the 17th and 18th centuries (until finally it was six months long), so did the time of their freedom.

Visitation reports suggest that certain communities took great advantage of their cloistered existence to break some of the rules in privacy. At Santa Maria dei Miracoli nuns were known to dress up as men and sing profane songs accompanied by lute and guitar, breaking the rule that all performers should be wearing religious garb.

Venetians regularly attended these performances against strict rules from the Patriarch at San Pietro, who forbade them from attending convent theatres. The Patriarch was also scandalised to learn that not only did the citizens of Venice attend these theatres, but they were also locking themselves in the convent, *'to talk with nuns at prohibited hours and were seen carrying backdrops and props backwards and forwards all day long in order to put on these tragedies and other plays, which occurrences cause confusion within the nunnery and great scandal without.'*

Guardì's painting of the fashionable parlour of San Zaccaria can be seen in Ca' Rezzonico (p.132).

The Ospedali

In the 17th and 18th centuries Venice was one of the most important musical centres in the world. The passion for music among all classes of society produced one of the noblest educational experiments of the Baroque era: the *ospedali* (hospices, or hospitals).

Funded in part by the church, and also by private donations, hospitals became homes for a growing number of orphans. These abandoned children needed to learn a viable trade so it was decided to train them as musicians at the ospedali. By the 16th century there were four ospedali in Venice: one in Dorsoduro and three in Castello. Vivaldi taught at the ospedale of Santa Maria di Pietà.

Boys and girls both received a musical education, but the boys left early to become apprentices in other trades. The girls had to stay on until they were adults – they could only leave to get married or join a convent. As married women they were not allowed to use their talent as professional musicians, so many chose to remain in the ospedali where they were free to perform and teach.

RIVA DEGLI SCHIAVONI

The performances were extraordinary. Paying spectators came from around the world to hear concerts in the ospedali, given by women and girls singing and playing behind grilles, out of sight from the audience. Many singers became internationally famous without ever leaving Venice. Indeed, they became famous for their voices alone, without ever being seen by the audience.

La Pietà (map 11, A2)

On the site where the former church and ospedale of Santa Maria di Pietà once stood, La Pietà is known affectionately as 'Vivaldi's church' and his music is still performed here.

Designed by Giorgio Massari in 1739, possibly influenced by suggestions from Vivaldi, the church was completed in 1745.

The best place to book tickets for performances of Vivaldi's music is:
Vivaldi Store
Campo San Bartolomeo
Fontego dei Tedeschi 5537/40
041 522 1343; map 5, B5

Antonio Vivaldi (1678-1741)

The composer and violinist known as 'the Red Priest' was the eldest of six children born to Giovanni Vivaldi and Camilla Calichio. Antonio's father was a barber before he became a professional violinist and his mother was a tailor's daughter. Giovanni was his son's first teacher, giving him violin and harpsichord lessons at home. They also performed on many occasions as a father/son duo, and they may have played together at Antonio's first serious concert performance in the orchestra of San Marco at Christmas in 1696.

Antonio was groomed for the priesthood and ordained in 1703. But he never truly exercised his profession and soon refused to say mass, claiming that it was impossible due to serious asthmatic attacks. However, this condition did not prevent Vivaldi from teaching several instruments, conducting choirs and orchestras, composing and travelling as a director of his own operas.

Vivaldi was appointed *maestro di violino* at the *Ospedale della Pietà,* where he taught violin and wrote two full *concerti* each month for the girls to perform. Vivaldi then entered the more profitable world of opera and he began travelling, often in the company of a lovely young singer Anna Giraud and her sister Paolina. Eyebrows were raised and trouble ensued: he was barred from the city of Ferrara in 1737 because of his relationship with Anna and his refusal to say mass.

The early successes in Venice did not sustain Vivaldi later in life; other composers became more popular. In 1740 he went to Vienna to revive his career in another great musical city. This was not to be. He died in a boarding house and was buried in a pauper's grave.

Vivaldi's genius was expressed in his concertos, sonatas, and sacred works. Today he is regarded as one of the foremost composers of the Baroque era, standing alongside Monteverdi, Telemann, Handel and J S Bach.

Museo delle Icone (Icon Museum)

Ponte dei Greci 3412
vaporetto San Zaccaria
041 522 6581
9.00-12.30, 13.30-16.30 Mon-Sat, 10.00-17.00 Sunday
admission €5
map 11, A1

Located beside the church of San Giorgio dei Greci, the museum is found on the first floor of the Hellenic Institute of Byzantine and Post-Byzantine Studies. Highly recommended for those who enjoy Byzantine art, the collection houses some of the finest portable Greek icons dating from the 14th-18th centuries. There is more life and expression in these paintings than is typically found in iconography.

The painting style and subject matter are part of the Eastern Orthodox faith, where icons are an essential part of worship. Rather than telling a story, each painting presents an image for meditation, prayer and devotion. This is a highly conservative art form, with minor developments taking place over the centuries.

In the 15th century there was a flowering of icon painting on the island of Crete. Artists were later influenced by Renaissance concepts of perspective and moved beyond two-dimensional representation. The majority of the works on display are products of Cretan workshops. There is a splendid painting of *St George* and another of the *Archangel Michael*. The museum also contains illustrated manuscripts and embroidered vestments.

Greeks in Venice

The Greek community in the lagoon began with a number of Greek artists who were invited to work on the mosaics at Torcello. When Crete became part of the Venetian Empire, along with other Greek islands and mainland ports, their numbers increased until some 4,000 were living in the city of Venice.

ΧΣ

ο ΑΓ
ΤΑΦΟC

Η ΑΓ ΜΑΡΙΑ ΗΜΑΔΑΛΙ
ΝΗ·

ΚΕ ΕΙ CY ΕΒΑCΤΑCΑC ΑΥΤ
ΨΗ ΜΟΙ ΠΒ ΕΘΗΚΑC ΑΥΤ
ΚΑ ΓΩ ΑΥ ΤΑΩ·

ΡΑΒΟΥΝΗ

Scuola di San Giorgio degli Schiavoni

Calle dei Furlani 3259/a
vaporetto San Zaccaria
041 522 8828
09.00-13.00, 14.45-18.00 Tuesday-Saturday, 09.00-13.00 Sunday,
14.45-18.00 Monday
admission €3
map 6, G6

Located a short walk away from the church of San Giorgio dei Greci, this Scuola is sometimes known as the 'Carpaccio Scuola' because it contains so many of the great artist's paintings. Founded by Dalmatian merchants in 1451 for the benefit of Slavonian seamen (*Schiavoni* means 'slav') the Scuola is still a focal point for the local Slav community – distributing charity and sponsoring scholarships.

Vittore Carpaccio (p.126) painted the lives of the Dalmatian saints George, Jerome and Triphun. He transposed their stories from the book, *The Golden Legend*, to a mysterious orient replete with palm trees, turbaned figures, and exotic animals.

St George slaying the Dragon
George confronts the dragon terrorising the inhabitants of Silene (in Libya). A Christian soldier, he is moved by the tears of a beautiful princess about to be the dragon's next victim. George mounts his steed, protects himself with the cross, and wounds the creature with his lance.

Triumph of St George, St George Baptises the Selenites
The wounded dragon is exposed in the city square to the frightened inhabitants. George vows to kill the dragon if they agree to be baptised. In the following scene of mass baptism an elegant greyhound can be seen, his head turned away from the proceedings, one of the many dogs Carpaccio liked to include in his paintings.

The Daughter of Emperor Gordian Exorcised by St Triphun
The eleven-year-old saint has cast out the evil spirit from

CARPACCIO: *VISION OF ST AUGUSTINE*

the emperor's daughter, Gordiana. The demon appears before them in the guise of a winged, horned beast.

St Jerome and the Lion

Jerome is among his brethren when a lion hobbles painfully into the monastery. The monks flee in terror. Carpaccio's sense of humour shows in the contrast between the pained lion and the panic stricken monks. Jerome removes the thorn and commands the monks to return and minister to the beast.

Funeral of Jerome

The death of Jerome is a far more serious piece, but the huge pince-nez of the monk reading the service suggests comic intent.

The Vision of St Augustine

Augustine receives a visitation from Saint Jerome. The phenomenon is represented by a ray of light pouring through the window, washing over Augustine. The light illuminates a very detailed Venetian interior and a slightly bewildered fluffy dog.

Santi Giovanni e Paolo (San Zanipolo)

Campo Santi Giovanni e Paolo
vaporetto Rialto, Fondamente Nove, Ospedale
07.30-18.30 daily
map 5, E4

After the Basilica San Marco and the Piazza, this church
and its campo are the grandest in Venice. Known by
locals as *San Zanipolo*, this enormous building is also
called the *Pantheon of Venice* because it houses so many
monuments to doges, war heroes and other famous
Venetians. It was here that the bodies of deceased doges
were transported for their last solemn honours, following
the official funeral service in San Marco.

Dedicated to two brothers who were martyred in Rome
in the 3rd century, the church was built by Dominican
friars on land donated by Doge Jacopo (Giacomo) Tiepolo
in 1234. Jacopo's sarcophagus is placed outside the door,
along with that of his son, Doge Lorenzo Tiepolo. After
an attempted revolt in 1310 by Bajamonte Tiepolo (p.64,
Council of Ten), the tombs were altered; such a shameful
rebellion meant that a new Tiepolo crest had to be
devised.

Begun in 1246 and demolished not long afterwards, new
construction began in 1333 and the church was finally
consecrated in 1430.

Amongst the many monuments and tombs are some
splendid paintings. Be sure to visit the *Cappella del
Rosario* (Rosary Chapel), to the left of the main altar.
There are several works by Paolo Veronese. Look for his
Annunciation, *Assumption* and *Adoration of the Shepherds*
on the ceiling.

The Bellini brothers Giovanni and Gentile are buried in
the *Cappella di Sant' Orsola* (Chapel of St Ursula, which
is now closed). Giovanni's painting *SS Vincent Ferrer,
Christopher and Sebastian* can be found in an altarpiece
along the aisle to the right of the main entrance. Further
along on the right, in the *Cappella di San Domenico*

(Dominican Chapel) is the ceiling painting *The Glory of San Domenico* by G.B. Piazzeta, who was Giambattista Tiepolo's teacher.

Outside the church is the equestrian statue of Bartolomeo Colleoni, a general in the service of Venice. Originally thought to be by Leonardo da Vinci, it was found to be the work of his teacher, Andrea Verrochio.

Ghost stories

Venetians tell stories about the ghosts of three doges that haunt the streets surrounding San Zanipolo: the Traitor Doge (Marino Falier), the Blind Doge (Enrico Dandolo) and the Prophetic Doge (Tommaso Mocenigo).

Behind the church, in the Calle Torelli della Cavalerizza, Doge Falier assembled his followers in a plot against the Republic. Falier was caught and beheaded. When he was buried, Falier's severed head was placed between his legs. At night, his body has been seen searching for his displaced head in the places where he used to meet his followers. Many Venetians claim to have heard his desperate cry at the rear of the church, near the stained glass windows.

Doge Dandolo led the Fourth Crusade in the sacking of Constantinople in 1204. Because Dandolo caused a lot of innocent bloodshed, his ghost carries a sharp sword by the blade, cutting his own hands. With two burning coals in place of his blind eyes, Dandolo is condemned to wander in search of Falier to avenge the honour of Venice. Legend says they come close occasionally, but they are unable to see each other.

In 1423, Doge Mocenigo predicted the downfall of Venice. His spirit is doomed to continuously pull a long roll of paper from his mouth, on which is printed the word '*Veritas*'. The paper wraps around his legs, making him trip and fall. It has been reported that the ghost will accept help to free his legs. This will cause his face to light up in gratitude and he will continue on his way.

Museo Storico Navale

Campo San Biagio
041 520 0276
8.45-13.30 Mon-Fri, 8.45-13.00 Sat, closed Sunday
admission €1.55
map 11, D3

Near the Arsenale, this museum contains one of the world's largest maritime displays and everything is well annotated in English. Spread over four floors, it is definitely worth a visit, and not just for the Venetian craft such as the Doge's grand *Bucintoro*. Of potential interest is a room with model junks, a Viking room and for children, a collection of seashells. Admission includes entrance to the nearby Padiglioni delle Navi, which houses more Venetian boats but is often closed.

Arsenale

Venice was the first city of medieval Europe to engage in capital investment on a wide scale, committing public funds to essential industries like shipbuilding. Naval war and marine commerce used two different types of ship: the long *war galleasses* and the round *merchant galleys*, both powered by a combination of oar and sail, and built at the Arsenale shipyards. Begun in 1104, the shipyards became the centre of military power in Venice – the engine that ran the empire, a great shipbuilding complex that was the world's first assembly line.

At its height in 1570, the Arsenale covered 46 hectares, was home to 300 shipping companies and employed up to 16,000 people who could produce and fully outfit 100 war galleys in eight weeks. New firearms and small arms were also developed here. The Lion of St Mark guarding the land gate does not display the customary words, 'Peace be unto you, Mark, my evangelist', as they were deemed unsuitable.

The Battle of Lepanto (1571) against the Ottoman Turks was the Venetian Empire's last great victory and the last major sea battle fought with oar power. Other European states had converted to sail and their control over trading routes increased. Venice did not keep up with new technologies, so the Arsenale fell into decline. By the time Napoleon arrived, shipbuilding had virtually ceased.

The Arsenale is still a naval base, repairing and refitting ships, but is mostly off limits to the public. Some of the buildings are now being used by the Biennale; others house a theatre and temporary exhibition spaces.

The Sack of Constantinople

The relationship between Venice and Constantinople had always been complex. A first treaty was signed in 800, early in Venice's history when she was a brand new republic seeking customers for her wares. Byzantium had been a great empire since the fall of Rome and the capital, Constantinople, was a very wealthy city.

Then the power balance shifted. As Constantinople fell into decline and decadence, Venetian trade and power increased. Her industry expanded to include iron and glass manufacture, jewellery making, cloth dyeing and most lucrative, shipbuilding. Venice developed a powerful war fleet to protect her trade routes against pirates. These ships also protected Byzantium in exchange for ever more generous trading privileges.

But Venice and Constantinople became direct rivals for Eastern Mediterranean trade during the 12th century. Venetians were hated for their arrogance and envied for their success. In 1171, Venetians living in the Byzantine Empire were arrested and their property confiscated. To resolve matters, the serving Venetian ambassador to Byzantium, Enrico Dandolo, went on a peace mission to Constantinople in 1172. The ambassador so annoyed the Emperor Manuel with his stubbornness that the ruler had him blinded.

In 1201 the armies of the Fourth Crusade became stranded on the Lido. Venice had agreed to supply ships and sail them to the Holy Land, but the Crusaders found themselves unable to pay. Venice stood to lose a substantial fortune. Enrico Dandolo, now Doge Dandolo, had a solution. He proposed that the Crusaders postpone payment until plunder should make good the debt. But in exchange for this concession, they must recapture for Venice the powerfully fortified town of Zara on the Dalmation Coast. When the papal representative tried to stop this assault on a Christian city, Dandolo threatened to cut off supplies to the army and refused to recognise papal authority. The papal legate was told to either minister to the Crusaders needs or return to Rome.

In October 1202, the blind Doge Dandolo, then 85 years old, unfurled the banner of St Mark at the head of a fleet numbering more than 500 ships – the largest ever amassed – and sailed out of the Venetian lagoon. The fleet attacked Zara in November and after two weeks of intense fighting, the city surrendered. Crusaders sent emissaries to Rome begging forgiveness. Pope Innocent granted supplicant forgiveness to the Crusaders but excommunicated the Venetians. The papal edict was kept secret and therefore had no punitive effect. But the Crusade continued and the Pope made no attempt to enforce his decree.

While in Zara, the Crusaders received a tempting proposal from the Byzantine prince Alexius whose father Emperor Isaac II Angelus had been usurped. The Emperor was imprisoned in Constantinople. Would the Crusaders help? Dandolo seized his chance for revenge. There were some who objected to fighting yet another Christian power when they had signed up to defeat the Muslims – but most stayed, motivated by the treasure chest that was Constantinople.

The most fortified metropolis in the world had never been successfully attacked. The Venetians transformed part of their fleet into floating assault weapons. By laying spars side by side and lashing planks across them, they created long sturdy gangways, flying bridges that could place warriors within reach of the defence towers.

When battle commenced, transport ships were sent in first, sending a shower of stones to cover the landing of troops. Then the assault ships neared the walls, with soldiers standing on the flying bridges, exchanging blows with enemy garrisons. Next came the war galleys, filled with Crusaders and bowmen. Captains of the fleet held back in fear until they saw the Doge, fully armed on the prow of his galley, holding the banner of St Mark and crying out to his men to drive their ships ashore if they valued their lives. The aged, blind Dandolo planted the flag on solid ground. Dandolo's captains rallied behind him and the first battle was won, on 17th July 1203.

Envoys sent by the fleet demanded the money that young Alexius had promised. The Crusaders, encamped on the Bosphoros, awaited payment. The prince betrayed them and attacked. He failed; later he was ambushed and murdered. His successor Alexius V also attacked the allies and met defeat.

On 12th April 1204, the Venetians and the Crusaders stormed Constantinople again. This time they gave full vent to their lust for blood and loot. In a three-day rampage of rape and murder, they looted a city with more wealth than the rest of Europe put together.

The Venetians were the most organised, stealing methodically for the glory of the Republic. Along with gold, jewels, priceless relics and artifacts, they took the four Roman horses, the *Quadrigo,* that now reside in San Marco. Venice became, and remains, the chief repository of Byzantine art.

Doge Dandolo also won land concessions for Venice. In addition to three-eighths of Constantinople, he acquired the best harbours of the Byzantine Empire for the Republic. Venice had won firm control of all shipping routes from the Adriatic to the eastern Mediterranean and into the Black Sea. The little marine republic now possessed an empire.

Castello Ghost Story

In September 1921, Vinicio Salvi claimed that he was searching for snails in the garden close to Garibaldi's monument (map 12, G3) when a 'red shadow' appeared, punched him in the arm and then vanished into thin air.

Salvi's arm was covered in bruises but the neighbourhood was divided: there were those who believed Salvi and those who claimed it was down to the red wine he liked to drink. People were uneasy and no one strolled the Via Garibaldi for several evenings. Then, exactly one week after the Salvi sighting, lovers embracing near the monument were attacked by a 'red shadow'.

A vigilante committee was established to keep watch on the monument. Fifteen men stood guard. All was quiet until the hour after midnight, the witching hour. Then, when two men approached the monument to give it closer inspection, a red lightning bolt hurled them to the ground. The vigilantes rushed to rescue their comrades, and suddenly the shadow took human form. A figure wearing a red shirt stared out in defiance. 'It's Bepi!' cried Tino, a seventeen-year-old boy considered to be 'simple' by the community. 'Bepi used to sit here and say: I will always guard my General's back. And when I'm no longer here I'll do it from Heaven,' said Tino.

As the men stared it became clear that the image that appeared before them was in fact Giuseppe Zolli (Bepi) who had fought in Garibaldi's legion. Zolli had died a few weeks previously and was keeping his vow of loyalty to his hero.

As news spread it was necessary for the vigilantes to guard the monument from the curious. By popular demand a new statue was added, facing away from Garibaldi. It is Bepi, guarding his General's back.

Isola di San Pietro

This is a working side of Venice, with boat repair yards
and simple homes. Those seeking quiet and a break from
other tourists will find peace on this little island. Aside
from the church and campanile, there are no major sights.

San Pietro di Castello

10.00-17.00 Monday–Saturday, closed Sunday
Campanile, 10.00-18.00 daily
admission fee chorus pass
map 12, I1

From the 11th century, San Pietro was the Cathedral of
Venice, the seat of Roman authority, located far away
from the centre of Venetian power in San Marco. Keeping
the cathedral at the edge of the lagoon enabled the
doge to ignore papal excommunications and political
interference from Rome (p.26).

The interior has been stripped of its former grandeur,
and is now a parish church serving its community. It
contains some interesting pieces by Veronese: *St John the
Evangelist* and *St Peter and St Paul*. On the right side of the
church, is the *Throne of St Peter of Antioch,* a marble chair
decorated with lines taken from the Koran.

Biennale

The Biennale was founded in 1895 from an idea jotted down on a napkin at Caffè Florian. Today it is the most prestigious contemporary art exhibition in the world. The exhibition is held bi-annually in summer, during odd numbered years, in the *Giardini Pubblici*. The exhibition pavilions are owned by the participating nations.

The Venice Biennale is just one of the cultural events organised by the *Società di Cultura La Biennale di Venezia*. The society is a public/private partnership structured along corporate lines with a Board of Directors, who appoint the Artistic Directors for all events under the Biennale umbrella including the art exhibition and the Venice Film Festival, music concerts and dance events.

ORDER TICKETS AND OBTAIN A SCHEDULE OF ALL EVENTS FROM THE BIENNALE WEBSITE AT WWW.LABIENNALE.ORG

Film Festival tickets are also available at ACTV outlets and on the day at the ticket office at the casino on the Lido.

THE ITALIAN PAVILION

Film Festival

The Venice Film Festival is held annually on the Lido during the first two weeks of September. The 61st edition was an unforgettable year for the new head Marco Mueller. It was the year that Al Pacino, starring as Shylock in *The Merchant of Venice*, was denied a seat for the screening of his own film. And it was also the year that Harvey Weinstein, head of Miramax, threatened to kill Mr Mueller.

Film companies require a location permit to shoot in Venice, with the ultimate authority residing with the mayor. The mayor also has a seat on the board of the Venice Biennale, the governing body for the film festival. In 2003, two British producers of *The Merchant of Venice*, also starring Jeremy Irons and Joseph Fiennes, approached then-mayor, Paolo Costa, for permission to shoot. He arranged for the Grand Canal to be closed for a day to facilitate the film. It was duly reported in the press that Mayor Costa was a great fan of Al Pacino.

Later in the year, Paolo Costa invited Pacino to a special opening of La Fenice opera house, which was attended by international celebrities, including Elton John. But Pacino did not appear and Costa felt the public snub.

Fast forward to the 2004 Venice Film Festival and the screening of *The Merchant of Venice*. Pacino had done his glad-handing and autograph signing on the red carpet. He was looking forward to sitting down to watch his film, but there was no seat. The cinema was full. Pacino was the star, but somehow a seat had not been allocated.

The resulting delay had a knock-on effect: the next film, made by Miramax and starring Johnny Depp, was not screened until after 2am. The celebrity dinner at the Doge's Palace, scheduled to follow the evening screenings, ended up being a cold breakfast. Producer Harvey Weinstein took the stage at his screening, saying he would first teach Marco Mueller the meaning of a schedule and '*then I'll drown him in the Lagoon*'.

ISLANDS

SAN GIORGIO MAGGIORE

San Giorgio Maggiore

vaporetto San Giorgio
041 522 7827
09.30-12.30, 14.30-16.30 open later in summer

The church, campanile and island occupy one of the most spectacular sites in the lagoon. The view from the campanile takes in Venice, the islands of the lagoon and beyond to the open Adriatic. There is small admission charge for the lift.

In 982, Doge Tribuno Memmo gave the island to Zuane Morosini. A Benedictine monastery was soon established and dedicated to St Stephen whose corpse was part of the loot from Constantinople (p.183). After an earthquake in 1223 destroyed the church buildings, George was again named the patron saint of the island, the position he occupied before Stephen's arrival. This is why both *St Stephen* and *St George* stand at the entrance to the church.

Designed by Palladio, with construction started in 1565, the present church was completed 45 years later. The white interior is simple and luminous. In the sanctuary are two of Tintoretto's best paintings *The Last Supper* and *The Gathering of Manna* completed when the artist was nearly 80. Tintoretto's final work *The Deposition* hangs in the Capella dei Morti.

Palladio (1508-1580)

Andrea di Petro della Gondola, nicknamed Palladio, was one of the most influential architects in the Western world yet he suffered for years under the shadow of his rival Sansovino (p.81). In the 1540s Palladio was designing villas for the nobility of Vicenza, without receiving similar work in Venice. Indeed, he was only granted the commission for his first church, San Francesco della Vigna, because Sansovino was in prison. Palladio's second church was San Giorgio Maggiore and his third, Il Redentore on Giudecca. A mathematician, he devised proportions based on strict formulas developed by ancient Roman architects. Palladio wrote *The Four*

Books of Architecture, which were widely translated and spread his ideas across Europe and America.

A papal election

Napoleon needed a pope to crown him as emperor. Pope Pius VI had been taken prisoner by Napoleon and died in exile in Valence. Napoleon would have appointed his own pope, but Cardinal Camerlengo insisted that an election be held. In 1799 the Cardinal summoned 37 other cardinals from around the world to San Giorgio Maggiore to elect a new pope. They deliberated for three months before appointing Niccolo Chiaramonti as Pius VII. The new Pope ingratiated himself with Napoleon and in 1804 crowned him Emperor at Notre Dame in Paris. Up a narrow staircase leading from the sanctuary, is the *Sala Capitolare*, where the election was held.

The balloon

In 1806 the monastery was suppressed and the island was handed over to the Austrian army as a barracks. Soldiers used the church as a workshop and it was here that Pasquale Andrioni designed a balloon to lift 70,000 pounds. Ten of these balloons were meant to take 10,000 men across the channel to assist in the invasion of Great Britain.

Andrioni's French assistant, Dupre, declared: '*The separation of Great Britain from the Continent has caused centuries of atrocities. The Romans, under Julius Caesar were the first to conquer her. May the French, under Napoleon, be her final conquerors. That is the prayer of Humanity.*'

Thousands came to see the launch, but the balloon would not rise.

Restoration

In 1951 Count Vittorio Cini acquired a 99-year lease on San Giorgio and lovingly restored the buildings in memory of his son, Giorgio, who was killed in a flying accident. Today it is possible to see exhibitions, attend concerts in the cloister or just enjoy the peace and quiet.

VAPORETTI FOR MURANO, BURANO AND TORCELLO LEAVE FROM FONDAMENTE NOVE IN CANNAREGIO.

Murano

Visit the glass museum, or the Basilica Santi Maria e Donato, or pop into a studio to watch glass being made. However, if you are visiting Murano only in the hope of a better price for glass you will be disappointed.

Museo del Vetro (Glass Museum)

Fondamenta Giustinian 8
041 739 586
10.00-18.00 in summer, 10.00-16.00 in winter, closed Wednesday
admission €5.50

Founded by Abbot Vincenzo Zanetti in 1861, the museum exhibits more than 4,000 pieces from all eras, and provides a good insight into glassmaking. On the ground floor is a small room with glass from the 1st and 2nd centuries. Here you will find some very simple and elegant pieces that illustrate how old the glassmaking tradition is in the region. Upstairs, there is a room with displays showing how glass is made, how colours are added and which tools are used. Unfortunately, this room is not labeled in English.

There is a giant candelabra on display and an elaborate

glass centrepiece of a fountain in a garden, made for the Doge's table. Another room exhibits more contemporary glass from the 1980s.

Basilica Santi Maria e Donato

Campo San Donato
08.00-12.00, 15.30-19.00 Monday-Saturday; 15.30-19.00 Sunday

Recently restored, this church has an incredible mosaic floor. Thousands of pieces of semiprecious stones, marble and glass are used to create geometric patterns. Look closely and you will see images of animals, flowers and fish. The floor of the Basilica San Marco is more spectacular, but it is covered by carpets and tourists.

Originally dedicated to St Mary, there has been a church on this site since the 7th century. This red brick version, with its Romanesque design, was built in the 12th century to hold the remains of Donato, patron saint of Murano. According to legend, the saint killed a dragon, and four of the dragon 'bones' are kept behind the altar.

Glassworks

Look for the sign *Fornace* (furnace), or visit:

Venini
Fondamenta Vetrai
041 739 955

Berengo Studio and Gallery
Fondamenta Vertrai 109A
041 739 453

Glass

In the 1st century AD, Pliny the Elder attributed the invention of glass to the Phoenicians, claiming that a ship carrying *nitre* dropped anchor near a beach. As the passengers prepared their dinner, cooking pots were stacked on nitre taken from the ship's cargo and a fire was lit under them. The mixture of fire, nitre and sand produced rivulets of a foreign liquid: glass. There are three main components in glass: silica, soda and lime. On Pliny's beach, the sand contained silica and lime, and nitre is a natural source of soda.

Modern historians say that glass was invented in Mesopotamia (Iraq) around 1500 BC. Glass-making techniques spread to Egypt in 1450 BC. In 332 BC, Alexandria was considered to be one of the most important centres for the production of glass *tesserae* (used in mosaics) and gold-banded glass flasks (for scented oils). The first known attempt to create a coordinated set of glass tableware occurred in Puglia, southern Italy.

To make glass, the basic ingredients are heated to a liquid state at 1,700°c. Fluxes or melting agents are added to lower the melting point, enabling the artisan to work the glass. This is a slow and detailed process: the glass is picked up with an iron blowpipe, then blown, spun, and twisted into shape. Beads are made from a long glass cane, cut into small pieces. Each piece of blown glass is unique because the hand gestures and movements of the glass artist cannot be exactly replicated.

Venice has one of the oldest glassmaking traditions in Europe. A document from the 3rd century details rivalries between glass producers and cutters in Aquileia in the Veneto. The foundations of a glass factory and the remains of three furnaces from the 7th century were found on Torcello. The glass industry was moved to Murano from Venice in 1291 when all furnaces were removed to the island to limit the hazard of fire in Venice.

Glassworkers enjoyed a privileged position in Venetian society and this reflected the economic importance of the goods they created. If a nobleman married the daughter of a glassmaker the noble's titles would pass to their children. Foreign glassworkers who practiced on Murano for 15 years were granted full Venetian citizenship.

The Venetian government, in recognition of the value of Murano glass and its place in the global market, strictly regulated production. To prevent an oversupply, furnaces were only permitted to operate for a specific period set by the government. Ateliers were forced to close for an annual vacation of up to six months. But should glass be required for Basilica San Marco or any other public building, special dispensation to keep the glassworks open was always granted.

All glassworkers had to belong to the guild *Capitolare dell'arte*. In 1285 the Great Council decreed that special authorisation from the doge was required before broken glass, sand, or any other material used in glassmaking could be exported. From 1295 any glassmaker who left Venice was banned from the guild forever. In 1301, the production of spectacles (and later mirrors) came under the jurisdiction of the guild and ateliers were also moved to Murano.

Those that divulged the secrets of Murano glass were subject to assassination. A favourite method was to stab the victim with a special knife made with a glass blade. The assassin would then snap the handle off, leaving the glass inside for a slow, painful death.

Murano glass reached a peak of creativity and global trade between the 15th and 17th centuries. By the fall of the Republic in 1797, all of the secrets had long been revealed. Other centres were on the rise and Murano glass went into a slow decline. Today, there are ateliers where the ancient traditions are kept alive and new artists are being trained. There is still beautiful glass being made on Murano.

Burano

A 40-minute vaporetto ride north-east from the city, Burano is a delightful contrast to the more ostentatious marvels of Venice. You can while away a happy hour or two just wandering around this miniature world of brightly coloured houses, canals and shady parks. The story is that all the houses were painted in distinctive colours, so that each fisherman could easily recognize his own home when returning home after a day out on the water.

The main street and the piazza facing the church of San Martino Vescovo are dedicated to Baldassare Galuppi (1706-85) a famous musician who was known as *Il Buranello*, the pride of Burano. A violinist and composer of opera, he set many of Carlo Goldoni's plays to music in a genre known as *opera buffa* (comic opera). If you are on Burano in the early evening, find your way to the Via Baldassare Galuppi to see the *passeggiata*, when the island residents come out for a stroll and a visit.

Lace

Burano is the historic capital of Italian lace production. As early as the 14th century, nuns were making lace exclusively for church use. The Duchess Morosina

Morosini, wife of the Doge, was so fond of Burano lace that she established a workshop employing 130 lace-makers. The lace was part of her personal wardrobe, and much of it was given to her friends in the grandest courts of Europe. When trade guilds took over the craft in the 15th century, lace became increasingly popular as a fashion item. Many famous portraits by Rembrandt and Van Dyke show noblemen wearing elaborate lace collars. During this time the women of Burano became so adept that they were paid large sums to leave and practice their lacemaking in Normandy.

Towards the end of the 17th century French and Dutch producers surpassed Burano and the craft went into decline. The Countess Adriana Marcello was responsible for its revival at the end of the 18th century. She was so moved by destitution caused by a bitter winter and a disastrous fishing season, that she established a school of lace, *Scuola di Merletti,* providing the islanders with a much-needed secondary source of income.

Today, young women do not want to learn the painstaking and intricate skills of lacemaking. This could lead to the craft dying out in the next generation.

Scuola di Merletti

Piazza B Galuppi 187
041 730034
10.00-17.00 daily April-October
10.00-16.00 daily October-March
closed Tuesday
admission €4

The Scuola is now a museum and shop. Sometimes on weekday mornings you can see older women making lace in the traditional way.

From Burano, it is worth walking over the long wooden bridge to the peaceful island of Mazzarbo.

Torcello

A VISIT TO BURANO AND TORCELLO IS A GOOD DAY OUT.

From Burano, catch the ferry to Torcello, and then stroll towards its centre along the path beside the canal. The only bridge on the island is Devil's Bridge, one without balustrades, similar to those in Carpaccio's paintings.

Turricellum

The *Altinati* arrived in the 7th century and named the island *Turricellum* after the tower in Altinum, their native village on the mainland. The new community flourished with the production of glass and trade in wool. The island also benefited from an increase in refugees from the mainland, especially stonemasons and carvers from Ravenna. Torcello once had a population of 20,000 with 20 parish churches.

As Venice grew, people began to leave the island in favour of the city. The buildings on Torcello were taken apart, stone by stone, with whole staircases and portals loaded on boats and moved to Venice. Eventually the island was almost completely abandoned. Today, people arrive to visit the two churches and the museum, or to dine at Locanda Cipriani, the only restaurant.

Basilica di Santa Maria Assunta

041 270 2464
10.30-17.30 daily March-October
10.00-17.00 daily November-February
admission €3 church, €2 campanile

Mosaics are the main features in the church. The floor is an extraordinary mosaic made of coloured marble. The *Madonna Teotica*, in the apse, with a large teardrop on her cheek, dates from the 12th century. Facing her, on the opposite wall, is *The Last Judgement*, an enormous mosaic made in two stages by Venetian-Byzantine artists in the 12th and late 13th centuries. It is divided into several bands: at the top is the *Crucifixion* and *Christ's descent into*

Hell; at the bottom there is a representation of Paradise inhabited by the saints and patriarchs. There is also a depiction of the medieval notion of Hell, no doubt rather frightening at the time.

A HEAD SET WITH COMMENTARY IN ENGLISH EXPLAINS THE SYMBOLISM CONTAINED WITHIN THE MOSAIC IN ENTERTAINING DETAIL.

It is worth paying the extra charge to climb to the top of the 11th century Campanile. Built a few yards east of the cathedral, to offer refuge to clergy in the event of armed attack, it offers an expansive view of the lagoon. Looking at the surrounding flat and marshy islands provides some insight into what the early settlers must have faced.

Opposite the Basilica is the church of Santa Fosca, and the Museo di Torcello, which exhibits a mix of paintings, coins, jewellery and architectural artifacts.

The Lido

vaporetto Santa Maria Elisabetta

Largest of the lagoon islands, serving as a beach resort and suburb, the Lido is a 12km long narrow strip of beach-fringed land that protects Venice from the Adriatic. Frequent waterbuses connect with the city and it is worth taking the journey just for the view of Venice. Cars are allowed on the Lido, giving it a very different character to Venice, and there is a bus service that runs the length of the island.

Originally this was a wild and windswept place. The poets Byron and Shelley went horseback riding here and were struck by the haunting desolation. Developed in the late 19th century as a fashionable resort, it became the playground of the idle rich as epitomised in Thomas Mann's *Death in Venice* and Visconti's filmed version of the same name. If Venice is the glorious *La Serenissima* the Lido today is a somewhat faded Hollywood star. Despite her elegant past, she does not quite live up to her former grandeur.

In Venice itself opportunities for sport and recreation are few and far between so, if you are looking for beaches, golf, tennis or cycling, the Lido is probably your best bet. However, it does become very crowded in the summer, particularly in July and August, and it can be a shock to

leave the car-free streets of Venice and suddenly encounter busy traffic and seaside paraphernalia. The best way to escape the crowds is to explore the Lido by bicycle – available for hire near the vaporetto stop.

The large hotels control many of the beaches, making them effectively private property. You will pay dearly for anything from a sun-lounger to an umbrella. The wide stretch at Alberoni is widely regarded as the best on the island and is also known as the gay beach.

Most of the palatial homes and hotels on the island were built at the turn of the century. There are some good examples of *art nouveau* (known as *Liberty style* in Italy) and *art deco* architecture that are worth seeking out. Look for the *Hungaria Hotel* and *Villa Monplaisir* on Gran Viale Santa Maria Elisabetta. This wide street leads from the lagoon on one side, to the sea on the other. It is the heart of the Lido and is lined with hotels, expensive shops and restaurants. *Grand Hotel des Bains*, the location for the film *Death in Venice*, faces the sea at the end of the street. Further west the *Grand Hotel Excelsior*, an exotic Moorish masterpiece, was the world's largest hotel when it was built in 1907.

The Lido hosted the first international film festival in 1932 and is still the location of the Venice Film Festival, an annual industry event held in September.

Cycling

Giorgio Barbieri
Via Zara 5, halfway along the
Gran Viale
041 526 1490
08.30-19.30 daily
open March-October, closed the
rest of the year
€3.00 per hour, €9.00 per day
Bikes and tricycles with
canopies for hire

Bruno Lazzari
21B Gran Viale
041 526 8019
08.00-20.00 daily,
March-September
08.30-13.00, 15.00-19.30 daily
October-February
€3.00 per hour, €9.00 per day
credit cards accepted
You must leave some form
of ID with this hire shop.
Payment is taken on return of
the bike.

Golf

Circolo Golf Venezia
Via del Forte Alberoni
041 731 333
08.30-18.00 Tuesday-Friday
08.30-20.00 Saturday, Sunday
April-September
08.30-18.00 Tuesday-Saturday
October-March
€50.00 per day Tuesday-Friday
€60.00 Saturday and Sunday
credit cards accepted
www.circologolfvenezia.it
This course on the southern
tip of the Lido is reputed to
be one of the best in Italy.
Non-members are permitted,
but need proof of membership
of another golf club.

Horseriding

Circolo Ippoco Veneziano
Ca'Bianco
041 526 8091
closed Sunday afternoon and
Monday
€116.00 for 5 lessons including
membership and insurance
Ride in their own arena, on
marked tracks and along some
parts of the beach.

Rowing

Canottieri Diadora
Ca'Bianco
vaporetto Lido then bus B
041 526 5742
Beginners can learn the art of
Venetian rowing.

Running, Jogging

The Lido is ideal for distance
jogging as there are long
stretches of beach and well
maintained roads.

Tennis

Tennis Club Ca'Del Moro
Via Ferrucio Parri 6
041 770 965
08.30-20.30 Monday-Saturday
08.30-20.00 Sunday
€8.25 per hour per person
€8.52 per court for 90 mins
pool - €10.00 for halfday.
€15.00 full day
No credit cards
Ten tennis courts are available.
It does have other facilities
including a swimming pool,
football pitches and a gym.

Chioggia

This is a charming fishing town at the south end of the lagoon, accessible by land or by combining a vaporetto and bus journey from Venice. By far the best way to arrive is by boat. Find your way to the Lido and take a No.11 bus for Pellestrina where you will board a boat to complete the journey. It takes 90 minutes each way and a through trip costs €5.

Chioggia was once the busiest fishing port in the Adriatic. Today it has an unpretentious and friendly atmosphere with charming bridges over small canals. The town's grid layout makes it easy to find your way around. The cobblestoned main square has been pedestrianised and is a lively place during passeggiata.

Fishing boats are residents' most cherished possessions, the flat-bottomed ones with colourful decorations are known as *bragozzo*. Carpaccio's last painting *St Paul* is in the church of San Domenico.

Rendezvous Fantasia
Via Roma 1445
30019 Sottomarina di Chioggia
041 551 0400 or mobile 330 24 73 31
www.rendez-vous-fantasia.com
Travellers with boating experience seeking a more adventurous way to visit the lagoon might consider hiring a houseboat in Chioggia. Equipped for eating and sleeping on board, these boats also come with a skipper if you need one. The company provides instructions, itineraries and docking places at each destination.

CARNEVALE

Carnevale

It begins in February, on the Sunday ten days before Lent. At noon, in the Piazza San Marco, a hush spreads over the crowd of some 500 costumed figures, 15,000 photographers and 100,000 onlookers. Then an angel appears, floating down out of the sky in a cloud of sparkling confetti. Shrouded in white, she melts into the swirling mist, the soles of her trainers visible, as she hovers in the air before dropping lightly to the ground. The annual party, the costumed fantasy that is *Carnevale*, is now officially open.

Other than a closing parade ten days later, on Shrove Tuesday, there is no formal programme. Many hotels organise dinners and balls, but for most people the fun is in the streets and bars, and in the Piazza San Marco. It's about dressing up, or watching and photographing those who are in costume. Annual participants come from around the world and, in order to be recognised, many will have already emailed a description of their costumes to the friends they made last year. Currently, those from France and Austria outnumber most other European nations – probably because they can more easily transport their elaborate costumes on the train.

Carnevale or Carnival relates to *carne levare*, which means 'leave carnal pleasures'. Evolving out of earlier pagan festivals, it was adapted to the Christian calendar, whereby the time leading up to Easter became a time to abstain, not only from eating flesh but from all of its desires as well. Prior to this ordeal, celebration and feasting are the order of the day. In Venice there was another social function: Venetian society was strictly hierarchical and dressing up at Carnevale gave the lower classes the illusion of equity with the ruling class. It was a part of Venetian life until 1848 (when it was banned to thwart Austrian tax policy) and then revived in 1979.

The two biggest and best-known carnivals are in Rio

de Janiero and Venice. In the tropical climate of Brazil, costumes are as scanty as possible, often consisting only of feathers. Venice is far too cold for such youthful erotic displays, with temperatures rarely above 12°c. Venetian costumes cover the entire body and are large enough to accommodate warm woollies underneath. This makes Venice a very democratic carnival. Anyone can participate, you don't have to be young, or gorgeous, or particularly wealthy. Book yourself a flight and a hotel and join in the fun. Arrive in costume and *you* are the show.

What to wear?

The type of costumes worn during Carnevale fall into two main categories: historical and fantasy, with the second type becoming more popular. The traditional Venetian costume is the *bauta* – a black veil fully covering the hair and draping around the shoulders, topped by a black tricorn hat and worn with a plain white mask. The mask has a triangular projection over the nose and mouth, designed to allow eating and drinking (it also changed the sound of a person's voice). It is often worn with a long black cloak, called a *tabarro.* The ensemble is intended to conceal not only the identity of the wearer but the gender as well. With this costume, anyone could misbehave with impunity and escape the consequences.

Fantasy costumes can assume any shape and size, limited only by the imagination. Deciding which costume to wear depends on your agenda: a full mask and headdress is best to attract attention in the Piazza, but it can impede your movement. A lighter costume with a half-mask that can be removed is more suited to drinking and conversing.

Independence of spirit is what carnival is all about. The object is to become a different person in costume. Posing, gestures and attitudes will come naturally. For the span of carnival, you can wear your costume as though it is your ordinary dress, at any time of night or day.

Masks

Traditionally the masks were made of leather, first boiled and then moulded into shape. Papier-mâché is preferred today, with the best masks derived from handmade moulds. Avoid plastic masks as they are impossibly hot. Always check that the mask is not split: if it is bent at the side, it may crack.

In a full mask you are advised to cut holes in the nostrils to allow you to breathe without condensation. If you have time to prepare your mask beforehand, paint the interior with two coats of gloss paint to waterproof the mask from the moisture in your breath. You may wish to reinforce the inside of the mask with bandage adhesives for extra strength. Also fit a foam pad to the very top of the inside of the mask if wearing a headdress. This will keep the mask from slipping under the weight.

For a simple costume that is easy to obtain, wear a half-mask with a vaguely 18th century military jacket, high black boots and a tricorn hat, worn with or without a giant feather. Add a black cape to complete the ensemble. If you are flying to Venice, you might like to bring most of the outfit in your suitcase, then buy the mask and rent the hat after you arrive.

The play is the thing

Most of the big events take place on or near the stage in the Piazza. There are performances of *commedia dell'arte*, a form of Italian theatre dating from the 16th-18th centuries and a long-standing part of Carnevale. Plots are improvised from established situations, with stock characters defined by their masks. As stereotypes, they are a comical reflection of Venetian society: *Pantalone* is the rich old merchant, *Balanzone* the know-it-all doctor, *Pulcinello* the work-shy clown, *Brighella* is a crafty servant, *Harlequin* is a daft acrobat and *Columbina* is a cunning wench. Aside from the staged plays, you will see people wearing costumes that represent these characters.

Performances of all kinds happen spontaneously: groups arrive in full costume, establish a space for themselves, and then perform. There are parades and, if you are in serious costume, you can join in without question. Your costume is your ticket to enter, and to being informed about the next place to go. Be prepared to be photographed; the short walk from the clock tower in San Marco to the water's edge can easily take half an hour, with photographers snapping all the way. The photographers often know exactly what kind of picture they want and will arrange photo sessions that will then become mini-events or spontaneous parades.

Money is no object

Carnevale has no admission charges unless you elect to go to one of the vastly expensive private balls (a lonely experience without a party of several friends). If you make your own costume your only cost will be that of being in Venice.

Recommended shops

BAUTA

masks
La Zanze Venexiana, p.112
La Bottega dei Mascareri, p.113
Ca' Macana, p.262
Papier Maché, p.264

costume
Atelier Pietro Longhi, p.113
Nicolao Atelier, p.263

For more information on Carnevale, or to book tickets to a ball, visit the website:

www.carnivalofvenice.com

Festa della Sensa

held in May on the Sunday after Ascension

The *Festa della Sensa* is also known as *The Marriage of Venice to the Sea*. It is the day when Venice honours her relationship to the sea with a symbolic marriage ceremony. The Mayor of Venice (taking the place of the doge) is rowed into the lagoon in the *Bucintoro,* a gilded ceremonial vessel, followed by a flotilla of hundreds of boats and gondolas. When the Bucintoro reaches the the Adriatic, the Mayor tosses a gold ring into the water and recites the words: *As a sign of your eternal domination, we, Doge of Venice, marry you, o sea!* The first of these weddings took place in 1177 and the last in 1798, after the fall of the Republic. The festival was revived in 1986. Today's ceremonies are reduced in pomp but still represent an important and historic bond between Venice and her eternal master.

Vogalonga

held on a Sunday in May

This rowing marathon was established in 1975 by Canadians living in Venice as a protest against the excessive number of motorboats on the canals. The regatta is open to all rowers, including foreigners, amateurs, professionals and gondoliers. The only entrance requirement is that your boat be powered by oar. At 9 am bells ring to announce the start of the festivities, oars are raised high in a salute to Venice and the old Republic. The race begins. The flotilla of row-boats passes San Elena, crosses the lagoon to San Erasmo, and then circles around Burano and Torcello. The race continues around Murano and returns to Venice via the canal of Cannaregio, to San Marco and the finish line at Dogana del Mar. The racecourse covers a total of 30 kilometres and takes between four and five hours.

Festa del Redentore

held on the third Sunday in July

The Festa del Redentore is one of Venice's plague-related festivals, marking the end of the epidemic of 1576. The festival is centred on Palladio's Church of the Redentore, which was built in thanksgiving for the city's deliverance from plague. A bridge of boats is erected from the Redentore church on Guidecca to the Zattere in Dorsoduro. On Saturday night hundreds of people row their boats into the lagoon for a picnic on the water. The evening ends with a grand fireworks display. Afterwards it is traditional to row to the Lido to watch the sunrise.

Regatta Storica

held on the first Sunday in September

This is the annual regatta and race of the city's gondoliers and other expert rowers. It starts with a procession of richly decorated historic craft along the Grand Canal. Boat crews are dressed in period costume. Bystanders are expected to join in the event and may even be issued with appropriate colours. The canal glows with the colours of the costumes, and gilded boats brought out of storage especially for the festival.

Festa della Salute

held on 21st November

The Festa della Salute is a memorial of the plague of 1630, which wiped out one-third of the city's population. Venetians walk in procession over a pontoon bridge, built especially for the occasion across the Grand Canal to the Salute. People light candles in the church to give thanks for another year of good health and pray for sick friends and relatives. The festival offers the only chance to see the Salute as its designers intended – with the main doors open and hundreds of people ascending and descending the steps.

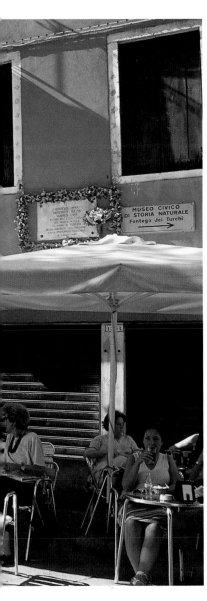

FOOD&WINE

AL PROSECCO, SANTA CROCE

The quality of food in Venetian restaurants has improved from decades past when the majority of establishments served unimaginative pasta and pizza to tourists. Just as there has been a rebirth in quality and craftsmanship amongst certain artists and artisans in Venice, there are now many imaginative chefs who are working to very high standards. Often they are adapting traditional dishes to create something distinctive.

Venetian cuisine relies on seafood from the lagoon and the Adriatic. Many dishes, such as *sarde in saor*, originate from the practical side of Venetian life. Seafaring Venetians needed a way of storing their sardines on long voyages: pickling them in vinegar was a good solution. Since the Veneto was never suited for growing wheat, pasta was not traditionally a part of the Venetian diet. Rice and maize corn are used to create *risotto* and *polenta* dishes respectively. For vegetables, Venetians have always favoured artichokes and celery, which are often used in unexpected ways.

Spices and herbs from the Orient and the Middle East influenced Venetian cooking until the 20th century, when Italian food generally became more homogenous and based around pasta. Some modern dishes still feature food and spice combinations not found in other cities, and there are chefs in Venice actively researching ancient recipes and reviving the old ways (p.239).

ARBA (*Associazone dei Ristoranti della Buona Accoglienza*) is a group of restaurants committed to offering quality cuisine, respecting a fair quality/price ratio and offering a varied wine menu. They publish a brochure that is available at the Tourist Information Offices and in member restaurants. Not all restaurants that belong to ARBA are mentioned in this book; we recommend many non-member restaurants that serve good food and cover all price ranges.

It has become fashionable for top-class restaurants to call themselves osteria and enoteca. This can be confusing, particularly if the restaurant concerned is the Osteria da Fiore, Venice's only Michelin-starred restaurant. All dining establishments are listed in this guide as restaurants.

A *bacaro* was once where working class people would go for a cheap glass or bottle of wine and a bite to eat. The cooking consisted of less desirable cuts of meat and fish offered at a low price. There are no longer any true *bacari* in Venice. The name now means establishments serving wine and *cicheti* – Venetian finger food such as stuffed olives, meatballs, *sarde in saor*, dried cod and other seafoods. Usually eaten standing at the bar, cicheti with a glass of wine is part of the Venetian experience.

You will need to ask for the bill because bringing it without your approval is considered rude.

Remember that you will usually pay less if you eat or drink standing. Expect to pay in cash in bars.

Types of Establishment

Ristorante
a restaurant, with dishes à la carte, at the higher end of the price range.

Trattoria
often family owned, offering moderately priced cuisine.

Osteria
a traditional wine bar, serving wine by the glass with snacks or simple meals.

Enoteca
a place to taste and purchase wine, often serving cicheti and wine by the glass.

Bacaro
an osteria, see left.

Bar (Café)
popular for breakfast, serving sandwiches at lunch, and drinks of all kinds throughout the day and evening.

Pasticceria
cake and pastry shop, sometimes selling savoury tarts and sandwiches.

BEWARE OF RESTAURANTS THAT OFFER A *'MENU TURISTICA'*. THIS IS ALWAYS THE SIGN OF A MEDIOCRE ESTABLISHMENT.

Dining in Venice

Venetians start the day with a *capuccino* or a *caffelatte* and a pastry. Italians insist that, after about 10.00 coffee should be an *espresso*. Those who must have milk can ask for a *macchiato,* espresso with a touch of milk, without embarrassment.

Lunch can be substantial: a full meal will feature *antipasti* (starter), *primi* (first course) of pasta or rice, *secondi* (second course) of meat or fish, often served with *contorni* (side dish) of vegetables, followed by *dolci* (sweet) or fruit and then finally, coffee. The trend today is to have only one or two courses. In a trattoria, lunch prices average €30-€40 for two, if a starter is shared and each person has a main course with a glass of wine.

In Venice, it is common to have *un aperitivo* at a local bar after work at around six or seven pm. This is often an aperitif of either *Prosecco*, a sparkling wine from the Veneto, or a *spritz*, the typical Venetian cocktail. Some will take a *giro di ombre*, a stroll around local *osterie,* sampling a glass of wine with *cicheti* (the Venetian version of *tapas*) in several places. An *ombra* is a glass of red or white wine drunk standing at the bar. The word comes from 'shadow', meaning a drink that is taken in the shade, or as the day wears on.

The evening meal is served earlier than in other parts of Italy, beginning at around seven-thirty pm. Many restaurants will not seat anyone after 22.30. Again, four courses are on offer, with most people opting for fewer. It is common to end a meal with a *digestivo* – either a liqueur or a *grappa.*

If you can manage it, try to eat Italian style, with a very minimal breakfast to ensure that come lunch time, when many shops, churches and attractions are closed, you are hungry enough to enjoy a leisurely Venetian lunch *al fresco* in a shady campo.

Typical Venetian Dishes

Venetian food is known for its simplicity. Fish and seafood dominates most menus along with rice and *polenta*. Below are some popular Venetian specialities.

Antipasti

Sarde in Saor
Sardines that are dusted in flour and fried, marinated in onions and vinegar, then sauteed with pine nuts and raisins.

Antipasto di Mare
A cold selection of seafood (usually squid, crab, mussels, prawns and octopus) dressed with olive oil and lemon juice.

Carpaccio
Thin slices of raw meat or fish, sometimes served with a rocket and parmesan salad.

Baccala
Dried cod often mixed with olive oil, parsley and garlic and served on slices of bread.

Primi

Risi e Bisi
Rice and peas, cooked with ham and Parmesan cheese.

Bigoli in Salsa
Large coarse spaghetti with butter, onions and anchovies.

Risotto in Nero
Risotto with cuttlefish cooked in its own black ink.

Raddicchio alla Griglia (in pasta)
Red chicory leaves grilled over a hot fire. Raddicchio adds a slightly bitter flavour.

Spaghetti alle Vongole
Spaghetti served with fresh clams in a garlic and chilli pepper sauce. *Caparozzoli* is a superior clam to *Vongole*.

Secondi

Fegato alla Veneziana
Finely chopped liver cooked with onions.

Fritto Misto
Mixed fried fish from the Adriatic. This can consist of anything from calimari to sardines, scampi and squid.

Seppioline Nere
Baby cuttlefish cooked in their own ink.

SOME RESTAURANTS CHARGE BY THE 100 GM FOR FISH.

Dolci

Bussolai
Ring-shaped biscuits from Burano, often served with sweet wine at the end of the your meal, which are meant to be dunked in the wine.

Local Wines

The hilly country leading up to the southern slopes of the Alps and the Dolomites is ideal for wine production and produces some of Italy's best known wines. The Veneto is part of this area and stretches from Lake Garda to northeast of Treviso. This region has the largest output of superior *Denominazione di Origine Controllata* (DOC) wines in Italy. However, no wines from this region are in the highest quality DOGC category.

Along with Veneto wines, those from Trento-Alto Adige and Friuli-Venezia Giulia are commonly found in Venetian restaurants. The only wines actually produced in the province of Venice come from the village of Pramaggiore in the Veneto. These are the white *Tocai di Lison* and red *Cabernet di Pramaggiore* and *Merlot di Pramaggiore.*

Red wine

Valpolicella and *Bardolino*, made predominantly from the *Corvina* grape, are produced in the region north-west of Venice between Verona and Lake Garda. The towns of Bardolino and Sant'Ambrogio di Valpolicella are in the heart of the area.

Valpolicella is a complex red with a delicate nutty scent. There are three basic styles: *Normale* (the table wine) *Recioto*, and *Ripasso.* Recioto (a rich, sweet wine) is expensive; *Recioto Amarone* (also costly) is smooth, dry and high in alcohol content. Ripasso is made by a unique method whereby colour and strength are increased by macerating the grape skins before pressing.

Valpolicella from Dal Forno, Quintarelli and Zenato are good, but for a real treat try the *Conti Neri Ripasso Classico 2001.*

Bardolino is a light summery wine, best drunk young. Top producers are Cavalchina, Montresor, Le Vigne di San Pietro and Zenato.

White wine

Soave comes from the town of the same name located east of Verona. It is made from the *Garganega* grape with small quantities of *Trebbiano* and sometimes *Chardonnay*. Soave has a tarnished reputation internationally, but locally it is often very good. The best Soave is usually Classico, especially those made by La Cappuccina, Fattori and Graney, Gini, Portinari and Tedeschi. Try *Bianco di Custoza*, a Soave-style white from the region west of Verona.

Pinot Grigio, a popular grape and wine of the same name, is grown in the north-east of Italy. Some of the best white wines come from Friuli and Alto Adige. Look for producers Vigna Baccana, San Michele Appiano, Borgo San Daniele.

Prosecco

A sparkling, dry white wine very popular in Venice, with a light, fruity bouquet. Prosecco is normally served as an *aperitivo* on its own, or as a base for a *spritz* or a *Bellini*. The best wines are the *Prosecco di Conegliano-Valdobbiàdene (DOC)* and there are several quality producers: Carpene-Malvolti, Adami, Bortolin, Canevel, Case Bianche, Gregoletto, Nino Franco, Ruggeri, Zardetto. Usually sparkling, Prosecco is also available in different styles: there is a still *secco* (dry), *amabile* (medium-sweet) or *frizzante* (semi-sparkling).

Grappa

A strong brandy distilled from grape *pomace* – the skins and seeds of grapes left over after pressing for wine. Juniper berries or plums can also be used to make grappa. The best local grappa comes from Veneto producers Carlo Gobetti, Vittorio Capovilla and Jacopo Poli. Be careful, grappa is extremely strong!

Bellini

Venice's most famous cocktail, created around 1940 in Harry's Bar, is made with Prosecco and fresh white peach juice.

The Venetian Spritz

If you see someone with a bright orange or reddish coloured drink, they are likely having a *spritz* – popular in Venice since the Austrian occupation. This is a very local aperitif, usually taken from 11.00 to lunch and then later as an *aperitivo*. The base is white wine (sometimes Prosecco), mixed with a good measure of bitter or sweet *aperitif,* topped with seltzer and garnished with a lemon twist and a large olive. There are several kinds: the classic *spritz al bitter* (favoured by men) is made with Campari, the sweet *spritz al Aperol,* and the in-between *spritz al Select.*

Beer

Chiara or *Biondi* is a pale lager; *Rossa* is more like a bitter with a reddish colour; *Scura* is a darker beer similar to stout; *Malto* is malt beer.

Alla spina is beer from the tap, while *in botiglia* means 'in the bottle'.

Coffee

Caffè doppio	a double measure of espresso
Caffè ristretto	extra strong
Caffè alto or caffè lungo	a weaker espresso
Caffè macchiato	black coffee with a dash of milk
Latte macchiato	a glass of hot milk with a splash of coffee
Caffè conpanna	with whipped cream
Caffè freddo	cold, unsweetened black coffee
Caffè coretto	with a drop of brandy or grappa
decaffeinato	decaffinated
bollente	boiling (coffee is often served lukewarm)

Restaurant Listings

Restaurants are listed according to price range, signified by the € symbol. Prices are average per person, for 2-3 courses including wine, and *coperto* (a cover charge for the table).

Listings are by sestieri, in descending order of price.

Restaurants and trattorie are listed first, followed by osterie and enoteche.

Smoking is banned in all bars and restaurants in Italy.

€€€€	€75 and over
€€€	€50 - €75
€€	€25 - €50
€	€25 and under

San Marco

Monaco-Gran Canal
Calle Vallaresso 1325
041 520 0211
12.00-14.30, 19.00-22.30 daily
credit cards accepted
booking advisable
map 9-10, E3
€€€€

This elegant and famous restaurant is located in the former Ridotto and the terrace has a splendid view of the Grand Canal and the Salute. The cuisine is excellent.The salmon and swordfish tartare and the crawfish salad are especially renowned. During Acqua Alta, the waiters serve in their wellies and guests elevate their feet on benches. Live piano music every evening except Tuesday.

La Cusina
Calle del Traghetto 2200
041 240 0759
lunch and dinner daily
credit cards accepted
booking advisable
map 9 D4
€€€€

Dine at the restaurant of the Europa e Regina Hotel with superb views over the Grand Canal, while enjoying a tempting and sophisticated menu. Try scampi marinated in raisins and onion, loin of lamb perfumed with oranges and paprika, or spaghetti with a scorpion fish sauce. La Cusina also offers a short but interesting low-calorie menu. For something lighter on the pocket, sit on the terrace of the adjoining hotel and sample the bar menu.

Harry's Bar
Calle Vallaresso 1323
041 528 5777
10.30-23.00 daily
credit cards accepted
booking advisable
map 9-10, E3
€€€€

A Venetian institution known for once having Hemingway as a regular customer. This is also the place where *carpaccio* was invented – thin slices of beef served raw with rocket salad. For some, having a Bellini or a Martini at the bar is an essential part of the Venice experience.

Quadri

Piazza San Marco 120
041 522 2105
09.00-midnight Tues-Sun
credit cards accepted
book for dinner
map 10, F2
€€€€

Find the entrance under the arches of the Procuratie Vecchie and enjoy a gorgeous view over the Piazza and Basilica while dining. A fine meal could start with a pear, rocket and parmesan salad, followed by pasta with crawfish and basil or grilled scallops with aubergine. The wine list is carefully selected to perfectly balance the food.

San Marco Osteria Enoteca

Frezzeria 1610
041 528 5242
10.30-23.30 Mon-Sat
credit cards accepted
book for dinner
map 9-10, E2
€€€

The chef is imaginative and the young staff are enthusiastic and knowledgable. There is an extensive wine list and a good choice of wines by the glass. Try a primi of *capesante i carciofi* (pilgrim scallops with

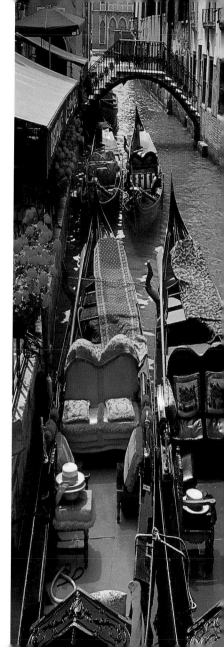

SAN MARCO

artichokes) or *pappardelle al
ragout d'anatra* (tagliatelli
with duck ragu); followed by
*coda di rospo con curry e maela
verde (*monkfish served with
a delicate curry sauce over
rice), or *costolette di cervo in
salsa mirtilli* (deer chops with
blueberry sauce). Pineapple
cossata with pistachio sauce is
recommended for dessert.

Acqua Pazza
Campo Sant'Angelo 3808
041 277 0688
10.00-23.00 Tues-Sat
credit cards accepted
booking advisable
map 9, B2
€€€

This is the place to dine *al
fresco* in one of Venice's most
central and airy campos.
Antonio makes his wonderful
pizzas with fresh tomato
and buffalo mozzarella, and
his other dishes are equally
delicious: bucatini pasta with
scorpionfish, linguine with
lobster and baked mussels
in pepper are just a few
examples.

Al Bacareto
Calle de le Boteghe 3447
041 528 9336
08.00-23.00 daily
closed Sat morn, Sun and Aug
credit cards accepted
booking advisable
map 9, B2
€€

Stand at the bar (the cheaper
option) and enjoy tasty
cicheti. Ask for an *ombra* of

unbottled Friulian wine.
In the dining room, try the
excellent *risotto alla pescatore*
(fisherman's risotto), *bigoli
in salsa;* or *seppioline nere
alla polenta (*cuttlefish and
polenta).

Cavatappi
Campo della Guerra 525
041 296 0252
09.00-24.00 daily
closed Sun eve and Mon
map 5, C6
€€

A modern wine bar tucked
away amid the tourist traps.
They serve a variety of wines
and cheeses from all regions
of Italy and at midday there
are good risotto and pasta
dishes. Dinner in the evenings
are a more formal affair with
swordfish and grilled tuna on
the menu.

Assassini
Rio Terà dei Assassini 3695
041 528 7986
11.30-15.00,18.45-23.30 daily
closed Sat morn and Sun
no credit cards
map 9, C1/2
€€

The atmosphere of this osteria
makes up for the small menu,
which changes daily. You will
find soup and white meat
on Mondays, special pastas
on Wednesdays and fish
on Fridays and Saturdays.
The pasta with radicchio is
especially creamy. Be advised
that pasta *alla nerveti* is pasta

served with veal cartilage – a tasty dish but not one to order unaware.

A la Campana
Calle dei Fabbri 4720
041 528 5170
11.00-15.00, 19.00-20.30 daily
closed Sun
no credit cards
map 9-10, E1
€

Busy at lunchtime but quieter in the evenings, this typical osteria serves a traditional menu. At midday the menu is less expensive offering quick meals to local office workers. Try *risotto radicchio* or *tagliolini canestrelli* (lagoon scallops) followed by grilled fresh fish.

Ai Rusteghi
Campiello del Tentor 5513
041 523 2205
09.30-15.00, 17.00-20.30 Mon-Sat
closed Sat in summer
map 5, B5
€

Delicious, soft panini are served here with different fillings such as shrimp and porcini mushrooms, egg and asparagus, and roast pork and chicory. With a few outside tables, this is an ideal place for a light lunch.

Bars
Vitae
Salizzada San Luca 4118
041 520 5205
09.00-01.30 Mon-Sat
closed Sat morn
map 9, D1

Come here for an aperitif or a cocktail and sample tasty titbits of tramezzini filled with olive, chicory, roast pork, tuna or vegetables. At lunchtime bar meals are served. Try octopus salad with celery, chicken bites with castraure or Spanish moquequa soup. Vitae attracts young professionals for whom it is an oasis in a busy business area. A lively place at night.

Club Malvasia Vecchia
Corte Malatina 2586
23.00-04.00 Wed-Sat
membership €15.00
map 9, C3

Tucked away in a courtyard, behind La Fenice, is this dance club. Purchase a membership for a one-off charge and dance to the music of the owner DJ. Drinks are reasonably priced.

Cakes and ice cream
Caffè Florian
Piazza San Marco 56
041 528 5338
10.00-midnight daily
credit cards accepted
www.caffeflorian.com
map 10, F2

Very expensive, this historic café has been home to the wealthy, noble and literati since it was established in 1720: Dickens, Goethe, Byron and Proust have all conversed at its tables. At one time, it was the only café in Venice to serve women and Casanova frequented it for that reason. They serve traditional and specialist coffees, afternoon tea (scones and sandwiches included), homemade ice cream, Prosecco and various aperitifs. There is a surcharge if the orchestra is playing, however brief your visit.

Le Café
Campo Santo Stefano 2797
041 523 7201
08.00-23.00 daily in summer
08.00-20.30 daily in winter
map 9, B3

A pleasant café offering a choice of sweet and savoury dishes, including salads that are good for a light lunch. The café has a pastry shop around the corner for a quick takeaway.

Rosa Salva
Campo San Luca 4589
041 522 5385
07.30-20.30 Thurs-Tues
08.30-20.30 Sun
map 9, D1

Serves excellent cakes and pastries. This is the main branch of a group of well-known *pasticceri*, although not as atmospheric as their outlet in Castello.

Marchini
Calle Spadaria 676
041 522 9109
09.00-20.00 Mon-Sat
map 10, F1

Delicious, expensive and irresistible to chocaholics; the smell alone will lure you in. Marchini serves a prizewinning *Torta del Doge*.

CAFFÈ FLORIAN

Paolin
Campo San Stefano 2962
041 522 5576
09.30-midnight daily
closed Thurs in winter
map 9, B3

In business since the 1930s, Paolin has a great setting with outside tables. Try its famous pistachio ice cream.

San Polo

Da Fiore
Calle del Scaleter 2202A
041 721 308
12.30-14.30, 19.30-22.30 daily
closed Sun, Mon and Aug
credit cards accepted
booking advisable
map 3-4, E4
€€€€

With a Michelin star, Da Fiore is rated by many as Venice's best gourmet fish restaurant. Maurizio and Mara Zanetti insist on the freshest lagoon-based seafood ingredients. Start with *saordi orate alla*

Marco Polo (marinated bream) then *risotto di scampi* for primi, and for secondi *rambo al forno in crosta di patate* (baked turbot in a crust of potatoes). There is always a fine selection of regional cheeses and the wine list is extensive.

Antiche Carampane
Rio Terà de la Carampane 1911
041 524 0165
12.30-14.30, 19.30-22.00 daily
closed Sun eve and Mon
credit cards accepted
map 4, G4
€€€

Although difficult to find, you will be amply rewarded by this peaceful restaurant in the former red-light district. The chef has a delicate touch, serving only the freshest fish. For primi try *linguine con lo scorfane* (pasta with fish in a light vegetable sauce) followed by monkfish in a crust of Parmesan cheese.

Antico Dolo
Ruga Vecchia S.Giovanni 778
0039 041 522 6546
closed Tues
credit cards accepted,
map 4, H4
€€€

Open for *cicheti* as well as meals, this cosy, friendly osteria serves typical Venetian seafood. Try the huge antipasti platter, *seppie* (cuttlefish)with *polenta* and *spaghetti al scoglio*.

Alla Madonna
Calle della Madonna 594
041 522 3824
12.00-14.30, 19.00-22.00 daily
closed Wed, Aug 4-17, Jan
credit cards accepted
reservations not accepted
map 3, I4
€€

This roomy, bustling seafood restaurant has been going strong for four decades and is beloved by locals and tourists alike. On the menu are scampi and tiny squid (*scampi e calamaretti fritti*) and a delicious *sarde in saor.* Try Venetian style liver with polenta or roast chicken. Their house white, Tocai, is very drinkable. Lunchtime is just slightly less busy. If there is a queue, it usually moves quickly.

Naranzaria
Erbaria di Rialto 130
041 724 1035
11.00-15.00, 18.00-01.00 daily
11.00-01.00 in summer
closed Mon
map 4, I4
€€

This popular new restaurant right on the Grand Canal is a gathering place for young Venetians, especially in the early evenings for aperitivo. The wines are from Brandino Brandolini in Friuli, a region noted for Pinot Grigio. Food is has Friulian flavour with San Daniele proscuitto served for antipasti.

Muro
Campo Bella Vienna 222
041 523 7495
08.00-15.00, 17.00-01.00 daily
closed Sunday
map 4, I3
€€

Also located in the Erbaria market, the outdoor tables here often spill over into the campo as people sip prosecco and greet their friends. Food is under the domain of Beppe the Bavarian who can have eclectic tastes. One signature dish is saffron penne with monkfish and liquorice, another is purple potato soup.

Vini da Pinto
Rialto Pescheria 367
041 522 4599
lunch and dinner daily
closed Monday
credit cards
map 4, H3
€€

A traditional wine bar located at the Rialto fish market established in 1890. Try the *Baccala Mantecato* (codfish prepared Venetian style).

Da Sandro
Campiello Meloni
041 523 4894
lunch and dinner Sat-Thurs
map 4, G5
€

Da Sandro consists of two restaurants. The one closest to the bridge is tiny and serves a good quality pizza at a reasonable price. The osteria opposite has more seating and a broad traditional menu. Cheap and cheerful.

Ruga Rialto
Ruga Rialto 692
041 521 1243
11.00-15.00, 18.00-24.00 daily
map 4, H4 (nr C.D Sturion)
€€

The menu may be limited and traditional but Venetians come here for the atmosphere created by three genial hosts: Marco, Giorgio and Giorgio who often organise themed evenings and offer live music on Friday.

Frary's Bar
Fondamenta dei Frari 2559
041 720 050
10.00-midnight daily
closed Tuesday evening
map 3, D/E5
€

Well-prepared Arab and Greek cuisine, including falafel, dolmades and souvlaki. Leave room for the delicious pistachio, date, raisin and rosewater ice cream.

Osteria alla Patatina
Calle del Saoneri 2741A
041 523 7238
09.30-14.30, 16.30-20.30
closed Sunday
map 3-4, E5
€

Good for cicheti, this osteria serves simple, well prepared food. Comfortable.

All'Arco

Calle dell'Occhialer 436
041 520 5666
08.00-15.00 daily
closed Sunday
map 4, H4

Tasty cicheti in a tiny, busy osteria near Rialto. A good range of unbottled wines.

Shri Ganesh

Fondamenta Rio Marin 2426
near Ponte del Cristo
041 719 804
12.30-14.00, 19.00-23.00 daily
closed Wednesday and
Thursday lunch
map 4, F4
€

Missing your Indian curry? Enjoy authentic dishes at reasonable prices on the canalside terrace.

Bars

Caffè dei Frari

Fondementa dei Frari 2564
041 524 1877
open daily
map 3, D/E5

A popular bar with the locals, this is the perfect place to have a spritz or a prosecco after a visit to the Frari. The bar also serves salads and light snacks. The decor is Parisian belle epoque and there is a charming upstairs gallery with seating.

Cantina do Mori

Calle dei do Mori 429
near the Rialto Bridge
041 522 5401
08.00-20.30 Mon-Sat

no credit cards
map 4, H4

A much-loved wine bar, founded in 1462 and now under new owners Giovanni Spaza and Rudy Sportelli. Do Mori offers a good selection of red wines by the glass and a variety of cicheti but beware, the prices of the tiny dishes can add up rapidly.

Osteria Bancogiro

Campo San Giacometto 122
041 523 2061
10.00-15.00, 18.00-01.00 daily
closed Sunday eve and Monday
map 4, I4

Beneath the porticoes of the Fabbriche Vecchie in the Rialto market area is a wine enthusiast's dream bar. Sample a delicious selection of Italian wine from Sicily to Trentino. Upstairs is a cosy restaurant serving food cooked fresh from the market.

Taverna Da Baffo

Campo Sant'Agostin 2346
041 520 8862
07.30-02.00 daily
closed Sunday
map 3-4, E4

A neighbourhood staple for cappuccino, *panino* and *aperitivo*. Giorgio Baffo was a poet famous in the 18th century for his risqué verse.

Cakes and ice cream

Bucintoro

Calle del Scaleter 2229
07.15-20.00 daily

closed Wednesday
map 3-4, E4
Traditional Venetian sweets
and pastries.

Rizzardini
Campiello dei Meloni 1415
041 522 3835
07.00-21.30 September to July
closed Tuesday
map 4, G5
A joyful place for every kind
of pastry. During Carnevale,
fritelle (fried doughnuts with
various fillings) are available.

Santa Croce

Al Vecio Fritolin
Calle della Regina 2262
041 522 2881
12.00-14.30, 19.00-22.30 daily
closed Sunday evening, Monday
closed January and August
credit cards accepted
booking advisable
map 4, G3

€€€
Bubbly Irina runs a cosy and
inviting trattoria, serving a
fresh seasonal menu and tasty
grilled scallops.

Il Refolo
C. S. Giacomo dell'Orio 1459
041 524 0016
10.00-01.00 daily
closed Monday, Tuesday
credit cards accepted
map 4, D/E3
€€€
This picturesque restaurant
with a lovely outside dining
area features a small menu
of high quality. Choose from
mozzarella in carrozza with
misticanza, marinated salmon
or tuna hamburger and other
dishes. Il Refolo also offers a
variety of beer.

Alla Zucca
Ponte del Megio, San Giacomo
dell'Orio 1762

CAMPO SAN GIACOMO DELL'ORIO

041 524 1570
12.30-15.00, 19.00-23.00 daily
closed Sunday
credit cards accepted
booking advisable
no smoking
map 3-4, E2
€€

The cuisine is inventive and caters for vegetarians. Meat eaters will enjoy the chicken fricassèe in tzatsiki sauce. The wine list is limited but of good quality.

Al Nono Risorto
Calle della Regina 2338
Sotoportego de la Siora Bettina
041 524 1169
12.00-14.30, 19.00-midnight daily
closed Wednesday
no credit cards
map 4, G3
€€

Sometimes hosting live jazz and blues, this friendly trattoria has a large dining area and a garden overhung with wisteria.

Bars

Al Prosecco
Campo S. Giacomo dell'Orio
041 524 0222
08.00-22.30 daily
closed Sunday
map 3, D/E3

Sit outside in the afternoon sun and watch the children play in the Campo as you enjoy an *aperitivo*. Al Prosecco has a large selection of the variety of Prosecco wines produced around the Veneto.

Ice cream

Alaska
Calle Larga dei Bari 1159
041 71 5211
08.00-13.00, 15.00-20.00 daily

map 3, C3
The owner of this ice cream bar obviously enjoys his work as he produces a wonderful variety of interesting flavours, all using fresh ingredients. Tucked away but worth seeking out.

Dorsoduro

Agli Alboretti
Rio Terà Antonio Foscarini 882
041 523 0058
lunch and dinner daily
closed Wed and Thurs lunch
booking advisable
map 8, H5
€€€

Formerly one of Peggy Guggenheim's favourites, the current prize-winning chef, Pierluigi Louisa, creates dishes that are much loved by local gourmets. Try the pumpkin risotto with diamonds of tarragon-flavoured cuttlefish. A superb wine list and cheese trolley, together with immaculate service throughout. Tables indoors and alfresco.

L'Incontro
Rio Terrà Canal 3062A
off Campo Santa Margherita
041 522 2404
lunch and dinner daily
closed Mon and Thurs lunch
credit cards accepted
map 8, F3
€€€

Paolo is now the owner of this restaurant serving Sardinian specialties and wines. Start

PAOLO AT L'INCONTRO

with a *primi* of *culurgiones* (pasta stuffed with potato, cheese and mint), followed by a *secondi* of grilled beef with rosemary. For *dolci* try *pecorino* and *parmigiano* cheese with *corbezzolo* honey, made from the flowers of the Lychee plant. Pieces of cheese are dipped in a pool of bittersweet honey, absolutely delicious. Afterwards you'll need a *digestivo* – *Mirto* is a Sardinian liqueur made from the myrtle plant, it is said to aid digestion, and it works.

Avogaria
Calle dell'Avogaria 1629
041 296 0491
lunch and dinner Wed-Mon
map 7, D4
€€€

A very stylish designer

eatery where the cuisine is as mouth-watering as the decor. Antonella is from Puglia and uses her childhood recipes to prepare her wonderful food. Try the pepper-baked mussels, or the pasta with a special Puglia sauce. The red Puglia wines are delicious – full bodied and fruity with a lovely buttery finish. Lunches are served at the bar.

La Rivista
Calle Larga Pisani 979A
041 240 1425
07.30-23.00 Tues-Sun
credit cards accepted
map 8, H5
€€€

Once the wine and cheese bar of the stylish Ca' Pisani Hotel, this restaurant has become a local favourite, offering an innovative meat and fish menu. True to its origins, there is a wide selection of good wines by the glass and an interesting selection of Italian cheeses. Dining both inside and out.

Osteria al Quattro Feri
Calle Lunga San Barnaba 2754A
041 520 6978
lunch and dinner Mon-Sat
credit cards accepted
map 8, F4
€€

A good restaurant serving only fish and seafood, the house specialty is tuna *in saor*. They serve a tasty vegetable and shellfish primi, and excel at fresh grilled fish. The wine list is adequate and the service friendly.

Oniga
Campo San Barnaba 2852
041 522 4410
lunch and dinner Wed-Mon
map 8, F3
€€

This restaurant is primarily known for fish, but there is meat on the menu, sometimes even a Hungarian goulash. Try pumpkin gnocchi with prawns or the seafood lasagna. The wine list is reasonable and waiters are friendly. In the summer you can sit out in the campo.

La Bitta
Calle Lunga San Barnaba 2753A
041 523 0531
18.30-23.00 Mon-Sat
no credit cards
map 7-8, E4
€€

A cosy dining room with tasty meat dishes, but no fish. La Bitta has excellent sausages served as *antipasti* or with polenta for *primi*. For *secondi* try roast duck. An excellent list of red wines to complement their dishes features wines from Veneto, Fruili and Trentino, as well as other parts of Italy.

Al Pantalon
Calle del Scaleter 3958
041 710 849
10.30-15.00, 18.00-22.00 daily
closed Sat morn, Sun

map 8, F1
€€
This restaurant tirelessly turns out good fare to local workers and students eager to satisfy their hunger. Choose to eat at the counter (the cheaper option) or at the tables. The menu includes seafood risottos, *seppie fritte* (fried cuttlefish) and its famous fried potato slices.

Pane, vino e San Daniele
Campo Angelo Raffaele 1722
041 523 7454
10.00-24.00 Thurs-Tues
credit cards accepted
map 7, C4
€€
A simple trattoria located opposite the church. They serve a selection of Friulian wines and the famous San Daniele prosciutto.

Al Chioschetto
Fondamenta Zattere 1406
07.00-01.00 daily
map 7-8 E5
This kiosk has a large seating area and is well located. While gazing over the Guidecca Canal enjoy an aperitif or a light snack.

Venus Venezia del Scalete
Calle del Scaleter 3961
041 715 004
10.30-15.00, 17.00-01.00 daily
closed Sun morn
map 8, F3
A friendly wine bar with pleasant decor.

Cantinone già Schiavi
041 523 0034
Ponte San Trovaso
08.00-20.30 Mon-Sat
no credit cards
map 8, G5
A well-known enoteca with a comprehensive list of wines. This is one of the few places in Italy selling *fragolino bianco*, a digestivo made from white strawberries.

Bars
Ai Artisti
Fodametta della Toletta 1169a
041 523 8944
08.00-22.00 daily
map 8. F4
Tucked away in the corner of Campo San Barnaba just beside the church is this friendly little bar that serves excellent sandwiches.

Pub Senso Unico
Near the Guggenheim
Calle della Chiesa 684
open till midnight
map 8, I5
Guinness has a concession in Venice, so many pubs serve Irish beer. This bar has a cosy little room in the back with a canal view.

Bar Margaret Duchamp
Campo Santa Margherita
09.00-02.00 Wed-Mon
map 7, E3
A stylish, modern bar with seats outside. They serve very good sandwiches. Open late.

Imagina
Rio Terrà, Campo S. Margherita
041 241 0625
08.00-02.00 Mon-Sat
map 7-8, E3
A lively modern bar that is popular with the local students at the university.

Venice Jazz Club
Ponte dei Pugni 3102
041 523 2056
concerts at 19.00
map 8, F3
Live jazz music on Mon, Wed, Fri and Sat.

Cakes and ice cream
Gobbetti
Rio Terrà Canal 3108B
07.45-20.00 daily
map 8, F3
Good chocolate and pastries just off Campo Santa Margherita.

Tonolo
Calle San Pantalon 3764
041 523 7209
07.45-20.30 daily
07.45-13.00 Sun
closed August
map 8, F1
Reasonably priced pasticceri, of good quality. Tonolo also produces cakes and pastries in small sizes for tasting.

Gelateria Nico
Fondamenta Zattere 922
041 522 5293
06.45-22.00 Fri-Wed
map 7-8, E5
A good place for ice cream after a stroll along the Zattere.

Cannaregio

La Colombina
Campiello del Pegolotto 1828
041 275 0622
18.30-02.00 Wed-Mon
credit cards accepted
booking advisable
map 2, F5
€€€

There is a regional flavour
to the menu in this quiet
courtyard restaurant run
by a father and son team
from Tuscany. The house
speciality is the classic *bistecca
alla Fiorentina* (grilled rare
Chianina beefsteak).You will
also find a good selection of
cheeses and Tuscan wines.

Anice Stellato
Fondamenta de la Sensa 3272
041 720 744
10.00-14.30, 19.00-22.00 daily
closed Mon
credit cards accepted
booking advisable for dinner
map 1-2, E3
€€€

This is an excellent fish
restaurant. The name means
'Star Anise'. It serves salmon,
tuna, seabream and seafood
risottos, all prepared with
tasty spices and aromatic
herbs. Try a mixed cicheti
for antipasti, followed by
cuttlefish with polenta. For
dolci, try a *bavarese* (delicious
vanilla custard served with
a tangy plum sauce). A good
wine list and friendly service.

Osteria Antica Adelaide
Calle della Racchetta 3728
open daily
map 5, A1
€€€

Traditional Venetian cuisine
in an old style restaurant with
a jovial atmosphere.

Vini da Gigio
Fondamenta San Felice 3628A
041 528 5140
12.00-14.30, 19.30-22.30 daily
closed Mon and Tues
credit cards accepted
booking essential
map 2, I6
€€€

Ideal for relaxing meals, this
popular restaurant is just
off Strada Nuova near the
church of San Felice. Staff will
suggest wines to go with your
meal. Leave room for dessert
and finish off with a grappa.

Osteria da Rioba
Fdm della Misericordia 2553
041 524 4379
lunch and dinner Tues-Sun
map 2, G4
€€

Don't be fooled by the simple
decor; the chef is inventive
and the food is excellent. Try
an *involtini of monkfish with
gamberoni* (layers of prawns
wrapped in monkfish, served
with a *timbale of radiccio di
Treviso)*. The wine list has
excellent choices from Friuli
and the Veneto.

I Quattro Rusteghi

Campo Ghetto Nuovo 2888
041 715 160
lunch and dinner
credit cards accepted
booking advisable
map 1-2, E4
€€

This restaurant is well worth a visit for those with an adventurous palate. Chicca combines fresh ingredients and oriental spices to create dishes that are unique and delicious. While the lunchtime menu consists of simple sandwiches, at dinner the unusual menu might include: *Fiocchette* (pasta balls stuffed with cheese and pears); grouper fillet in orange sauce with pine nuts;

CHICCA

or smoked breast of goose served with butter and apple cream. Chicca also likes to serve grilled vegetables with sesame and cinnamon oil. Her menu changes weekly and the staff are attentive. Highly recommended.

Chicca
(pictured above)

Chicca left Venice as a young woman and travelled the world, stopping long enough to live in Kenya and the USA. When her father died and left her the family business, she returned to Venice and the restaurant in the Campo Ghetto Nuovo. (see details above)

Chicca says: 'Venice was a place where many cultures lived together. So the old method of Venetian cooking employed a 'criss-cross' style, using lots of spices from different culinary traditions. But most of the dishes created when Venice was an imperial power have been forgotten.' Authentic Venetian dishes that have survived are risotto, polenta, and some of the seafood specialties.

Cicchas's cuisine follows a Middle-Eastern philosophy. She has studied the cuisine of the Eastern Mediterranean from the period 1000 to 1200 and rediscovered recipes that were used in Venice between 1300 and 1700. As well as recreating some of these dishes, this philosophy is inspiring her own creations.

RESTAURANTS

Al Bacco
Fdm de la Capuzine 3054
041 717 493
07.00-23.00 Tuesday-Saturday
12.00-15.00 Sunday
map 1, D3
€€
The menu is as traditional as
the wooden decor, and the
warm welcome.

Enoteca do Colonne
Rio Terà S. Leonardo 1814c
041 524 0453
closed Saturday
map 1-2, E5
€€
Excellent sandwiches and
nibbles for a reasonable price.

Trattoria all'Antica Mola
Fondamenta d. Ormesini 2800
041 717 492
lunch and dinner Thurs-Tues
map 2, F4
€€
A friendly restaurant that is
popular with tourists. Serving
well-prepared traditional
Venetian dishes. The house
wine is very drinkable and
there is a small garden at the
rear.

Dalla Marisa
Fondamenta San Giobbe 652B
041 720 211
lunch and dinner Tues-Sat
closed Wed eves and in Aug
no credit cards
booking advisable
map 1, A4
€
Coming from a long line of
butchers, Marisa offers an
authentic meat-based menu
with dishes that are always
freshly cooked with seasonal
vegetables. Even though this
trattoria has become very
popular in recent years, the
standards continue to be high.
Outside tables are available.

Un Mondo Divino
Salizada San Canciano 5984a
041 521 1093
10.00-15.00, 17.30-21.30 daily
closed Mon
map 5, B4
€€
Cora and Raffaele are a
charming young couple who
serve delicious fresh seafood
and have over 40 wines by
the glass. Excellent for a quick
snack or a sit down dinner.
The oven baked mussels are
wonderful.

Ca d'Oro-alla Vedova
Ramo Ca' d'Oro/
C.D Pistor 3912
041 528 5324
11.30-14.30, 18.30-22.30 daily
closed Thurs, Sun and Aug
no credit cards
map 4, H2
€€
Brother and sister, Mirella
and Renzo Doni run this
historic and beautiful osteria
off Strada Nova, which their
family have owned and run
for 130 years. They serve an
extensive range of cicheti and
unbottled wines by the glass.
You will need to book if you
want to sit at a table.

Da Alberto
C. Larga Giacinto Gallina 5401
041 523 8153
10.00-15.00, 18.00-22.00 daily
closed Sun
credit cards accepted
map 5, D4
€€

Friendly osteria with a large array of cicheti including fried sardines and excellent meatballs. There is a dining room at the back. The warm pasta served with cold tomato and basil salsa makes a perfect lunch on a hot day.

La Cantina
Campo San Felice 3689
041 522 8258
11.00-22.00 Tues-Sat
map 4, H1; map 2, H6

A great spot to people-watch as you sip your Prosecco or down a mug of draught beer. Sample the delicious crostini and small panini with their fresh and imaginative range of fillings.

Algiubagiò
Fondamente Nuove 5039
041 523 6084
06.30-23.30 Wed-Mon
closed January
map 5, D1

Enjoy a coffee or draught beer, and a *panini* on this terrace at the vaparetto stop for the islands of Murano, Burano, Torcello and Sant'Erasmo. A few hot dishes are also available.

Bars

Paradiso Perduto
Fdm della Misericordia 2640
041 720 581
18.00-02.00 Thurs-Mon
map 2, H5

Expect the unexpected at this late-night spot. There could be jazz, reggae or even an art exhibition. The food is expensive and not particularly good, drinks are reasonable.

Al Parlamento
Fondamenta Savorgnan 511
041 244 0214
map 1, B4

A good local bar with panini, cocktails and music in the summer.

Cantina Iguana
Fdm della Misericordia 2515
041 713 561
18.00-02.00 Tues-Sun
map 2, H5

A lively Mexican late-night venue; the sounds are mainly

salsa, although rock and jazz bands play here at the weekends. There is a happy hour from 6-8pm when some aperitifs are two for the price of one. Eat spicy tortillas and tacos washed down with a Corona.

Fiddler's Elbow
Corte dei Pali 3847
041 523 9930
17.00-midnight daily
map 4, H2
A well loved Irish Pub serving draught Guinness, with pleasant seating outside.

Cakes and ice cream

Kosher Bakery
SP. dei Ghetto Vecchio 1143
07.00-13.00, 16.30-19.00
map 1, D4
Known by locals to be the best bakery in Cannaregio.

Pasticceria Puppa
Calle Spezier 4800
07.00-13.30, 15.30-20.30 Tues-Sat
07.00-20.30 Sun, closed Aug
map 1, C6
This traditional pastry shop is also a café and bar.

Castello

Al Covo
Campiello della Pescaria 3968
behind Rivi degli Schiavoni
041 522 3812
12.30-14.00, 19.30-22.00 daily
closed Wed, Thurs
no credit cards
map 11, C2
€€€€

ARBA Consortium. This fish restaurant reinvents traditional recipes to enhance the ingredients. Cesare Benelli's imaginative cuisine includes tagliolini with oysters and tempura style *fritto misto,* and additional seasonal vegetables. The wine list is extensive. Save room for chocolate cake with dark chocolate sauce made by the chef's American wife, Diane.

Il Nuovo Galeon
Via Garibaldi 1308
041 520 4656
open lunch and dinner daily
closed Tuesday
credit cards accepted
map 12, F3
€€€
ARBA Consortium. Highly recommended for fish and seafood. The décor follows a nautical theme; a Venetian fishing boat has been sawn in half to create the bar. The staff are cheerful and helpful. For antipasti try the *scampini,*

STAFF AT IL NUOVO GALEON

baby shrimps with baby artichokes (it is very Venetian to have these tiny artichokes with seafood). Also try octopus and celery in a salad. For primi try *tagliolini* with tuna, olives and capers, followed by a secondi of turbot with scampi. The Pinot Grigio Livio Felluga is some of the best Pinot Grigio available.

Santa Marina

Campo Santa Marina 5911
041 528 5239
lunch and dinner daily
open Mon for dinner only
closed Sun,closed Aug and Jan
booking essential
map 5, C5
€€€

Run by two young couples, this fish restaurant has achieved a good reputation amongst local gourmets. More unusual fish dishes are *scampi in saor*; octopus sauteed with onion; and spiced tuna. Tables outside are pleasantly located.

Alle Testiere

Calle del Mondo Novo 5801
between Salizzada San Lio and
Campo Santa Maria Formosa
041 522 7220
12.00-15.00, 19.00-23.00 Tues-Sat
closed Aug
credit cards accepted
booking essential
map 5, D6
€€€

This small restaurant has only eight tables but unfailingly produces good food and wine.

Each part of the team takes great care over their domain; Bruno ensures the quality of the ingredients, his mother prepares lovely desserts and Luca supervises the wine (a small but select list) and speciality cheeses. A good choice for dinner *a deux*.

Corte Sconta

Calle del Pestrin 3886
041 522 7024
12.30-14.30, 19.00-22.00 Tues-Sat
closed Jan, Aug
credit cards accepted
booking advisable
map 11, C1
€€€

Tucked away in a *sconta*, this friendly osteria serves skilfully prepared traditional fish cuisine. The menu is extensive particularly in its range of starters and the list of wines and grappas is equally impressive. There is a tranquil courtyard dining area overhung with vines.

Alla Mascareta

C. Lunga S. Maria Formosa 5183
041 523 0744
19.00-02.00 Fri-Tues
map 5-6, E5
€€€

A warm and welcoming enoteca, which has an additional quiet room with tables. Wine tasting can be accompanied by meats and cheeses. A good place to sample wines of the Veneto.

Da Remigio

Salizada dei Greci 3416
041 523 0089
lunch and dinner daily
closed Mon evening, Tues
credit cards accepted
booking advisable
map 11, A1
€€

This is a very pretty trattoria popular with the locals. Da Remigio serves excellent fish and seafood at reasonable prices. Try *spaghetti alla busara* (pasta in a brandy-based garlic and paprika sauce) or thin spaghetti with butterfly prawns.

Al Diporto

Sant'Elena
Calle Sengio 25-27
041 528 5978
lunch and dinner Tues-Sat
map overview G4
€€

If you become peckish while visiting the Biennale Gardens, this simple trattoria is a short ten minute walk away. It is on the corner of Calle del Cengio and Calle del Pasubio near Campo der Grappa, off Viale Quattro Novembre. Al Diporto serves a typical Venetian menu with an emphasis on fresh seafood washed down with crisp house white wine. Located near the sports stadium, it can become busy on match days.

Da Sergio
Calle del Dose 5870A
041 528 5153
08.30-15.30, 18.00-21.30 daily
closed Sat eve, Sun
map 5, D5
€
This is a family run business,
very popular with people
working locally. Da Sergio
serves favourites such as
minestrone, roasts, steak and
pasta.

Al Portego
Calle de la Malvasia 6015
Between S. Lio and Santa Marina
041 522 9038
10.00-15.00, 19.00-22.00 Mon-
Sat
map 5, C5
€
Small, cosy osteria where
you can stand at the bar and
enjoy cicheti with a glass
of wine or sit at one of the
tables. Customers are friendly
so don't be surprised if you
strike up a conversation with
the people seated next to you.

Birreria Forst
Calle delle Rasse 4540
041 523 0557
10.00-23.00 daily
closed Sat in winter, closed Aug
map 10, H2
€
A great oasis for a snack and
draught beer very close to
the Doge's Palace. Wonderful
black bread *tramezzini* with
pork, beef or frankfurters and
mustard. Also try their French

rolls and excellent *prosciutto
crudo* from Parma. Coffee is
not served.

Angiò
Ponte della Veneta Marina 2142
041 277 8555
07.00-midnight daily in summer
closed Tues
map 11, D3
€
If you are near the Arsenale
or San Biogio, this is a good
place to sit and enjoy the view
over the lagoon. Angiò serves
panini, salad, cold meats
and cheese, together with a
selection of wine or Irish beer.

Bars
Olandese Volante
Campo San Lio 5658
041 528 9349
11.00-01.00 daily
closed Sun am
map 5, C5
With a large outside seating
area, this sandwich and beer
bar is good for evening drinks
and snacks and keeps late
hours. Meals are available
at midday.

Cakes and ice cream
Da Bonifacio
Calle degli Albanesi 4237
Behind the Doge's Palace
041 522 7507
07.30-20.30 Fri-Wed
map 10, H2
A tiny cake shop and bar that
sells freshly made traditional
cakes, pastries and mini
pizzas, great for a takeaway

245

picnic. A nice place also for breakfast or an aperativo.

Didovich
Campo Santa Marina 5987A
041 523 9181
08.00-20.00 Mon-Sat
map 5-6, C5

This bakery makes Venice's tastiest *salatini* (savoury vegetable tarts). It is also the author Donna Leon's favourite pasticceria for *zaletti* (soft biscuit with raisins).

Boutique del Gelato
Salizada San Lio 5727
041 522 3283
10.00-20.30 daily
map 5-6, C6

The ice cream at Silvio's place is always good.

Rosa Salva
C. SS. Giovanni e Paolo 6779
041 522 7949
07.30-20.30 Thurs-Tues
08.30-20.30 Sunday
map 5-6, E4

A beautifully restored branch of this well known group of pasticceri. The terrace offers a good view of the church.

Giudecca

Hotel Cipriani
private launch from Piazza San Marco opposite Doge's palace
041 520 7744
map p.291, E5

Known as 'the Cip' (*chip*) this 5 star hotel is located at the tip of the island. Set in lush gardens, the hotel has three restaurants: the formal Fortuny Restaurant and Terrace has a dress code in the evenings; Cip's Club is an elegant yet informal marine-style eatery with an outdoor terrace; and the casual Seagull poolside bar has views of Venice.

Harry's Dolci
Fondamenta S. Biagio 773
vaporetto: Sant-Eufemia
041 522 4844
12.00-23.00 Wed-Sun
lunch and dinner
overview map B5
€€€€

Harry's well-known cuisine is served here as well as his famous sweets. A romantic setting with superb views across the canal to Dorsoduro.

Los Murales
Fondamenta Zitelle 70
vaporetto: Zitelle
041 523 0004
09.30-midnight Thurs-Tues
overview map D5
€€

A simple bar serving good Mexican food including burritos, tacos and fajitas. Relax on the terrace and enjoy the stunning views across to San Marco.

Lido

Pachuka
Spaggia San Nicolò
041 242 0020
08.30-04.00 daily
closed Tuesday in winter
€€

This establishment is a self-service pizzeria at lunch, serves fresh fish at dinner and turns into a disco during the later part of the evening. Located at the mouth of the harbour near the beach, the shady terrace offers a pleasant respite from the heat.

Bar Trento
Via Sandro Gallo 82
041 526 5960
07.00-21.00 Mon-Sat lunch & cicheti
during Film Festival dinner is served and bar is open Sundays
€

Traditional Venetian fish dishes are well prepared for the typicallyworking class clientele. Good sausages and risotto.

Murano
Busa alla Torre
Campo Santo Stefano
041 739 662
open daily, lunchtimes only
credit cards accepted
€€

Situated in a pleasant, airy campo, this seasonal fish restaurant is run by Lele, a friendly bearded giant. The seafood pastas are good and his *moeche* (shore crabs) are legendary.

Burano
Al Gatto Nero
Fondamenta Giudecca 88
041 730 120
12.00-15.00, 19.00-21.00 Tues-Sat
credit cards accepted

€€€
This charming trattoria is tucked away off the main square across the canal from the fish market. Try the creamy seafood risotto for lunch, and then relax on the grass and enjoy the view.

Da Romano
Via Galuppi 221
041 730 030
lunch and dinner daily
closed Sun eve and Tues
credit cards accepted
€€€

Located in a former lace school, this trattoria is easy to find on Burano's main street and is popular with locals and tourists. The ingredients are fresh but the cooking can be unimaginative.

Torcello
Locanda Cipriani
Piazza Santa Fosca 29
041 730 150
lunch and dinner daily
closed Mon eve and Tues
closed mid Jan-mid Feb
credit cards accepted
booking recommended
€€€€

The garden terrace is a serene setting for a summer lunch of *risotto all Torcellana* (risotto with Torcello vegetables), followed by delicate fillet of sole with artichokes. The wine list is extensive and the host, Bonifacio, is always happy to advise. For dolci, try their exquisite meringue.

Menu reader

Italian-*Venetian*-English

con, alla refers to how meals are prepared and/or the type of sauce

A

acciughe sott'olio anchovies in oil
aceto vinegar
acqua water
affettato misto cold sliced meats
aglio garlic
agnello lamb
al forno baked
albicocche *armelin* apricot
alla cacciatora with a red wine and mushroom sauce
alla diavola deep fried
ananas pineapple
anatra *ànara* duck
anguilla eel
antipasti starters
aragosta lobster
arancia orange
aringa herring
arrosto roast
articiòco artichoke
asparagi asparagus

B

baccalà dried cod
bagnacauda raw vegetables in oil & lemon
baìcoli tea biscuits
baìcolo baby sea bass
basilico basil
bavarese ice-cream cake with cream

barbòn red mullet
bevarássa cockle
bigoli thick spaghetti
birra beer
bisàto adult eel
bisi peas
bistecca beef steak
bollito *bòsega* boiled
bovoléti escargot
braciola di maiale pork steak
branzìno sea bass
brodo clear broth
bruschetta bread rubbed with oil
burro *butiro* butter
bussolài ring-shaped biscuits

C

caffè coffee
calamari squid
calda hot
calzone folded pizza
canella cinnamon
cannelloni stuffed pasta
canestrèlo queen scallop
canòce mantis prawn
capesante fan shell scallop
cappelle di funghi mushroom caps
capretto kid, goat
carciofi artichokes
carne meat
carote carrots
carpaccio sliced raw meat or fish
carré di maiale pork loin
castagne chestnuts
castràure spring artichokes
cavoletti di Bruxelles brussels sprouts

cavolfiore cauliflower
cavolo cabbage
cefalo mullet
cernia grouper
cicheti tapas
cicoria chicory
cilege cherries
cime di rapa sprouting broccoli
cinghiale wild boar
cioccolata chocolate
cipolle onions
coniglio rabbit
contorni vegetables
coperto cover charge
cotoletta veal, pork or lamb chop
cozze mussels
crema custard
crespelle pancake
crostata tart
crostini bread rounds

D

datteri dates
degustazione tasting
digestivo liqueur or grappa

F

fagioli *fasiòl* beans
fegato *figà* liver
fenòcio fennel
fettuccine pasta
fichi figs
folpèto octopus
formaggi cheese
fragole strawberries
frìtola doughnut with raisins
frittata omelette
fritto misto mixed fried seafood
frutta fruit
frutti di mare mixed seafood

funghi mushroom

G

gamberetti shrimp
gamberi prawns
gazzosa lemonade
gelato ice cream
gnocchi potato pasta
gorgonzola blue
   cheese
granchio *gransèola*
   dressed crab
granita a drink with
   crushed ice
grigliata grilled

I

indivia endive
insalata salad

L

lasagne layered pasta
latte milk
lattuga lettuce
legumi legumes
lenticchie lentils
lepre *lièvaro* hare
limone lemon
lingua tongu

M

maiale pork
mandorla almond
manzo beef
marroni chestnuts
marsala sweet wine
marzapane marzipan
mascarpone cream
   cheese
mazzancòlla shallow
   water prawn
mela apple
melanzane
   aubergine
melone melon
menta mint
meringhe meringue
merluzzo cod

minestrone
   vegetable soup
moèca soft shell crab
mozzarella soft
   white cheese
musèto pork snout
   sausage

N

narànsa orange
nocciole hazelnuts
noci walnuts
nodino veal chop

O

olio oil
ombra glass of wine
   consumed at the bar
oràda sea bream
origano oregano
ossocòlo collar of pork
ostriche oysters

P

panada venexiana
   bread soup
pancetta bacon
pane bread
panino filled roll
panna cream
parsèmolo parsley
pasta noodles
patate potato
pecorino sheep
   cheese
penne pasta quills
peòci mussels
pepe pepper
peperoni peppers
peperoni ripieni
   stuffed peppers
pera pear
pesca peach
pesce fish
piselli peas
polenta cornmeal
pollo chicken
polpette meatballs

polpettone meatloaf
pompelmo grapefruit
pomodori tomatoes
porri leeks
prezzemolo parsely
primi piatti first
   course
prosciutto cured ham
prugne plums
puìna ricotta cheese
puré di patate
   mashed potatoes

Q

quaglie quails

R

radicchio chicory
ragù tomato sauce
rapa white turnip
rapanelli radishes
ravioli stuffed pasta
razza skate
ricotta cottage cheese
ripieni stuffed
risi e bisi a soup of
   rice and peas
riso rice
risotto rice dish
rosmarino rosemary

S

salame salami
sale salt
salmone salmon
salsiccia sausage
salvia sage
sarde sardines
sarde in soar
   marinated sardines
scaloppine veal
   escalopes
sècoe beef meat from
   the spine
sedano celery
senape mustard
seppie *sèpe nère*
   cuttlefish

servizio service
sgroppino a dessert of lemon
  sorbet, vodka and Prosecco
sogliola *sfògio* sole
speck smoked ham
spezzatino stew
spinaci spinach
spritz Venetian aperitif
stracchino soft cheese
stracciatella soup with beaten
  eggs
succo juice

T

tacchino turkey
tagliata finely sliced beef fillet
tagliatelle egg pasta
tagliolini noodles
tartufo truffles
tavola table
tè tea
tetina cow's udder
tonno tuna
torta tart flan
tortellini stuffed pasta
trippa tripe
trota trout

U

uccelletti small birds wrapped
  in bacon
uova eggs
uva grapes

V

verdura vegetables
vino bianco white wine
vino rosso red wine
vitello veal
vongole clams

Z

zafferano saffron
zucca pumpkin
zucchine courgette
zuppa soup

A Venetian Recipe

*'The secrets in the kitchen are the
secrets of Pulcinella, burdened
by obesity.'*
Nino Artale*

Pulcinella, a hopeless gossip,
could never keep a secret. What
Nino means is that good recipes
should be shared, but weight
gain may be the result. Here
is his personal recipe, which
contains the secret to making
perfect rice in a risotto dish.

*Nino Artale is a Venetian, a
gourmet chef and the author of
Ricettacolo, a book of short
stories with recipes. Those who
are fluent in Italian, with a sense
of humour and a love of food, will
enjoy his book, published by
L'Autore Libri Firenze
ISBN 88-517-0181-4

For a memorable experience,
you can sample Nino's excellent
Venetian and southern Italian
cooking in a unique Venetian
environment: the home of Nino
Artale and Nini Morelli. Two
courses and dessert start from
€35 per person, with wine and
aperitivo included. Dinner only;
Tuesday-Sunday, Sept-June.
This is not a restaurant service,
so bookings must be made at
least one day in advance and
groups cannot exceed seven in
number. No credit cards.
Tel: +39 348 544 3793
(call or text)

Prawn Risotto (serves 6)

1 kg fresh prawns
500 gm *vialone nano* risotto rice
4 tbsp olive oil
2 tbsp butter
4 tbs dry white wine
250 ml Prosecco
5 cups water
3 sticks of celery
2 medium onions, chopped
3 cloves garlic, chopped
chopped fresh parsley
2 tbps tomato purée
5 tbsp grated parmesan cheese
salt and freshly ground pepper

Slice the celery thinly. Heat 2 tbsp of oil in a saucepan and fry the celery gently, adding the white wine after 2 minutes. Let it simmer for a minute and then add one onion. Cook slowly, uncovered, for 10 minutes, then turn off the heat.

Heat the remaining oil in a non-stick frying pan. Add the garlic and the second onion. Fry gently for 2 minutes then add the prawns and stir for one minute. Stir in the Prosecco and the tomato purée. Simmer for 3-5 minutes. When the prawns are cooked, remove them to a plate using a draining spoon. Empty the remaining mixture into a saucepan, add the water with 1 tbsp salt and bring to a boil. After the prawns have cooled, remove heads and tails, keeping the prawns separate. Put the heads and tails into the boiling water. Boil for a minute, reduce the heat and simmer for 5-10 minutes.

Pour the celery and onion mixture out of the first saucepan. Melt 1 tbsp butter in the pan and then, with the heat turned high, add the rice. **The secret is in toasting the rice:** Stir constantly for 4-5 minutes, being careful not to burn it. Reduce the heat to medium, then add the celery and onion mixture. Strain the stock and pour in half the liquid. Stir occasionally and add more stock in stages, stirring all the while. The risotto should be the right consistency in 20 minutes.

To finish: chop the prawns into pieces and add to the rice, with the chopped parsley. Turn off the heat, add 1 tbsp butter, stir, and mix in the cheese. Add salt and pepper to taste. Let the risotto sit covered for a few minutes before serving.

SHOPPING

GIFT SHOP, CAMPO SAN BARNABA

When to shop

Shop hours in Venice are generally 10.00-13.00, 16.00-19.00. Most will close for lunch though this can vary depending on the shopkeeper's mood and the time of year. Food shops tend to open earlier than artisan shops, are often open during lunch, but then may close earlier than other shops.

VENICE IS FULL OF SHOPS. IF YOU SEE SOMETHING YOU LIKE, BUY IT. YOU MAY NOT BE ABLE TO FIND YOUR WAY BACK TO THE SAME SHOP.

What to buy

Aside from costumes and masks, Venice is most famous for glass, paper and lace.

Glass

The reputation of Murano glass has suffered because of Oriental imports flooding the markets and shops of Venice. The cheapest glass trinkets are often made in China. A consortium has been formed to support authentic Murano artisans and help shoppers identify Murano glass. The *Vetro artistico di Murano* trademark is your guarantee that you have purchased authentic Murano glass.

Established by the Region of the Veneto and a group of Murano glass artisans, *Vetro Artistico Murano* has been promoted since 2001. Only ateliers producing glass on the island of Murano can apply for the trademark. These artisans join the list of concessionary companies featured on the website www.muranoglass.com

They receive special labels to apply to their products. Shops selling authentic glass will often display the trademark logo in their windows.

IT IS NOT NECESSARY TO MAKE A TRIP TO MURANO TO BUY GLASS, AND YOU WILL NOT GET A BETTER PRICE IF YOU VISIT A GLASS FACTORY.

Paper

Papermaking began in Asia and travelled to Europe during the Middle Ages. Venice, at the crossroads of Europe and Asia, was the first place where the art of papermaking and bookbinding became established.

Venetian bookbinding dates back to 1450, with the advent of the first books printed with movable type. Aldus Manitius was one of the most influential publishers, whose *legatoria* (workshop) typeset many scholarly books in Latin and Greek. He is credited with the invention of Italics, the comma and the semi-colon.

Early books were bound with leather covers, but the facing pages would become damaged and discoloured. Marbleized paper was invented to conceal the damage. As leather bindings became more expensive, bookmakers used these decorative papers as covers, saving the leather only for the spine.

There are a number of shops selling marbleized paper and decorative stationary in Venice. Many are machine printed but there a few *legatorie* are still making paper by hand using traditional methods.

Lace

Hand-made lace falls into two main types. The first is known as needle or point lace, which has always been a speciality of the Veneto. The second is known as bobbin or pillow lace.

Much of the lace for sale in Venice and Burano are cheap imports. The genuine time-honoured traditions survive and authentic lace is worth seeking out. Expect to pay around €100 for a lace doily that is handmade and around €15 for the machine-made equivalent.

Many of the old establishedshops found in the Piazza San Marco sell authentic Venetian lace.

San Marco

Berengo Fine Arts
glass
C. Larga di San Marco 412/413
041 241 0763
map 10, G1
A popular producer of glass sculpture.

Venini
glass
Piazzetta dei Leoni
0414 522 4045
map 10, G1
Now owned by Royal Copenhagen of Denmark, sells elegant tableware.

L'Isola
glass
Campo San Moisè 1468
041 523 1973
map 9-10, E3
Unique pieces designed by Carlo Moretti, who has created an exciting range of multicoloured celebration goblets and flutes.

A Mano
lamps
off Merc. San Salvatore
041 528 6881
map 5, B6
A pretty little shop selling hand-made lamps. For their workshop see p.112.

Livio de Marchi
wooden sculptures
Salizzada San Samuele 3157
041 528 5694
map 9, A2
For those that like something unusual, this shop sells detailed wooden sculptures of articles of clothing.

Domus
tableware
Calle dei Fabbri 4746
041 522 6259
map 9-10, E1
A large range of crockery and tableware for every occasion.

Rigattieri
ceramics
Calle dei Frati 3532/6
041 523 1081
map 9, B2
Traditional Bassano ceramics, glassware and tableware with a large variety of serving platters, bowls and spoons.

Linda Gonzales
stationery, handmade books
Campo San Fantin 1854
041 528 5563
map 9, D2
This tiny shop sells hand-bound notebooks of all kinds with leather covers, marbled paper, whatever your fancy. Located just across from La Fenice.

Legatoria Piazzesi
marbled paper
Campiello Feltrina 2511
041 522 1202
map 9, C3
Reputed to be the oldest retailer of paper products in Venice. They use traditional methods to hand print beautiful papers, including wallpaper.

Il Papiro
stationery, marbled paper
Calle del Piovan 2764
041 522 3055
map 9, B3
Calle della Bissa, 5463
041 241 1466
map 5, B5
A traditional stationers that sells hand-bound books, pens and cards.

Libreria Goldoni
books
Calle dei Fabbri 4742
041 522 2384
map 9-10, E1
A general bookstore with a comprehensive stock of books about Venice in different languages.

Studium
books
Calle della Canonica 337/C
041 522 2382
map 10, G1
A good stock of books in English including Venetian food, culture and guidebooks.

Il Tempio della Music
music
RM del Fontego dei Tedeschi, 5368
041 523 4552
map 5, B5
Near the Rialto Bridge, Il Tempio sells every kind of music but specialises in classical, opera and jazz.

Vivaldi Store
music
Campo San Bartolomeo,
Fontego dei Tedeschi 5537/40
041 522 1343
map 5, B5
The best place to look for all things Vivaldi as well as concert tickets.

Trois
Fortuny fabrics
Campo San Maurizio 2666
see p.87

Venetia Studium
Fortuny fabrics
Calle Larga XXII 2403
see p.87

MURANO GLASS JEWELLERY

Bevilacqua
handwoven fabrics
Ponte della Canonica 337B
see p.87

Jesurum
lace
Piazza San Marco 60-61
041 520 6177
map 10, F2

Since Victorian times, this beautiful emporium has been selling high quality household linen at prices to match. You can purchase faithful replicas of traditional lace designs.

Rolando Segalin
shoes
Calle dei Fuseri 4365
041 522 2115
map 9, D1
Handmade shoes to order. An interesting window display features Rolando's more eccentric creations.

Perle e Dintorni
glass beads
Calle della Mandola 3740
041 520 5068
map 9, C1/2
Buy a ready-made piece of jewellery or beads individually in this treasure trove of glass.

San Polo & Santa Croce

Amadi
glass
Calle Saoneri 2747
see p.112

Constantini Rossella
glass jewellery
Calle dei Saoneri 2735
041 713 002
map 3-4, E5
The settings are modern and the prices are reasonable.

Glass Paradise
glass jewellery
Rio Terrà 2600a
041 522 6875
map 3-4, E5
A wide selection of bracelets.

La Zanze Venexiana
icons, masks, boxes
Calle 2A Saoneri 2657
see p.112

La Bottega dei Mascareri
masks
Calle dei Saoneri 2720
see p.113

Defina Ennio
wood carving
Calle dei Saoneri 2672
see p.112

Gilberto Penzo
model boats
Calle dei Saoneri 2681
see p.113

A Mano
lamps
Rio Terrà 2616
see p.112

MODEL BOATS IN SANTA CROCE

Antichita Rocca
antiques
Calle 2A Saoneri 2658
041 714 500
map 3-4, E5
Interesting high quality
antiques.

Il Mercante di Sabbia
antique lamps
Rio Terrà 2600
041 713 494
map 3-4, E5
This shop sells lamps and
mirrors, together with good
quality second-hand and
antique jewellery.

Cenerentola
traditional lampshades
Calle dei Saoneri 2718
map 3-4, E5
Classic lampshades made
with antique embroidered
cloth.

Sabbie e Nebbie
modern ceramics
Calle dei Nomboli 2768B
041 719 073

map 3-4, E3
Japanese and Italian ceramics
are sold here, together with
other well selected craft items.

Arca
modern ceramics
Calle del Tintor 1811
041 710 427
map 4, F2
Teresa della Valentina uses
vibrant colours in her tiles,
vases and objets d'art.

Legatoria Polliero
bookbinding workshop
Campo dei Frari 2995
041 528 5130
map 3, D5
A traditional bookbinding
workshop overstuffed with
albums, leather-bound books,
folders and other stationery.

Mare di Carta
nautical charts and books
Fdm dei Tolentini 222
041 716 304
map 3, A4
Also has information on boat

rentals and cruises.

Arte & Design
stationery
Campiello Mosche 53A
041 710 269
map 7-8, E1
Moleskin notebooks in bright colours. Also in Dorsoduro.

Interpress Photo
film development
Campo delle Beccarie 365
041 528 6978
map 4, H3
It is not easy to find cheap film development in Venice but this outlet is competitive, with a one hour service.

Atelier Pietro Longhi
costume hire
Rio Terrà 2604B
see p.111

Fanny
gloves
Calle dei Saoneri 27/23
041 522 8266
map 3-4, E5
This fun shop has the most unusual gloves and bags in lovely bright colours.

Zazu
womenswear
Calle dei Saoneri 2750
041 715 426
map 3-4, E5
Silk dresses and jewellery.

Aliani
delicatessen
Ruga Vecchia 654-5
041 522 4913
map 4, H4
An excellent delicatessen

selling a variety of cheeses, meats and prepared dishes.

Mascari
delicatessen
Ruga dei Spezieri 381
041 522 9762
map 4, H3
Sells a fine variety of condiments (including those made with white truffles), spices and the finest saffron, pinenuts and dried *porcini.*

Targa
pasticceria and bar
Ruga del Ravano
041 523 6048
map 4, H4
Pastries here are light and flaky. A quiet place for coffee near the market.

Rialto Biocentre
health foods
Alimenti Biologici
Campo Beccarie 366
041 523 9515
map 4, H3
Sells natural and organic products, vitamins and herbs.

Dorsoduro

L'Angolo del Passato
Murano glass
Calle del Cappeller 3276A
041 528 7896
map 8, F3
This shop sells lovely antique Murano glass and also some excellent modern pieces.

Legno e Ditorni
wooden models
Fondamenta Gheradini 2840
041 522 6367

map 7-8, E/F3

Intricate wooden models of buildings and monuments that appeal to all age groups.

Dittura

shoes

Calle Nuove Sant' Agnese 871 (off Rio Terrà Foscarini)
041 523 1163
map 8, H5

Dittura sells *furlane*, the traditional gondoliers' velvet shoes, ideal as slippers.

Libreria Toletta

books, stationery

Calle de Toletta 3
041 523 2034
map 8, G4

Three shops; two on one side of the street, one on the other. Good prices but English selection is limited. Art books, maps and the Venetian A-Z: *Calli, Campielli e Canali.*

Ca' Foscarina

books

Calle Foscari 3259
041 522 9602
map 8, F2

A very good shop for books in the English language.

Arte & Design

stationery

Fondamenta dei Cereri
Dorsoduro 2408H
041 718 898
map 7, B2

Also in Santa Croce.

Cartoleria Accademia

art supplies

Campo Santa Margherita 2928

041 520 7086
map 7-8, E2/3

A good selection of materials is available at this old store, established in 1810.

Capricci Vanita

women's clothes and lace

San Pantalon 3744
041 523 1504
map 8, F1

Giovanna Gamba runs this charming shop near the church of San Pantalon. In summer she sells handmade womens clothing. In winter she sells lace, including tablecloths, curtains and bed linen. Her clothing is influenced by Asian designs.

Annelie Pizzi e Ricami

lace

Calle Lunga S Barnaba 2748
041 520 3277
map 7-8, E4

An endearing shop that sells lace of a superior quality. Annelie has lace nightgowns, pinafores, tablecloths and lace-trimmed bed linen.

Tessuti di Helene
handmade silk scarves
Calle della Chiesa 683
map 8, I5
Handmade silk print scarves.
Lovely designs in rich
colours.

San Vio
jewellery
Campo San Vio 669
041 520 8136
map 8, I5
Two sisters, Susanna and
Maria Sent produce stunning
modern jewellery and
ceramics.

Gualti
jewellery
Rio Terrà Canal 3111
041 520 1731
map 8, F3
Interesting and dramatic
designs, made from synthetic
resin and tiny beads.

Antichità
glass beads
Calle Toletta 1195
041 522 3159
no credit cards
map 8, F4
Antique hand-painted
glassbeads, lace, jewellery
and children's clothes abound
in this little store.

Erboristeria il Melograno
health foods and remedies
Campo S. Margherita 2999
041 528 5117
map 7-8, E2
The lady who runs this shop
is known locally as a healer
who understands the herbal
requirements to treat various
afflictions. She sells herbal
remedies, vitamins, pot
pourri, soaps and fragrances.

Cantinone 'gia Schiavi
wine
Fondamenta Priuli 992
see p.232
This shop is also an enoteca
so you can taste before you
buy.

Cannaregio

Ca' Macana
masks
Rio Terra San Leonardo 1374-75
041 718 655
map 1-2, E5
A very large selection of
unique masks, handmade
from papier mache in the
traditional method. Prices
are reasonable. Masks with
cheerful faces are difficult
to find, but this shop has a
selection of clowns, suns and
moons, and other original
face masks that won't scare
the children.

La Campagnia delle Perle
murano glass
Calle Dolfin 5622
041 520 6969
map 5, B4
This is where you can
purchase a nice Murano
glass necklace for a relatively
inexpensive price.

Laboratorio Blu
children's books
Campo Ghetto Vecchio 1224
041 715 819

LA CAMPAGNIA DELLE PERLE

map 1, D4
A well stocked children's bookshop, with books for all ages in English and Italian.

Mori & Bozzi
shoes
Rio Terà Maddalena 2367
041 715 261
map 2, G5
All the most fashionable shoe trends with copies of designer names.

Nicolao Atelier
costume hire
Calle del Magazin 5590A
near Campo SS. Apostoli
041 520 9749
09.00-13.00,14.00-18.00 Mon
www.nicolao.com
map 5, B4
A famous costume showroom which has supplied wardrobe for films such as *The Wings of the Dove*. You can also see costumes being made at the workshop nearby at Calle del Bagatin 5565 (by appointment only, 041 520 7051)

Coin
department store
Salizzada San Giovanni
Grisostomo 5790
041 520 3581
09.30-19.30 Mon-Sat
11.00-19.30 Sun
map 5, B4
There are few department stores in Venice, so this one specialising in reasonably priced clothing may be welcome.

Cibele
health foods
Campiello Anconetta 1823
041 524 2113
map 2, F5
A comprehensive selection of vitamins, health foods and cosmetics.

Giacomo Rizzo
food and drink
C. S. Giovanni Crisostomo 5778
041 522 2824
closed Wednesday afternoon
map 5, B4
A good selection of local produce and fine balsamic

vinegar and they stock white truffle paste. You may find something interesting to take home amongst their enormous variety of pasta, including gondola shapes. You can also buy imported products like marmalade and a wide range of spices.

Tuttocasa
cookware
Campo Santi Apostoli 4518
041 523 8585
map 5, B3
A well-stocked kitchen shop with a good assortment of vegetable peelers and garlic presses. They have a variety of coloured plastic ware and Italian lucite, useful for picnics and dining al fresco.

Castello

Luigi Benzoni Atelier
glass
Fondamenta de Pintor 3874
041 528 1660
map 11, C1
Creative contemporary glass, situated near the Arsenale.

Anticlea Antiquariato
antiques
Calle San Provolo 4719A
041 528 6946
map 10, H1
Glass beads, lace and interesting antiques.

Laboratorio del Gervasuti
antiques
Campo Bandiera e Moro
041 523 6777
map 11, B1

A tempting array of antiques fills this family workshop opened in the late fifties by master craftsman Euginio Gervasuti whose son now carries on the tradition. There is also an antiques warehouse (viewing by appointment).

Papier Maché
masks
Calle Lunga Santa Maria Formosa 5175
041 522 9995
map 5-6, D/E5
Inspired by artists such as Kandinsky, Tiepolo and Klimt, these masks are distinctive and original.

Agile
toys
Campo San Lio
041 923 705
no credit cards
map 5, C5
A troupe of jugglers, weather permitting, run this outdoor stall that sells all kinds of toys including yo-yos, puppets and hats.

Ratti
kitchenware
Calle delle Bande 5825
041 240 4600
map 5, D6
A comprehensive stock of household goods, including adaptors, security items and a key cutting service.

Il Papiro
stationery
Calle delle Bande 5275
041 522 3648

map 5, D6

Beautiful, handmade marbled paper items

Giovanna Zanella

womenswear, accessories

Campo San Lio 5641

041 523 5500

map 5, C5

Unique designs using lovely fabrics.

Bottiglieria Colonna

wine

Calle della Fava 5595

041 528 5137

map 5, C6

This shop sells a variety of wine and an assortment of grappa, as well as a selection of olive oil and balsamic vinegar.

Supermarkets

Billa

Dorsoduro

Zattere Ponte Lungo 1491

041 522 6187

vaporetto: San Basilio

08.30-20.00 Mon-Sat

09.00-20.00 Sunday

Credit cards accepted

map 7, D5

Fruit and vegetables and other staples.

Standa

Cannaregio

Strada Nova 3659

08.30-19.20 daily

map 5, A3

Combination Woolworths and supermarket.

Su.Ve

Castello

corner of Salizzada San Lio and Calle Mondo Nuovo

map 5, D6

Staples including bottled water, near San Marco.

Coop

Giudecca

Calle dell'Olio 484

041 241 3381

vaporetto: Palanca

08.30-13.00, 15.30-19.30 Mon-Tues. and Thurs

08.30-13.00 Wed and Sun

08.30-19.30 Fri-Sat

credit cards accepted

A large new supermarket with reasonable prices.

CANNAREGIO

SAN MOISE AND BOTERO

This section contains a selection of interesting churches and galleries not included in the main chapters.

Opening and admission

Opening hours of churches are generally as follows:

10.00-18.00 Monday-Saturday
12.00-15.00 closed for lunch
many churches are closed on Sunday
closed 1st January and Christmas
single admission €2

Chorus pass €8

Chorus is dedicated to restoring and maintaining Venice's churches. The pass allows you visit its 15 member churches for one admission. Available at the churches, VELA ticket offices, and tourist information offices.
www.chorusvenezia.org

San Marco

Santa Maria Zobenigo

(or del Giglio)
entrance fee chorus pass
map 9, C3
Dedicated to *Madonna of the Lily* (*del Giglio*) and financed by the Barbaro family to glorify their naval and diplomatic achievements. A Rubens' *Madonna* is inside.

San Moise

Campo San Moise
map 9-10, E3
The elaborate Baroque facade was completed in 1668 when San Marco was the centre of opera, gambling and decadence.

San Salvatore

Campo San Salvador
open 09.00-12.00, 15.00-18.00
map 5, B6
This large well-lit Renaissance church has two paintings by Titian: *Annunciation* and *Transfiguration of Christ.* The floor is quite beautiful.

Santo Stefano

Campo Santo Stefano
entrance fee chorus pass
map 9, B2
The Gothic interior has a ship's keel ceiling with carved tie-beams. In the dark sacristy is Tintoretto's *Evangelists.*

San Giuliano (Zulian)

Campo San Zulian
09.30 Sunday, service in English
map 10, F1
The church (by Sansovino) was financed by the physician Tommaso Rangone who had praises to himself inscribed on the facade.

San Polo

San Cassiano

Campo San Cassiano
map 4, G3
In the sacristy are three Tintorettos: *Crucifixion, Descent into Limbo, Resurrection.*

S. Giovanni Elemosinario
Ruga Vecchia San Giovanni
entrance fee chorus pass
map 4, H/I 4
In the high altar is *St John the Almsgiver* by Titian.

San Polo
Campo San Polo
entrance fee chorus pass
map 4, F5
Founded in the 9th century the large church contains Tieopolo's *Stations of the Cross* and the *Last Supper* by Tintoretto. At the base of the bell tower are two lions: one holds a serpent between its paws, the other a human head.

San Rocco
Campo San Rocco
map 3, C5
The church is often passed by in favour of the Scuola. *St Roch curing the Plague Victims* in the chancel is worth seeing.

Santa Croce

San Giacomo dell'Orio
Campo San Giacomo dell'Orio
entrance fee chorus pass
map 3, D/E3
Founded in the 9th century, the church is a mix of styles with a sumptuous ceiling in the sacristy by Veronese.

San Nicolo da Tolentino
Campo dei Tolentini
map 3, A/B
Located near the Papadopoli gardens, this church was built in the Palladian style.

San Stae
Campo San Stae
entrance fee chorus pass
map 4, F2
Financed by the Mocenigo family, the church often hosts concerts and *Biennale* exhibits.

Dorsoduro

Gesuati
Fondamenta Zattere ai Gesuati
entrance fee chorus pass
map 8, G6
The Rococco church has a Tiepolo ceiling fresco *The Life of Dominic* and an altarpiece *Virgin with Saints.* (p.151)

San Barnaba
Campo San Barnaba
map 8, F3
This church once had unusual parishoners called *Barnabotti* – nobles reduced to begging because laws forbade them to work. Laws also decreed that nobles should dress in silk even if it was tattered.

St. George's Anglican
Campo San Vio; map 8,I5
10.30 Sunday, Sung Eucharist
18.00 daily Vespers
Bequeathed in 1892 to Venice's English community by Sir Layard. Contains the tomb of Consul Smith. (p.126)

Santa Maria dei Carmini
Campo dei Carmini
map 7, D/E3
The interior is spacious and features good carvings by the school of Sansovino. The Scuola has Tiepolo's paintings.

San Nicolo dei Mendicoli
Campo San Nicolo
map 7, A4
The winged lion on the Nicolotti banner pre-dates St Mark. The parish elected their own *doge*, or clan chief. The interior is lavishly decorated with carvings and sculpture.

San Pantalon
Campo San Pantalon
map 8, F1
The ceiling is covered by a gigantic painting depicting the life and martyrdom of the physician St. Pantalon. After 24 years painting this masterpiece, the artist Gian Antonio Fumiani fell to his death from the scaffolding.

San Sebastiano
Campo San Sebastiano
entrance fee chorus pass
map 7, C4
Veronese's paintings fill the church and tell the story of Esther, Queen of Xerxes I of Persia, who saved the Jewish people. Titian's *St Nicholas* is hung over the high altar.

San Trovaso
Campo San Trovaso
map 8, F/G5
This was neutral ground between rivals the Castellani and Nicolotti (p.78) who each had a separate entrance.

Cannaregio
San Giobbe
Campo San Giobbe
map 1, A4

Pietro Lombardo carved the Renaissance doorway. Inside are ceramics by della Robbia.

San Giovanni Crisostomo
Campo S Giovanni Crisostomo
map 5, B4
A pretty terracotta church near the Rialto with Bellini's *St. Jerome with St. Christopher and Augustine* in the first altar.

San Marcuola
Campo San Marcuola
map 2, F6
The Last Supper by Tintoretto, is the first painting of what became his favoured subject.

Sant'Alvise
Campo Sant'Alvise
entrance fee chorus pass
map 2, F2
Tiepolo's paintings suffer damage from the dampness of the church and are being continually restored.

Santa Maria di Scalzi
Fondamente degli Scalzi
map 3, A2
The Scalzi were Carmelite friars who came to Venice during the 1670s. Inside is a Tiepolo fresco *St Theresa*.

San Marziale
Campo San Marziale
map 2, H5
Tobias and Raphael by Titian is back in its home church after residing at the Madonna dell' Orto during restorations.

Santi Apostoli
Campo dei Santi Apostoli
Lutheran services

EX CHIESA DELL'ABBAZIA

10.30 on 2nd and 4th Sundays
map 5, B3
The Communion of St. Lucy by
Tiepolo is in the chapel.

Castello

La Pietà
Riva degli Schiavoni
041 523 1096
open only for concerts
map 11, A2
see p.170

San Francesco della Vigna
Ramo San Francesco
map 6, H5
The church was began by
Sansovino, but given over
to his rival Palladio when
Sansovino was jailed over the
collapse of the library vault.
The beauty of the interior
proved Palladio's talent. Near
the cloister is Giovanni Bellini's
Madonna and Child.

San Giorgio dei Greci
Fondamenta dei Greci
map 11, A1
The leaning campanile is the
most striking feature.

San Giovanni in Bragora
Campo Bandiera e Moro
map 11, B2
The church has carvings and
paintings by lesser known
artists. Vivarini's *Madonna
and Child with Saints* and
Conegliano's *Baptism of the
Christ* are influential pieces.

San Lorenzo
Campo San Lorenzo
map 6, G5
One of the four musical
ospedali, this church is now
part of the Ospedale Civile.

Santa Maria Formosa
Campo Santa Maria Formosa
entrance fee chorus pass
map 5, D6
Palma il Vecchio's *Santa
Barbara and Saints* depicts the
voluptuous Santa Barbara,
Venice's ideal of beauty.

The Lagoon Islands
Giudecca
Il Redentore
Campo Redentore
entrance fee chorus pass
map overview C5.
Considered by many to
be Palladio's masterpiece.
The church was built in
thanksgiving for the end of
the 1576 plague and is the
scene of the romantic summer
festival *Festa del Redentore*.
The interior is somewhat
disappointing compared to
the magnificent exterior.

Museums & Galleries

Museum Pass

A pass for €18 allows entrance to all of the following museums:

Museums of St Mark's Square (single admission €12)
  Palazzo Ducale (Doge's Palace)
  Muso Correr (Correr Museum)
  Biblioteca Marciana (also called the Libreria Sansoviniana)
  Museo Archeologico

Museums of 18th century culture
  Ca' Rezzonico
  Ca' Mocenigo
  Casa di Goldoni

Museums of Modern Art
  Ca' Pesaro
  Museo Fortuny

The Island Museums
  Glass Museum at Murano
  Lace Museum at Burano.

SENIORS WITH EU PASSPORTS MAY BE ENTITLED TO DISCOUNTS.

San Marco

Gallery Contini

Calle de Spezia 2765 San Marco
10.00-13.00, 15.30-19.30
041 520 4942
www.continiarte.com
map 3-4, E6

This is Botero's gallery. It is a private gallery and it is possible to buy drawings by Picasso, paintings by Chagall, Miro and, of course, works by Botero.

Palazzo Contarini del Bovolo

Corte Contarini d. Bovolo 4299
041 270 2464
10.00-18.00 daily April-October
10.00-16.00 Saturday-Sunday November-December
entrance fee
guided tours available
map 9, D1

There is a graceful external spiral stairway in this palazzo built by the Contarini family.

Museum of Erotica

834 Calle dei Fabbri
041 520 3900
10.00-23.00 daily
€10, reductions €6
map 9, E1

Venice has always had a reputation among those with an interest in the erotic arts. Indeed in the 18th and 19th centuries, Venice was known as the bordello of Europe. However the museum prides itself in making a distinction between erotica and pornography, and exhibits drawings, paintings, sculpture and literature.

San Polo

Casa di Goldoni

Palazzo Santani, Calle Nomboli
041 244 0317
10.00-17.00 Monday-Saturday April-October;
10.00-16.00 Monday-Saturday November-March

closed Sunday and holidays
€2.50; wheelchair access
map 8, H1
Carlo Goldoni wrote over 250
comedies and his plots became
popular in opera librettos. The
house displays his writings
and other works.

Santa Croce

Fondaco dei Turchi
Museo Storia Naturale
Canal Grande
041 275 0206
partly closed for renovation
map 3-4, E1-2
Venice's natural history
museum is housed in a former
warehouse for Turkish traders.
There is a collection of stuffed
animals, crustaceans, dinosaur
fossils and a section on lagoon
life.

Ca' Mocenigo
Museo del Tessuto e del Costume
Salizzada San Stae 1992
041 72 1798
10.00-17.00 Tuesday-Sunday
April-October
10.00-16.00 Tuesday-Sunday
November-March
closed 1 January and Christmas
€8
map 4, F2
A beautifully preserved 18th
century palazzo that once
belonged to the Mocenigo
family. The museum contains
antique fabrics and exquisitely
made costumes.

Ca' Pesaro
The Galleria d'Arte Moderna
Museo Orientale
Canal Grande 2076
041 524 0695
€5.50
10.00-17.00 Tuesday–Sunday
map 4, G2
The Pesaro family were
patrons of Titian. The art
gallery was founded in 1897
to contain prizewinning
works from the Biennale. It
exhibits works by Bonnard,
Matisse, Miro, Klee, Klimt
and Kandinsky, in addition to
works by Italian artists of the
19th and 20th centuries.

Dorsoduro

Galleria Ca'Rezzonico
Palazzo Contarini Michiel
041 528 0035
10.00-13.00, 16.00-19.00 daily
www.galleriacarezzonico.com
map 8, G3
A private gallery that is easy
to find and well worth a
visit. Step off the vaporetto at
Ca'Rezzonico and walk into
the gallery. Exhibits combine
contemporary art with
antiques.

Cini Collection
Palazzo Cini, San Vio 864
041 521 0755
10.00-13.00, 14.00-19.00
Tuesday-Sunday
closed August, December-March
entrance fee
map 9, A5
Tuscan Renaissance paintings
and illuminated manuscripts.

TRAVEL BASICS

GONDOLIER ON THE GRAND CANAL

Baggage

When you pack your luggage, bear in mind that wheeled suitcases will have to be carried and you will probably walk through narrow lanes and over stepped bridges to reach your accommodation. Hotels are often some distance from the vaporetto.

Climate

January and February are the coldest months (0-7°c). It is a damp cold, so pack layers and thermals. Skies can be either clear or misty. Snow is rare.

Spring and Autumn are the best times to visit, with many sunny days, but it can rain and *acqua altas* are frequent.

Summers tend to be humid (around 30°c), but there is often a breeze from the water.

Documents

•Passport Agency
0870 521 0410
www.passport.gov.uk
•Italian Consulate
0208 235 9371
•Foreign, Commonwealth office
www.knowbeforeyougo.co.uk
0208 235 9371
Passports should be valid for six months after travelling. A visa is not necessary for British and EC passport holders. Non-EC citizens should check with their own, or with the Italian Consulate.

Arriving in Venice

Marco Polo Airport
www.veniceairport.it
041 260 6111
recorded flight information
041 260 9260 in English
arrivals 041 260 9240
departures 041 260 9250
lost property 041 260 6436

THE APPROACH TO MARCO POLO IS FROM THE SOUTH. SIT ON THE STARBOARD (RIGHT) SIDE OF THE PLANE FOR AN AERIAL VIEW OF VENICE AND THE ENTIRE LAGUNA FROM CHIOGGIA TO TORCELLO.

Marco Polo is clearly signed and well organised with arrivals on ground level and departures on the first floor. Cashpoints, shops and cafes are available on both levels.

After baggage claim, turn right to find the First Aid station, a bar, cashpoint and post office.

Travelling into Venice
The kiosk selling tickets for travel into Venice is to the left after baggage claim. You can get to Venice by land and by water, on public transport or by private taxi. Buses depart from the front of the airport, boats from the yellow pier. A free shuttle goes to the pier.

By land
•ATVO direct bus departs every 20-30 minutes from the front of the airport, costs €3 and takes 20 minutes.

- ACTV stopping bus takes 40 minutes and costs €1.50.
- Taxis are available outside the terminal building and cost about €30.

By water
- Alilaguna fast ferries cost €10 for a one hour journey. Boats depart every hour from the yellow pier. There are two lines, red and blue.
- Red Line stops at Murano, continues to the Lido, then stops at Arsenale, San Marco and Zattere.
- Blue Line stops at Murano Colonna and Fondamenta Nove, on its way to San Zaccaria and San Marco.

Water taxis (p.31)
041 522 2303
Water taxis accept payment in cash only and are expensive. Expect to pay upwards of €80 depending on your destination.

Water taxi safety
- Hand your luggage to the driver before stepping into the boat.
- Wait until the driver has stowed your luggage before stepping into the boat.
- Do not stand astride the landing stage and boat when handing over cases.
- Give your hand to the driver when stepping in the boat.
- Smoking is not permitted.
- Do not stand at the back of the boat while in the San Marco basin or in the lagoon.
- When disembarking, be careful at low tides, the green covered areas are slippery.
- Life jackets are stored under the seating areas.

Treviso Airport
www.trevisoairport.it
0422 230 393

Currently used by Ryanair for departures from Stansted, the airport is approximately one hour from Venice.
- ATVO Eurobus to Piazzale Roma costs €4.30 one-way or €7.60 return (valid one week). The bus schedule is timed to align with flight arrivals and departures. Pay on board.

By train:
Santa Lucia Station

Two vaporetto stops are located outside the station:
- Lines 1 and 52 are on the right, line 82 is on the left.
- After 22.30, line N (night route) departs from the stop to the left. After 23.00 purchase tickets on board.
- If your luggage is over 75cm in any dimension it is charged as an extra person.

Parking

The Ponte della Liberta is the only road access into Venice, leading to car parks at Piazzale Roma and Tronchetto. Be advised that holiday weekends cause

huge traffic jams. Reserve in advance, bookings can be made online.
•Piazzale Roma and mainland carparks
www.urbislimen.net
•Tronchetto carpark
www.veniceparking.it

Piazzale Roma

Autorimessa Communale
041 272 7301, fax 041 723 131
€19 for 24 hours
fees can be higher in summer
open 24 hours, 365 days

Tronchetto

€18 per day (3 to 24 hours)
www.veniceparking.it
You can park a large camper or motorhome here, but be prepared to pay higher rates.
•Take the Tronchetto exit off the right lane of the Venice causeway, just before you reach the city.
•open 08.00-20.00 (extended during high season). Toilets, food and shops are near the cashier's office.
•Vaporetto Line 82 connects Tronchetto to San Marco and Venice.

Mainland car parks

Parking on the mainland avoids the traffic on the causeway to Piazzale Roma.
•Mestre
Parcheggi Mestre, €9 per day located near the train station
•Terminal S Giuliano, €7 per day next to the causeway by the lagoon, with ferries to Venice.

Getting around

Essential information is found on pages 16-39 of this book.

Vaporetti (p.28)
www.actv.it
041 528 7886

Main vaporetti routes

Line 1 covers all the stops along the Grand Canal. It runs from Piazzale Roma down to San Marco, then continues along the Riva Degli Schiavoni, out to the Lido, and returns.

Line 82 is a circular route with limited stops and is a faster way to get from the train station to San Marco. Starting from San Zaccaria it runs to the island of San Giorgio, up the Giudecca Canal, round Tronchetto and then down the Grand Canal. At peak times extra services run only from Rialto to Piazzale Roma and back, and these may also be extended from San Zaccaria to Lido.

Line 41/42 is the circular route from Murano to Fondamente Nove, through the Cannareggio canal to the train station (Ferrovia), and then down the Giudecca Canal to San Zaccaria. From here it cuts through St Elena back onto the Fondamente Nove and out to Murano. Line 41 runs anti-clockwise, line 42 clockwise.

Line 51/52 circumnavigates the island of Venice, starting and finishing at the Lido. Line 51 runs anti-clockwise, line 52 clockwise.

Line 61/62 runs from Piazzale Roma through the Giudecca canal to the Lido and returns.

Line 71/72 runs from San Zaccaria to Murano, then to the train station and Tronchetto and returns.

Line 12 to Murano, Burano and Torcello, leaving from Fondamente Nove.

Line 13 runs to Murano and Sant' Erasmo, leaving from Fondamente Nove.

Traghetti (p.31)

Tourist information

Venice has three public tourist information offices:
•Santa Lucia Railway Station
041 529 8727
•San Marco, near the gardens
041 522 5150
•Piazzale Roma
041 529 8746
Also visit
www.aguestinvenice.com

Tourist passes

Ask at the tourist offices for details. EU senior citizens may be entitled to discounts.

Chorus pass entry into 15 churches for €8 (p.268)

Museum Pass entry into 11 museums for €18. Pass is valid for three months, one entry per museum. (p.272)

VENICEcard does not offer a saving but combines a transport and museum pass. Book in advance online:
www.venicecard.com
Telephone 48 hours in advance
041 2424
or enquire at the tourist offices
•Blue VENICEcard covers public transport and VESTA serviced toilets.
•Orange VENICEcard includes Museum Pass, public transport and toilets.
•discounted for under 30s
•VENICEcards can also include the ferry to the airport and/or reserved parking space at San Giuliano carpark.

Collect VENICEcards from VELA offices in Marco Polo, Santa Lucia station, Piazzale Roma, Tronchetto or the Terminal di Punta Sabbioni.

Rolling Venice is a card for those aged 14-29, offers discounts on food, entertainment, transport and museums. A passport and a colour photograph are required. Cost €2.60.

Assessorato alla Gioventu
Corte Contarina 1529, San Marco
041 274 7650

Disabled travellers

Venice is not very wheelchair friendly and it is worth contacting **Informahandicap**, a helpful advice organisation regarding accessability in Venice. They will answer your queries in English by email or telephone.

Viale Garibaldi 155, Mestre
041 534 1700
informahandicap@comuneven ezia.it

• A map of wheelchair accessible areas of Venice is available to download from:
www.comune.venezia.it/mappe/ disabili/piantina.asp
The website also includes suggested itineraries.
• The tourist office will loan a key to wheelchair lifts in Venice.
• Vaporetti Lines 1 and 82 are wheelchair accessible, as are two-thirds of the routes.
• Routes operated by motoscafi are not accessible.
• many 3 and 4 star hotels have installed lifts.
• Popular state-run museums institutions are installing lifts. Enquire before visiting.

Medical and dental

Medical treatment
Dial:
• 118 emergency
• 041 523 0000 ambulance boat

Ospedale Civile
Campo San Giovanni e Paolo
vaporetto Ospedale
041 529 4111
casualty 041 529 4516
The hospital is located next to the church SS. Giovanni e Paolo. *Pronto Soccorso* means A & E.

Ospedale al Mare
Lungomare D'Annunzio 1, Lido
vaporetto Lido
041 529 4111
casualty 041 529 5234
A small hospital located on the seafront at the bottom of the Grand Viale. It has a small casualty department with limited services, but will transfer patients to Ospedale Civile if necessary.

The E111 form entitles UK residents to free medical and dental treatment and to pay local rates for prescriptions. It is available at UK post offices and must be carried with you. In Italy it should be exchanged at *Unita Sanitaria Locale* for an Italian certificate.

Chemists

Most chemists will have a list of doctors and dentists.

Chemists are usually open 09.00-20.00, closing for lunch in rural areas. Many pharmacists speak English and can assist with minor ailments. In Italy, medicine is often given by suppository *supposta* to avoid harming the digestion. Be sure to ask the chemist.

Consulates

• UK
Palazzo Querini, Accademia
Dorsoduro 1051, Venice
041 522 7207
• Ireland
Piazza Campitelli 3, Rome
06 68 30 73 16
• USA
Via Vittorio Veneto 119, Rome
06 46741
• Canada
Via GB de Rossi 27, Rome
06 68 30 73 16
• Australia
Via Alessandria 215, Rome
06 445 981
• New Zealand
Via Zara 28, Rome
06 441 7171

Police and fire

A Carabinieri office is located
on Piazzale Roma on the far
side near the car park, or just
off San Zaccaria in Castello.

Personal security

Credit card contact numbers
open 24 hours. Prefix 0044.

• Abbey National	908 344 900
• American Exp	1273 696 933
• Barclays Bank	1604 230 230
• Clydesdale	1132 881 403
• Egg	1268 298 807
• First Direct	1132 345 678
• Giro Bank	1519 441 220
• HSBC	1442 422 929
• Lloyds TSB	1702 278 270
• Nat West Bank	1132 778 899
• RB of Scotland	1268 298 929
• TSB Trustcard	1273 204 471

Police report

Depending on the severity
of the incident, you may
decide it is not wise to waste
precious holiday time at a
police station. Stolen items
are rarely recovered and
most credit card companies
are usually satisfied with a
telephone report from the
cardholder. However, if a
large amount was stolen,
and you will be making an
insurance claim, a police
report will be required.

Italian Police

In Italy there are many types
of police:
• Polizia Urbana
Traffic and parking police
• Polizia Stradele
Patrol motorways
• Police Statale
Thefts and petty crime
• Carabinieri
Serious crime, public order

Dial:
•113 Police or ambulance
•112 Carabinieri
•115 Fire Brigade, *Vigili d. Fuoco*

Tobacconists

Cigarettes can only be
purchased from licensed
tobacconists identified
by a white T on a black
background (*Tabacchi*). These
shops often close by 20.00.

Some bars will sell cigarettes
after hours and there are
vending machines tucked into

doorways, but these often charge premium prices.

SMOKING IS BANNED IN BARS AND RESTAURANTS IN ITALY.

Postage

Postage from Italy to the UK currently costs 41 cents for letters and postcards. Stamps may be bought at post offices or tobacconists. Post offices are marked on our maps.

Cashpoints

Cashpoints are plentiful and transactions can usually be made in English. Amounts can be withdrawn as needed from your account, which is better for personal security. Bank charges per transaction vary between £1 and £2.

Marco Polo airport has cashpoints in the terminal so it is possible to wait until arrival to withdraw holiday cash. Carry a few euro coins for carts or coffee. Cashpoint withdrawals are quicker than cashing traveller's cheques at a bank and may offer a more competitive exchange rate.

Credit card purchases may net a better rate of exchange than cashpoint withdrawals from your bank account. However, many transactions in Italy are paid in cash only.

Mobile phones

To access mailbox and answering services you need to set up a PIN number before you depart. Calls made to your mobile are charged at the local rate to the caller. However you will be charged for receiving the call while abroad. Screening calls can save considerable expense, as can text messaging.

To call UK mobiles from abroad, dial 0044 and mobile number but drop the zero at the front of the number.

To call Italy from abroad, dial 0039 then the number including the area prefix. Within Italy, drop 0039 dial the full number and the zero.

Public telephones

Hotels in Italy usually apply an expensive surcharge to telephone calls. A telephone card (*scheda*) may be obtained from a Tabacchi. Remove the perforated corner before using. A red flashing light indicates that a telephone is out of order.

Directory enquiries:
•Italy, 12
•Europe, 176
•Rest of world, 170
•Country direct, 172
dial 172 and then 0044 to speak to an operator in your own language.

Internet cafes

Net House
Campo San Stefano 2958-67
San Marco, map 9, B3
08.00-02.00 daily
open 24 hrs Fri-Sun, May-Sept

Internet Point
Calle dei Preti 3812/a,
Dorsoduro, map 7, D5
09.15-20.00 Mon-Sat

Planet Internet
Terrà San Leonardo 1519,
Cannaregio, map 1, E5
09.00-24.00 daily

Network café
Campo San Giacomo 124,
San Polo, map 4, I4
10.00-23.00 Mon-Sat

Toilets

Ladies' toilets in many
restaurants are set low to the
ground and have no seats.
There is rarely a handrail to
assist in raising or lowering
oneself. Toilets in museums
and public buildings are
usually at the normal height.

Look for green, blue and
white AmaV signs for
public toilets (cost 50 cents).
Otherwise, if the need arises
go to a bar, enquire if there
is a toilet and purchase
something before availing
yourself of the facilities.

Vaporetti are not equipped
with toilets.

Tipping

Tipping is left to your
discretion but, as a guide,
approximately €5 per week
for hotel maids and €6 per
guest per week in the hotel
restaurant is acceptable .

In restaurants a service
charge is normally included,
so anything extra is at your
discretion. Leave some
change at a bar.

Railway and airport porters
charge a fixed tip of €3-5
per piece of luggage. This is
also the amount to tip a hotel
porter.

Cinema

Giorgione Movie d'Essai
Rio Terra dei Franceschi 4612
vaporetto Ca' d'Oro
041 522 6298
no credit cards
map 5, B2-3
Art house cinema.

Swimming pools

In Italian pools, swimmers
must wear caps and flip-flops
or thongs in the shower room.

Sant'Alvise
Sant'Alvise, 3161 Cannaregio
041 713 567
map 2, E2

Sacca Fisola
Campo San Gerardo, Giudecca
041 528 5430
This swimming pool has a
beautiful view of the lagoon
through the glass wall.

Walks and garden tours

Venice Walks and Tours offer a range of guided walks on different themes including 'Ghost Venice' and 'Secret Gardens of Venice'. Book on their website before you go. www.venicewalksandtours.com

Boat Hire

It may sound like fun, but even with boating experience you will have great difficulty trying to navigate the narrow canals in the centre of Venice. Locals are also getting tired of rescuing tourists who have run aground in the lagoon. However, if you know the rules it is a fine way to see the Grand Canal and the surrounding islands of Venice. Be advised that boat rental operators will test your docking abilities before they let you hire a boat.

Brussa
Ponte delle Guglie 331,
Cannaregio
041 715 787
07.00-17.30 Mon-Fri
07.00-13.00 Saturday
map 1, D5
Rent small skiffs with 15 hp motors by the hour or by the day.

FOR MORE INFORMATION ON HIRING A BOAT IN VENICE VISIT MARE DI CARTA (P.259).

Marco Polo Departures

Overland buses and taxis stop in front of the terminal. This is a no-waiting, drop-off area.

Watertaxis and the Alilaguna waterbus from San Marco arrive in front of the old airport building, from where a free shuttle service operates to the departure area. Shuttles leave approximately every 15 minutes and the journey takes 12 minutes. Although it is possible to walk the distance in half the time, this will not be easy if you have heavy luggage. Trolleys are available free of charge at the terminal.

If you have time once you have checked your baggage, it is more pleasant to sit in the restaurant to the right in the main departures hall, than to go immediately through security. In the restaurant you can sit by the window and look across the runway to Venice. There are monitors to keep you informed of your flight departures.

Once through security there is a coffee bar, which closes by 20.00 and some duty-free shops but it is more relaxing to wait for your departure in the main hall.

Index

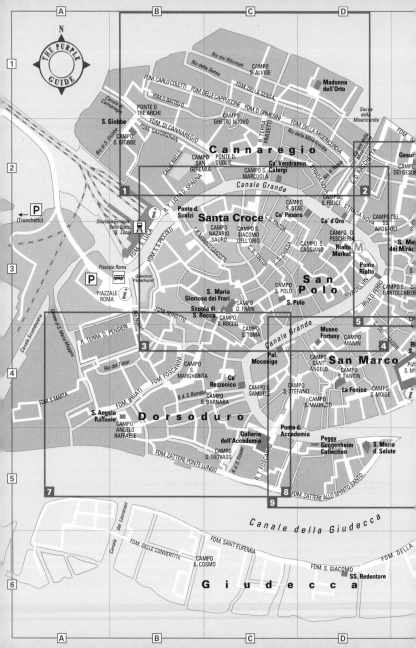

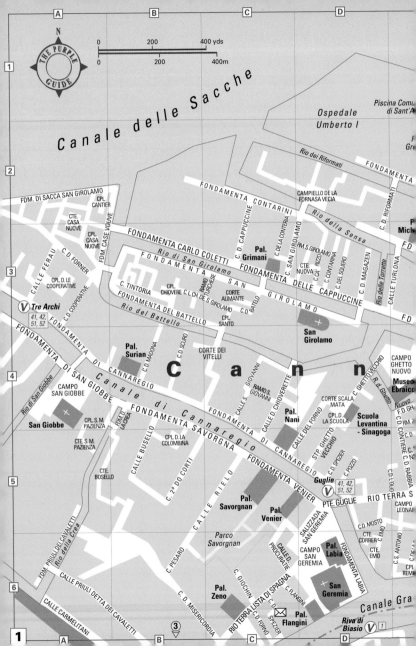

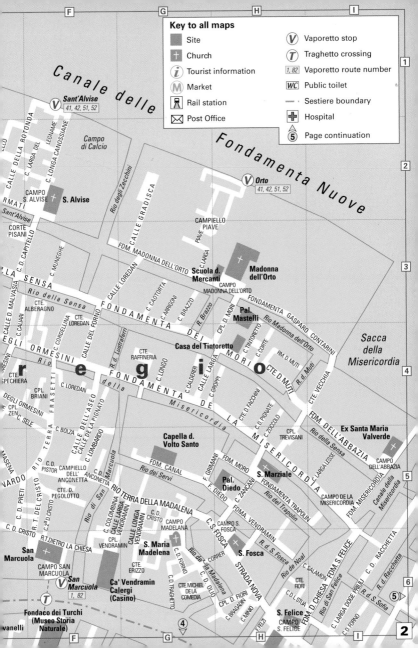

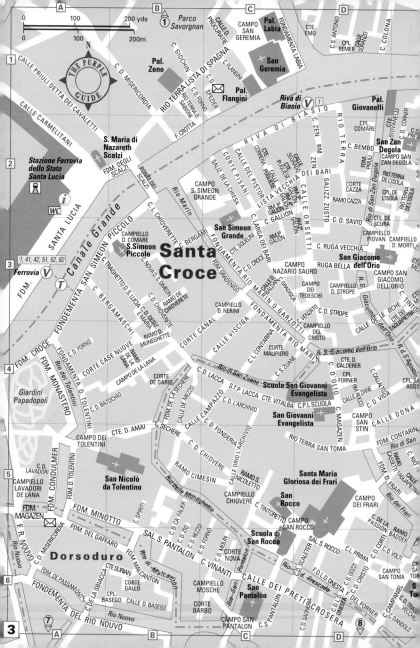

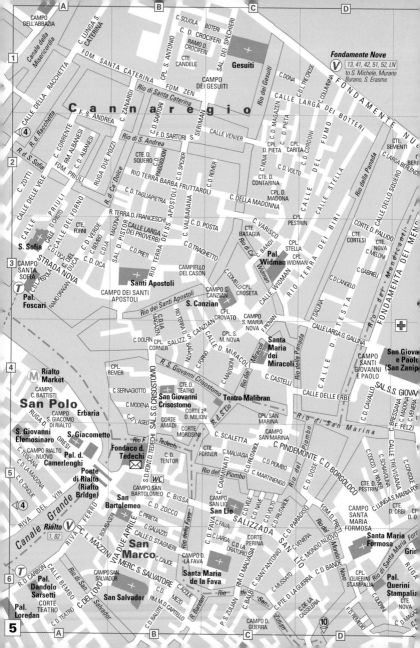

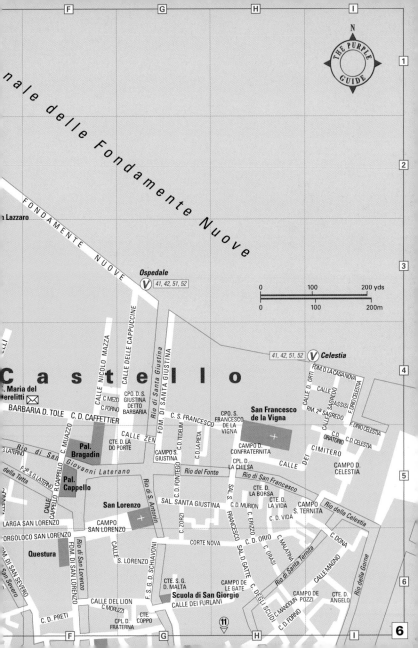

N THE PURPLE GUIDE

1

2

nale delle Fondamente Nuove

n Lazzaro

FONDAMENTE NUOVE

3

Ospedale
Ⓥ 41, 42, 51, 52

0   100   200 yds
0   100   200m

41, 42, 51, 52 Ⓥ *Celestia*

4

Castello

FDM. D. LA CASA NOVA

Maria dei
erelitti ✉
BARBARIA D. TOLE   C. D. CAFFETTIER

CALLE NICOLO MAZZO

CALLE DELLE CAPPUCCINE

CPO. D. S. GIUSTINA DETTO BARBARIA

Rio di Santa Giustina

FDM. DI SANTA GIUSTINA

C. MEZO
C. FORNO

C. S. FRANCESCO

CPO. S. FRANCESCO DE LA VIGNA

San Francesco de la Vigna

FDM. D. ORTI

CALLE D. ORTI

RM. 2ª SAGREDO

CALLE SAGREDO

F. DRIO CELESTIA

C. SASSISI

F. DRIO CELESTIA

CALLE C. D. CELESTIA

C. D. ORATORIO

CIMITERO

Rio di San

Rio di San

CALLE ZEN

CALLE MUAZZO

F. 2ª S. G. LATERNO

della Tetta

CALLE CAPPELLO

C. CAPPELLO

Pal. Bragadin

Pal. Cappello

CTE. D. LA DO PORTE

Giovanni Laterano

CAMPO S. GIUSTINA

FDM. DI S. GIUSTINA

C. D. FONTEGO

C. D. LA PIETA

Rio del Fonte

CAMPO D. CONFRATERNITA

CPL. D. LA CHIESA

Rio di San Francesco

CALLE DEI

CAMPO D. CELESTIA

CAMPO D. CELESTIA

5

LARGA SAN LORENZO

ORGOLOCO SAN LORENZO

Questura

RM. DI SAN SEVERO

FDM. DI SAN LORENZO

Rio di San Lorenzo

San Lorenzo

CAMPO SAN LORENZO

SAL. DI S. ANTONIN

C. ZORZI

SAL. SANTA GIUSTINA

CORTE NOVA

CTE. D. LA BORSA

C. D. MURION

SAL. S. FRANCESCO

CTE. D. LA VIDA

C. ERIZZO

C. D. ORIO

C. D. VIDA

CAMPO S. TERNITA

Rio della Celestia

C. DONA

CTE. D. ANGELO

Rio delle Gorne

6

C. D. PRETI

CALLE DEL LION

C. MORUZZI

CPL. D. FRATERNA

CALLE S. LORENZO

F. S. G. D. SCHIAVONI

CTE. S. G. D. MALTA

CTE. COPPO

Scuola di San Giorgio

CALLE DEI FURLANI

CAMPO DE LE GATE

C. DEGLI SCUDI

C. DI GATTE

C. D. ORASI

C. MALATINA

C. MANDOLIN

C. D. FORNO

CAMPO DE POZZI

Rio di Santa Ternita

CALLE MAGNO

⑪

F   G   H   I

6

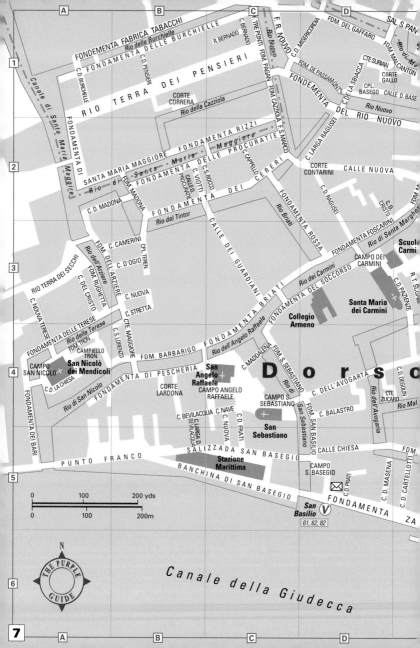

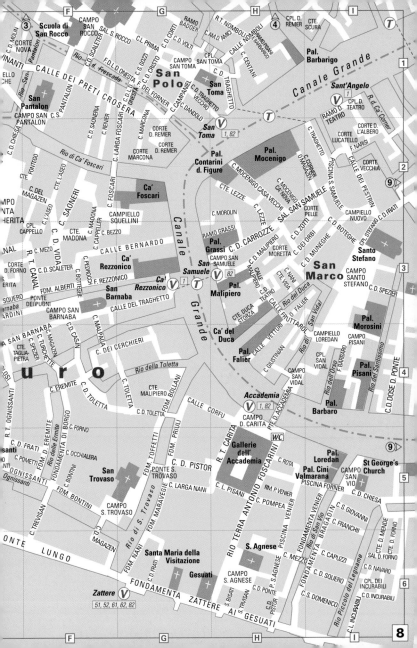

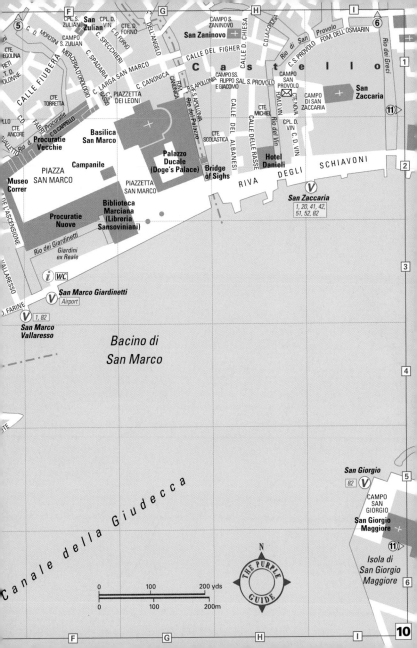

Arsenale Vecchio
Sant'Antonin
Museo delle Icone
San Giorgio dei Greci
San Zaccaria
C a s t
CPL. D. FRATERNA
C. D. MADONNA
C. D. MAGAZEN
SAL DEI GRECI
F. D. FURLANI
C. D. FORNO
C. D. MUNEGHETTE
PISC. S. MARTIN
C. GROSSO
Rio delle Gorne
SAL. SANT'ANTONIN
C. DELL'ARCO
Rio di S. Martin
CORTE VENIER
F. PENNINI
Rio dei Greci
C. BOSELLO
CTE. BOSELLO
CTE. QUERINI
CTE. BOLLANI
MORTE
C. D. L.
SAL. D. PIGNATER
C. D. CORAZZERI
CALLE DEL PESTRIN
F. TINTOR
CAMPO S. MARTIN
C. ARSENALE
CAMPO ARSENALE
C. TERAZZERA
CAMPO BANDIERA E MORO
STP. D. PRETI
C. DIETRO LA PIETA
San Giovanni in Bragora
San Martin
CTE. D PAPA
C. CROSERA
C. D. CA' GRITTI
C. DRIO ERIZZO
ERIZZO
FDM. D. POBAN
C. D. PEGOLA
FDM. D. ARSENALOTTI
F. D. MADONNA
La Pieta S. Maria d. Visitazione
CALLE D. PIETA
Rio della Pieta
CALLE D. DOSE
CPL. D. PIOVAN
CALLE DEL FORNO
CPL. D. LA PESCARIA
C. CA'
C. MEZO
C. MOROSINI
C. D. LA PESCARIA
C. CAGNOLETTO
Rio Ca' di Dio
C. D. FORNI
CPL. D. TAGLIAPIETRA
CTE. D. TAGLIAPIETRA
C. D. VIDA
F. D. ARSENALE
CAMPO D. TA
RIVA DEGLI SCHIAVONI
RIVA CA' DI DIO
Arsenale
1, 41, 42
FDM. D. FORNI
Rio dell' Arsenale
Museo Storico Navale
C. S. BIAGIO
CAMPO SAN BIAGIO
San Biagio
RIVA SAN BIAGIO
CTE. FORMEN
Canale di San Marco
San Giorgio
82
CAMPO SAN GIORGIO
San Giorgio Maggiore
Isola di San Giorgio Maggiore
A
B
C
D
1
2
3
4
5
6

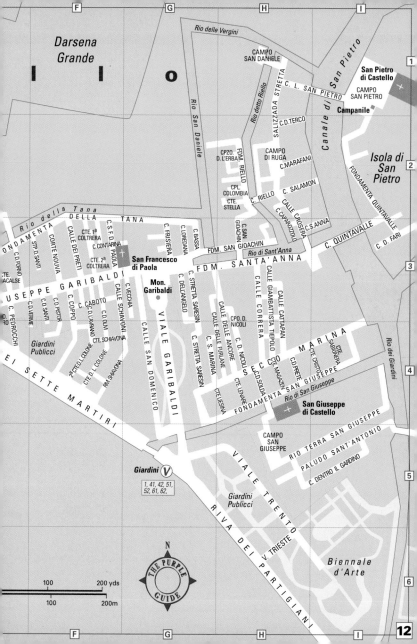

Essential Shopping Italian

Open	**Aperto**	*ah-***pehr***-toh*
Closed	**Chiuso**	*kee-***oo***-soh*
How much is this?	**Quanto costa questo?**	**kwan***-toh* **koh***-sta* **kwes***-toh?*
Can you write down the price?	**Puo scrivere il prezzo?**	*pwo skree-***veh***-reh eel* **preh***-tso?*
Do you take credit cards?	**Prendete carte di credito?**	*pren-***deh***-teh* **kar***-teh dee* **kreh***-dee-toh?*
I'd like to buy . . .	**Vorrei comprare . . .**	*voh-***ray** *kom-***prah***-reh*
Do you have anything . . .?	**Avete qualcosa . . .?**	*ah-***veh***-teh kwahl-***koh***-sah*
larger	**piu grande**	*pyoo* **grahn***-deh*
smaller	**piu piccolo**	*pyoo* **pee***-kohl-oh*
Do you have any others?	**Ne avete altri?**	*neh ah-***veh***-teh* **ahl***-tree*
I'm just looking.	**Sto solo guardando.**	*sto* **soh***-loh gwar-***dan***-doh*

Size Chart

Women's dresses, coats and skirts

Italian	40	42	44	46	48	50	52	
British	8	10	12	14	16	18	20	
American	6	8	10	12	14	16	18	

Women's shoes

Italian	36	37	38	39	40	41	
British	3	4	5	6	7	8	
American	5	6	7	8	9	10	

Men's suits

Italian	44	46	48	50	52	54	56	58 (size)
British	34	36	38	40	42	44	46	48 (inches)
American	34	36	38	40	42	44	46	48 (inches)

Men's shirts (collar size)

Italian	36	38	39	41	42	44	46	48 (cm)
British	14	15	15½	16	16½	17	17½	18 (inches)
American	14	15	15½	16	16½	17	17½	18 (inches)

Men's shoes

Italian	39	40	41	42	43	44	45	46
British	6	7	7½	8	9	10	11	12
American	7	7½	8	8½	9½	10½	11	11½